RADICAL PHILOSOPHY

2.16
Series 2 / Summer 2024

Editorial **Radical Philosophy Collective**	3
Writing Gaza during a genocide **Atef Alshaer**	6
In tune with their time **Nasser Abourahme**	13
Against singularity **Sami Khatib**	21
The urgency of anti-imperialist feminism **Walaa Alqaisiya**	33
Shock without awe **Abdaljawad Omar**	47

REVIEWS

Review article: How settler colonialism ends **Rahul Rao**	62
Samuel Moyn, *Liberalism against Itself: Cold War Intellectuals and the Making of Our Times* **Jessica Whyte**	74
Bernard Geoghegan, *Code: From Information Theory to French Theory* **Gus Hewlett**	78
Ruth Wilson Gilmore, *Abolition Geography: Essays Towards Liberation* **Jennifer Rycenga**	82
Sara Ahmed, *The Feminist Killjoy Handbook* **Hannah Boast**	85
Karl Marx, *Critique of the Gotha Program: New Translation* **Chris Newlove**	89
Christopher J. Arthur *The Spectre of Capital: Idea and Reality* **Rebecca Carson**	91
Sam Dolbear and Esther Leslie, *Dissonant Waves* **Paul Rekret**	94
Hiroki Azuma, *Philosophy of the Tourist* **Isabel Jacobs**	97
Nick Seaver, *Computing Taste* **Glen Billesbach II**	101

Editorial collective
Brenna Bhandar
Victoria Browne
Isabell Dahms
Lucie Mercier
Hannah Proctor
Rahul Rao
Chris Wilbert

Cover image
Palestine Action
https://palestineaction.org

Engineers

CC BY-NC-ND
RP, Summer 2024

ISSN 0300-211X
ISBN 978-1-914099-05-2

Editorial

Radical Philosophy Collective

The destruction of the means necessary to sustain life takes many forms. But while the numbers of those maimed and killed in Gaza fail to represent by themselves the scale of devastation, they do bear repeating. At the time of writing, they include over 40,000 recorded Palestinians killed by the Israeli military forces (of whom over 16,000 are children) and many thousands more people maimed or wounded. No-one yet knows how many bodies remain buried under the 40 million tons of rubble that now litter Gaza's landscape, the result of some 70,000 tons of high explosives. As Rasha Khatib, Martin McKee and Salim Yusuf recently argued in the *Lancet*, the actual death toll may well surpass 186,000 once it accounts for 'indirect deaths' caused by other elements of Israeli strategy – the deliberate encouragement of famine and disease via near-total restrictions on aid, medical supplies, water and food. Virtually the entire population of Gaza has been displaced, often several times over.

No set of numbers alone, of course, can measure the wider human suffering and environmental devastation. Yet, at the same time, a different set of numbers was quickly fixed and defined, in scale, date and implications, on 7 October 2023 and thereafter. According to the most recent Israeli records, Hamas-led militants took 251 hostages and killed 1,139 people: 373 were members of the security forces, 71 were foreign nationals and 695 were Israeli civilians, including 36 children. On that day Israel also killed 1,609 of the assailants and captured another 200 (who joined the many thousands of Palestinians already crowded into Israeli jails). Searching questions have been asked about Israel's representation of these events, and about the role its own military played in them, but these questions have had little impact on the discourse of the dominant. Some motives for the attack were claimed by its leadership, others were attributed to it, but its classification as terrorism was automatic and unequivocal, as was justification of Israel's response as an exercise in counter-terrorism and self-defence.

Characterisation of Israel's assault poses particular challenges given this political consensus. Did it begin abruptly on 8 October? Or did it continue, with unprecedented intensity, a long-running campaign that has all too many precedents? Did it begin with the bombings that responded to the Unity Intifada of May 2021? With the sniper attacks that literally shot the legs out from under the Great March of Return in 2018? With the aerial bombardments of 2014? Or of 2012? Of 2008-9? Should we include Israeli responses to the first and second intifadas? The conquests of 1967? The original ethnic cleansings of 1948? The Balfour declaration that began this hundred years' war? Even more troubling is the most obvious and most consistently evaded question that looms over this whole history of violence: when and how, if ever, might it end?

The sheer scale and range of the kinds of violence inflicted on Palestinians over recent years has generated a set of new terms that try to describe their specificities: ecocide, urbicide, educide and scholasticide, to name a few. The term scholasticide, coined by Karma Nabulsi after the 2009 Israeli assault on Gaza, refers to the long-running assaults on Palestinian educational institutions that have been a routine component of Israel's occupation since the Nakba. In April 2024, UN analysts expressed grave concern over the destruction of Gaza's education system, noting that the arrests, detention and targeted killings of teachers, students and staff amount to its systematic obliteration. As of early July, to cite a summary compiled by a branch of the UK's University and College Union, 'at least 95 university professors, and hundreds of school teachers and educators have been killed by Israeli forces in Gaza; all 12 universities in Gaza have been damaged or destroyed, along with well over 300 hundred schools and colleges, as well as cultural centres, archives, libraries, and museums.'

Established in 1978, the independent Islamic University of Gaza (IUG) was the first degree-awarding body to be set up in the Gaza strip, with eleven faculties including Medicine, Nursing, Engineering, Law, Education and Arts. Israel bombed it six times in December 2008, and again in August 2014. The scholar, professor, poet and activist Refaat Alareer reflected on the 2014 bombing in an essay he published two years ago.

> [W]hy would Israel bomb a university? Some say Israel attacked the IUG just to punish its twenty thousand students or to push Palestinians to despair. While that is true, to me IUG's only danger to the Israeli occupation and its apartheid regime is that it is the most important place in Gaza to develop students' minds as indestructible weapons. Knowledge is Israel's worst enemy. Awareness is Israel's most hated and feared foe. That's why Israel bombs a university: it wants to kill openness and determination to refuse living under injustice and racism.

In the 2014 attacks, Israeli bombs also killed Alareer's brother along with six other members of his family. Following appearances on the BBC, ABC News and *Democracy Now!* to discuss the 7 October attacks, on 6 December 2023, Alareer himself was killed by a carefully targeted Israeli airstrike, along with his sister, brother and four of their children. His eldest daughter, her husband and their newborn child were subsequently killed by another Israeli airstrike on 26 April 2024. In December 2023, IUG's president, physics professor Sufian Tayeh, was killed along with his family in an Israeli strike on Jabalia refugee camp. The main buildings of IUG were all destroyed by massive airstrikes just four days after 7 October. The whole of Israa University's main campus was flattened by the Israeli military in a single operation on 15 January 2024. Alareer's final poem 'If I Must Die' has become a point of reference at pro-Palestinian rallies all over the world.

If scholasticide is a relatively new entry in the terminology of destruction, the generic term that best describes the violence in Gaza is of course perfectly familiar. According to the 1948 UN Convention on the Prevention and Punishment of the Crime of Genocide, any accusation of genocide must be able to demonstrate an 'intent to destroy, in whole or in part, a national, ethnical, racial or religious group, as such.' As any prosecutor knows, proof of intention is usually the most difficult part of any genocide case. Surveying the declared intentions of Israeli leaders in the aftermath of 7 October, however, the Israeli genocide scholar Raz Segal immediately recognised that their response should be classified as a 'textbook case of genocide'. Many hundreds of qualified scholars and lawyers have repeatedly confirmed his assessment. As the South African government prepared its landmark case at the International Court of Justice in January 2024, it could draw on a compilation of hundreds of declarations of intent made by government ministers, state officials, legislators, military leaders, and so on, gathered by the group Law for Palestine. Defence Minister Yoav Gallant, for instance, repeatedly announced that 'I have removed all restraints' and promised 'no electricity, no food, no water, no fuel […]. We are fighting human animals and we are acting accordingly.' 'We will eliminate everything.'

As the legal arguments at and around the ICJ continue, the body count increases by the hour. The ICJ's provisional measures ruling of January 2024, that Israel's conduct in Gaza constitutes a 'plausible risk' of genocide, quickly became both touchstone and catalyst for dozens of legal actions, policy briefs and activist demands. The fact that further provisional measures were sought in May 2024, however, points to the futility of international legal proceedings in the face of what remains the most basic fact of the situation, a fact sanctioned by this very legal order itself: the impunity of Israel and its allies. The post-war international legal and political system – which since its inception has either been ignored or manipulated by powerful states and their clients to justify whatever actions they might want to take – is not so much being torn to shreds as being superseded altogether.

Meanwhile the international legal principles that might inform critical discussion of the events of 7 October, or Palestinian resistance in general, have effectively been erased from political memory. The additional protocols adopted in 1977 to supplement the Geneva Conventions of 1949 extended their scope to include 'armed conflicts in which peoples are fighting against colonial domination and alien occupation and against racist régimes in the exercise of their right of self-determination' (article 1, section 4); and in 1982, the UN General Assembly's resolution 37/43 further confirmed 'the legitimacy of the struggle of peoples for independence, territorial integrity, national unity and liberation from colonial and foreign domination and foreign occupation by all available means, including armed struggle.' The right to resist occupation with the use of force was recently reaffirmed in the opinion of Justice Hilary Charlesworth in the ICJ's advisory opinion of 19 June 2024, which considered the legality of Israel's occupation of Gaza, Jerusalem and the West Bank. The ICJ found Israel's occupation of the Palestinian Territories, recognised by the Court as a contiguous territory, to be unequivocally illegal on multiple bases of international law, and one which must end immediately. Whether this ruling becomes part of the political arsenal to achieve some form of Palestinian liberation, or suffers the same fate as so many previous UN Resolutions on the same, remains to be seen and acted upon.

In his opening remarks at the UN COP28 climate summit, Colombian President Gustavo Petro warned that 'What we are seeing in Gaza is a rehearsal of the future.' The Israeli genocide offers one vision of the future, but, despite ongoing censorship of so many educational, political and cultural institutions and violence against protestors, the resurgence of a global solidarity movement proposes another. This movement is a refusal of what the war on Gaza portends, and a total rejection of the impunity that has emboldened Israel and its allies to pursue their course of annihilation. In Palestinian steadfastness, the global solidarity protests, the student encampments, dissenting discourse and direct actions and demonstrations of all kinds, lies the articulation and enactment of a politics and ethics that, as Samera Esmeir describes, seek to 'say and think a life beyond what settler colonialism has made'.

Writing Gaza during a genocide
Atef Alshaer

The night before October 7, I sent an article I had read in the *Guardian* newspaper to an orthopaedic doctor acquaintance in Birmingham.[1] The article reported on the new techniques that Israeli soldiers were using on the borders with Gaza in order to shoot Palestinian protestors in both ankles at the same time, causing life-long problems to their mobility. As someone who grew up in Gaza and was shot in my own ankle when I was ten years old, I was struck that the technique had advanced from the time of the first Palestinian Intifada (1987-1993). The new automatic rifles which have two triggers now allow for two targets at once, hence the infliction of injury on both ankles. My mind flashed back to 2018, the last and only time I was in Gaza since 1999, when I left to study at Birzeit University in the West Bank. I remembered walking with my wife near the now-destroyed Shifa Hospital in Gaza, and seeing several young Palestinian men on crutches lining one street with amputated legs after being shot by Israeli soldiers during the Great March of Return protests (2018-2023), when Israel intensified its sniper campaign, targeting children, health workers, journalists and people with disabilities, something which the UN at the time described as 'a war crime against humanity'. It is estimated that more than 6000 unarmed Palestinians protestors were shot by military snipers, targeting sensitive areas that cause life-long injuries and immobility, such as knees and ankles.[2] One sniper boasted that he shot '42 knees in one day'.[3]

Sending the article was the last thing I did that evening, and I remember a night full of vague dreams, underscored by deep sleep. Upon waking, I checked my phone to find a stream of messages from friends asking me about what was happening in Gaza. At that point, I had zero knowledge. I surveyed the main news channels and settled on listening to Al Jazeera, which was broadcasting live from the surroundings of Gaza (originally all part of Gaza until the armistice line of 1949 when Israel gulped it all up) that had been penetrated by Hamas fighters and other citizens from Gaza. A few hours later, I received a call from one of the BBC radio stations asking me to comment on the situation. At that point, the magnitude of the event was not clear, so I spoke about the Palestinian desperation in Gaza and described the event as an attempt to break free from the enormous open air prison that Israel had created for Gaza and its long-suffering people. Subsequently, I spoke to BBC TV and felt that my interviewer was actually quite open-minded and, in the immediate aftermath of the event, gave me time to explain Palestinian conditions in order to establish some understanding of what had happened.

Meanwhile, I grew alarmed as to what was likely to unfold for the people in Gaza. The subsequent days and weeks proved catastrophic, and I was catapulted into a strange sort of media world on an almost daily basis, particularly via the various BBC radio stations in the UK. Almost immediately, October 7 became the preamble to every conversation and any departure from this supposed 'point zero', accounting for Israel's massive and unrelenting attacks against Gaza, and the systematic targeting of civilian infrastructure including hospitals, ambulances, schools, mosques, churches, bakeries, restaurants, water supplies, food supplies, medicine depots, and so on, was explained away by what happened on that date. History started then and only then. The horrifying reality imposed on Gaza up to that point was hardly accounted for, while the 'mighty vengeance' promised by Netanyahu saw thousands of Palestinian children and homes incinerated with American-made bombs.

Unsurprisingly, by the time I appeared on one of Radio 4's flagship programmes, the Moral Maze, soon after October 7, the other panellists were thoroughly uninterested in engaging with my point that history did not simply start on that date, dismissing the argument with remarks that 'we know the history', as if this meant that it did not matter. The contributors to the show – who included a priest, a university professor, a well-known pundit and a Rabbi who spoke from Jerusalem – expressed outrage and disgust at Hamas, yet ignored totally that, as they were speaking, Israel was bombarding and killing people in Gaza indiscriminately and relentlessly. 'Morality' was invoked as if this resided with Israel alone, despite so many gruesome massacres and deaths of Palestinians at the hands of Israel over the years. Except for the considered and humane discourse of another Palestinian guest and an Israeli speaker who both lost members of their families in the conflict, the tone was one-sided, loaded with dehumanising language directed against the Palestinians, every issue reduced to the word 'Hamas'. That prior to October 7 Israel was killing Palestinians in the West Bank, as well as Gaza, targeting their livelihoods, that its firebrand minister Itamar Ben Gvir was supervising torture sessions against Palestinian prisoners, that land and resources were constantly confiscated from Palestinians by settlers, worship at al-Aqsa mosque was being restricted and intimidating attacks and abuses by Jewish settlers were routinely faced by Palestinians in Jerusalem and elsewhere in the West Bank, that the 17-year-old blockade of Gaza was deepening the desperation there, and that Netanyahu and his government were sidelining Palestinian demands to such an extent that they were made effectively irrelevant to Israeli discourses – none of this was any kind of explanation for the October 7 attack, but was presented as a barrage of justification for it. Instead, the dehumanisation of the Palestinians was to be doubled down upon, so that bombing and attacks with the most advanced weapons on the planet against their bodies and institutions, against Palestine as a nation and community, could be justified and legitimated.

Above all, supporters of Israel from media pundits to the White House and Downing Street could not fathom the possibility that captives might seek to resist their captors, could rise, organise and inflict damage on their occupiers: how dare this heap of human dust form a storm against their occupiers? The few maintaining this self-evident point, such as the remarkable Norman Finkelstein, were a minority in the media, amidst the ceremonial chorus of condemnations and cheerleading for the massacres against the Palestinians in Gaza and the West Bank. As always, Israel was assured of total impunity. Unlike their Palestinian adversaries, Israeli commanders could order attacks without repercussions, and defy international law by cutting off water and food supplies to the target populations, while western leaders poured into Israel, expressing sympathy with Netanyahu and his government, and ignoring the non-stop devastation that Israel was visiting upon neighbouring Gaza and its people. When Keir Starmer, the leader of the Labour Party in the UK (and its Prime Minister at the time of writing), was asked if Israel had the right to cut off water and food supplies from the Palestinians, which Israel controls as part of its effective occupation of Gaza, he simply replied: 'Israel has this right'. Thus, the leader of one of Europe's largest 'left-wing' parties apparently concurred with the Israeli defence minister, Yoav Gallant, who described the Palestinians in Gaza as 'human animals' to justify the cutting off of water, fuel and food supplies to Gaza.

As a humanist, I have always been keen to make clear that I do not justify attacks against civilians. I argued in an article that I published anonymously soon after October 7 that in fact Hamas had miscalculated the Israeli response and did not read the geopolitical situation well. My understanding was that Hamas wanted to exchange Israeli prisoners with Palestinian prisoners and that its attack no doubt exceeded the limits set on it by its leaders in Gaza. Indeed, Hamas itself later admitted as much in a lengthy document. Much of the killing and destruction that took place against the civilian communities in Israel seems to have been undertaken by rogue elements, including from within Hamas itself and other movements that saw an opportunity to avenge the killing of their families or members of the same political groups by Israel. At the same time, as is now widely recognised, at least some of the killings were the responsibility of the Israeli army itself, which shot at Israeli properties to prevent the kidnapping of Israeli citizens; something that has now been admitted by Israeli sources themselves. Part of the picture of that day should also recognise that some Hamas fighters treated some Israeli civilians, including old women and children, well. None of this, however, fit with Israel's and its allies' narrative of absolute Palestinian savagery and barbarism, including now widely debunked stories of rape and baby-killing. There is little doubt that utterly inhumane and irresponsible acts were committed on October 7. I was horrified to see Israeli old women and children wheeled to Gaza, including a young woman with two babies, and was only mildly relieved when the spokesperson of the military wing of Hamas said something to the effect that they were willing to return them to Israel quite quickly in return for the release of Palestinian minors and women in Israeli prisoners. Yet Israel did not respond to the proposal, only to accept it after more than fifty days of unrelenting bombing and destruction in Gaza, which saw over forty Israeli civilians being returned as part of a deal that Hamas more or less suggested in the early days of the Israeli assault. By then, several Israeli captives had been killed by the Israeli bombardment, including the lady I had seen footage of with her two babies. As far as the Israeli civilians taken on October 7 are concerned, the picture is grim and inexcusable. Yet the damage could have been mitigated through negotiations had it not been for Israel's characteristic *modus operandi* of using extreme violence against the Palestinians in general in order to avenge an event which, tragic as it was, has been exploited beyond all reason to justify horrifying crimes against humanity.

I

It is over 250 days since the Israeli genocide began – a genocide effectively evidenced by the Israeli government and military's own statements, which do not hide their intent to render Gaza uninhabitable by unrelenting bombing and by the production of famine throughout the region, described as the fastest man-made famine in modern history by several human rights organisations. My feelings at seeing my birthplace maligned and destroyed to the extent that it has now been have induced daily bouts of suffering and despair. I engaged with this unimaginable situation through almost weekly writing for an Arabic newspaper, *Al-Arabi Al-Jadded*, in which I reflected on the ongoing grief over the tragic loss of doctors, journalists, teachers, children, women, and other devastations that reduced the much cherished Gaza of my memory to rubble. I also lamented the responses of official western governments and inept and corrupt Arab ruling elites, focusing on their discourses about, and disregard for the life of, Palestinian civilians who have borne the brunt of the devastating Israeli attacks. I concluded, as this situation pressed itself against the last vestiges of my mental well-being, that my faculties are simply not prepared or equipped or qualified to deal with so much senseless death and destruction.

It offers no relief here to think of evil, as Hannah Arendt thought of it, as 'banal'; that evil, in this case, is no more than a person simply doing their job. As she famously writes of Eichmann: 'I was struck by the manifest shallowness in the doer that made it impossible to trace the incontestable evil of his deeds to any deeper level of roots or motives. The deeds were monstrous, but the doer … was quite ordinary, commonplace, and neither demonic nor monstrous'.[4] I might concur, difficult as this is, that Israeli pilots and soldiers indiscriminately killing large numbers of people including children, and destroying hospitals to render life impossible in Gaza, are simply doing a job assigned to them. Yet, I find it hard, too, not to see the extraordinary levels of engineering of discourse that entrench ideologies of killing and normalise them to such an extent that they become positively *heroic* actions for the society that conducts such crimes. This discourse-engineering extends from the seats of the Israeli government and media to White House spokespersons to newspaper columns and headlines that uncritically support the Israeli state, which often portrays itself as victim and victimiser in the same breath. The default positioning of such discourse is not only to obscure the humanity of the Palestinians, and their reasons for resistance, unsavoury as some aspects of this might be, but to render them invisible under rubrics such as 'terrorism'. To this end, 'evil' is a deliberate system, produced and reproduced to such an extent that it takes on the appearance of banality, of an utterly disturbing ordinariness, which reflects an extraordinary level of historical concealment of its gruesome, abnormal and inhumane character. Yet, the 'doers' who uphold this system are neither simply ordinary nor commonplace. They are well-informed and well-trained, using the latest technologies of killing through devastating weapons to cause untold suffering and destruction against a civilian population with very little to nothing to defend itself.

It is noticeable in this regard that since October 7, so many Israeli figures in the Hebrew media in Israel have called openly for the massacring of Palestinian people in Gaza and happily expressed their delight and pleasure at seeing the destruction and death in Gaza. Equally, of course, there are always people who dissent from and reject such positions, including brave Israeli youth, limited as their numbers are, who prefer to go to jail rather than take part in the occupation and violence Israel routinely deploys against the Palestinians. Nonetheless, what is clear is that Israel has grown more callous and reckless about its image, with its settlers and their leaders frequently broadcasting their crimes in a newly heightened state of sadistic glee and confidence in their own unaccountability, while protestors take part in preventing essential supplies from getting into Gaza and soldiers post pictures on social media celebrating their cruelty. Israeli soldiers blow up houses and schools, terrorise doctors in hospitals, destroy hospital wards, trample upon dead Palestinian bodies with tanks and bulldozers, humiliate minors and old people, execute unarmed civilians, all while broadcasting their crimes to the world. Such crimes have been committed since 1948 when Israel was established, but the scale, and the shamelessness, with which they have occurred since October 7th have been extraordinary, inaugurating a new sense of dread and fear of a coming world where grim practices of torture and killing come to be regarded and accepted as normal and even necessary.

Dehumanised and brutalised, portrayed as irredeemably irrational fanatics, the Palestinians are, at the same time, entirely excluded from normative politics as determined by the United States and its allies. Terms such as 'the peace process' or 'the two-state solution', which are bandied about on every occasion, become meaningless gestures in a discourse over which the Palestinians themselves can have no say. As the Palestinians' conditions have worsened over the years, so too has any horizon whatsoever for their legitimate rights to be recognised further receded. Tareq Baconi, writing in the *New York Times*, has expressed the matter succinctly:

> Repeating the two-state solution mantra has allowed policymakers to avoid confronting the reality that partition is ... illegitimate as an arrangement originally imposed on Palestinians without their consent in 1947. The concept of the two-state solution has evolved to become a central pillar of sustaining Palestinian subjugation and Israeli impunity.[5]

II

Over the last few months, I have taken part in fundraising activities to help families related to mine and others staying with them in Rafah to survive. I felt moved by the protests in which I took part in London, where hundreds of thousands marched against the genocide in Palestine, expressing solidarity and feeling heartbroken by the mounting humanitarian disaster that Israel has engineered with the help of its allies. If nothing else, the situation has clarified the stark distance between many governments and political elites and the majority of their populations, whether in the West or in many Arab countries. There has rarely been a case where basic humanity and decency should so obviously have prevailed as this one. Yet in official media, Palestinian commentators and others have almost always found themselves pressed to argue even this most basic of points. In one of the interviews I had with BBC Five Live, I found myself puzzled, sensing that my interviewer demonstrated personal decency, giving me ample time to respond to his questions and develop my point, as the matter at hand required. Yet his questions were loaded with the mindset and culture of the institution he represented, repeating back to me the distorted narratives of the Israeli and American official bodies as if they were holy rites not to be doubted, from claims of hospitals in Gaza being used as human shields to the number of children killed being justified as part of the 'horrors of war', to commenting on antisemitism as if this was the main motivation of the Palestinian struggle rather than liberation from a brutal occupation. So much distraction, twisted moralisation and justification to wash away blatant crimes against humanity being committed daily.

Franseca Albanese, the UN Special Rapporteur on the Occupied Palestinian Territories, did not mince her words when she stated that 'the world now sees the bitter fruits of the impunity afforded to Israel. This was a tragedy foretold.'[6] If the ongoing tragedy in Gaza, stemming from 'the impunity afforded to Israel', was indeed foretold, the question persists as to why Israel is afforded such leverage and clout in western capitals that it feels immune from accountability, with so many of its officers and soldiers feeling free to broadcast their grisly crimes.[7] The Republican Party in the US, buoyed up by elements of the Christian Right, is so closely aligned with Israel today that its leaders attend meetings and gatherings with the likes of the Meir Kahane movement, previously proscribed as a terrorist organisation by the US and at one point described as racist by the Israeli parliament but which is now represented in the current Israeli government by the ministers Ben Gvir and Bezalel Smotrich – a movement whose expressed ideology calls for the forced deportation of the Palestinians or even their enslavement.[8] Such meetings have called, among other things, for the destruction of Al-Aqsa Mosque in Jerusalem and its replacement with the Jewish Temple. To some extent, this is replicated by the Democratic Party side of American politics, where a large component of that party has grown up sentimentally attached to Israel and to Zionism as redeeming of the guilt of Europe from the Holocaust inflicted on world Jewry during World War II. They are also attached to Israel, having built a state which on the face of it subscribes to western normative values, including electoral democracy and civil institutions that they recognise as akin to theirs. And they do not have much sympathy for the lives of Palestinian Arabs, who are seen through a civilisational prism developed from nineteenth-century orientalist and colonialist tropes. Put simply and crudely, the civilisational measure does not accord the same value to the life of a Palestinian or Arab or Muslim as it does to a western life of white European origin, and Israel is represented as part of that civilisational ideology in terms of life-value.

This absolute support for Israel is a significant achievement of one of the key intellectual figures of Zionism and the founder of the extremist Likud Party at the beginning of the twentieth century, Ze'ev Jabotinsky. Jabotinsky's strategy for Zionism, to which the ultra-right in Israel, including Benjamin Netanyahu, subscribes, consisted of two main considerations. First, for Israel – described by Jabotinsky as 'a bulwark against Asia' – to survive in the Middle East, it must ensure that it is literally and figuratively protected by an iron wall that keeps any potential enemies away. Accordingly, it is sheer power, not peace or political compromises, that matters. Second, Israel must be connected to the international power of the day, aligned with a major power that considers Israel's security its own; this was Britain in the past, and since the 1950s has been the United States. Jabotinsky's wish was ultimately fulfilled after the 1973 war between

Egypt and Israel when the United States made sure that Israel was secured against its (Arab) enemies, and that it would always have an advantage over them through 'iron-clad American support'. So has the 'impunity afforded to Israel' been established and guaranteed, with all that follows from this. A tragedy foretold.

III

My brothers in Europe and I have often analysed the situation at night, when we all returned from our work, despairing about the complicit parties, while taking refuge in each other's shared feelings. Sometimes the situation has got the better of me. I have found myself quietly crying, occasionally in front of strangers, while impulsively asking them 'what do you think of what is happening in Palestine-Israel?'.

Days are burdened by fears: is the family still there? Is my nephew Hassan still there? (He is my regular contact to check up on everybody.) Is my brother Saeed still smiling? How is my mother-in-law with her phobia of loud noise, and her vivacious five-year-old grandkid who speaks the language of adults now, coping with all this? Do they all have enough water? Enough food? Pointless to ask. Pointless to answer. Pointless to imagine. But we live in a pointless world right now.

To grieve it all, I occasionally write poetry, perhaps the most pointless master of all grief:

They prepared for their weddings

Those who die now
from my country
with the sun on their faces
and a horizon betraying them.
Those who die
with the bullets of Israel
and die from the promises of Israel
they die at the gatherings of roads
and from the weightless burden of the sky
they die
in houses bereft of light
in hospitals emptied of cures
they die.
Death visits them more than poetry,
hunger aethers their children,
and they prepare for their weddings
under collapsed roofs
over dead bodies under the rubble.
They die without mirrors
and walk in roads unashamed of their narrowness
those who die now
from the youth of my country
they are
without a doubt
concealing in their bodies
the barest sparks of a fire.

The body is a bounded space, bounded by its biological dynamics and psychological horizons. Short of death, it adapts. Suffering gives way to despair, where the mind flutters in aimless spaces.

It has been quite strange to hear the name of my city Rafah being repeated endlessly in the media and the mouths of politicians, including President Biden, as the next station for Israeli ground invasion and destruction. My city has become a cause celebre for all the wrong reasons. Rafah, this sleepy city, kissed and lashed by the Mediterranean Sea, has suddenly become a point of forced gathering for Palestinian civilians from the north and middle of the Gaza Strip, fleeing the horrors of Israeli invasions there. Rafah is now a site of immense suffering and hardship, teeming with refugees from the north in overcrowded tents and little to no means of sustaining life. As Israel now systematically destroys my city, I lament the fate of my family in tents. All hemmed in with thousands of other families, struggling all day long to provide food, water and other necessities of life for their families. There are not enough words of lamentation to express my sadness over you my beloved city.

More than one hundred people, mostly children and women, from my immediate and extended family have been killed in the ongoing Israeli genocide, as well as houses destroyed, livelihoods decimated and festering traumas created. My uncle's wife, Intisar Alshaer, who normally lives in Egypt and was visiting her family in Palestine, was killed along with scores of others in one gruesome Israeli bombing, where eight people, including an old man, two of his daughters and his three children, were killed. Ten other cousins were killed; one of them because of the unavailability of medicine for the minor injuries he sustained from an Israeli bombing. Another child was killed, while his father – a friend of mine – was at the oil presser. My nephew tells me that 80% of the neighbourhood of Hayy As-Salaam in Rafah where I grew up has been destroyed. Hundreds of houses were destroyed for no reason, other than to make the city unliveable for its inhabitants. I know of no family in Gaza that has not suffered the terrible and barbaric carnage Israel has been inflicting on them.

I remember looking at the face of a new friend I met at a meeting organised by a Palestinian family in London. He looked withdrawn and in utter despair. Upon asking about him, he told me that he had lost all his family members in Deir Al-Balah in the middle of Gaza in one Israeli bombing where twenty-one family members were sheltering. Such immense losses. Such immense consequences that mountains could not bear.

When I hear Israeli leaders say repeatedly that they are waging a war of civilisation in Gaza against barbarism, I see the images of all those innocent relatives, all the beautiful children, and can only think: 'fuck your civilisation'.

Yet, while I despair, I also remember my childhood in Gaza, and the children with whom I used to play on the beach of Gaza, many of whom have doubtless already been killed. I look closer and there I refuse to surrender to despair. As an act of will, in honour of my people and my childhood friends in Palestine, I hope for hope.

> To suffer woes which Hope thinks infinite;
> To forgive wrongs darker than death or night;
> To defy power which seems omnipotent;
> To love, and bear; to hope till Hope creates
> from its own wreck the thing it contemplates
> Life may change, but it may fly not;
> Hope may vanish; but can die not;
> Truth be veiled, but still it burneth;
> Love repulsed – but it returneth.[9]

Atef Alshaer is Reader in Arabic Language and Culture at the University of Westminster. He is the author of Language and National Identity in Palestine: Representations of Power and Resistance in Gaza *(2022) and* Poetry and Politics in the Modern Arab World *(2016), as well as co-author of* The Hizbullah Phenomenon: Politics and Communication *(2014).*

Notes

1. See Bethan McKernan and Hazem Balousha, 'Gaza Strip protesters received bullet wounds to ankles, medics report', *Guardian*, 4 October 2024, https://www.theguardian.com/world/2023/oct/04/gaza-strip-protesters-received-bullet-wounds-to-ankles-medics-report.
2. See 'UN: Possible Israel crimes against humanity in Gaza', *Al Jazeera*, 28 February 2019, https://www.aljazeera.com/news/2019/2/28/un-possible-israel-crimes-against-humanity-in-gaza.
3. See '"42 knees in one day": Israeli snipers brag about deliberately crippling Gaza protesters', *The New Arab*, 7 March 2020, https://www.newarab.com/news/israeli-snipers-brag-about-deliberately-crippling-gaza-protesters.
4. Hannah Arendt, *The Life of the Mind* (New York: Harvest/HJB Books, 1978), 4.
5. Tareq Baconi, 'The Two-State Solution is an Unjust, Impossible Fantasy', *New York Times*, 1 April 2024, https://www.nytimes.com/2024/04/01/opinion/two-state-solution-israel-palestine.html.
6. 'Rights expert finds "reasonable grounds" genocide is being committed in Gaza', *UN News*, 26 March 2024, https://news.un.org/en/story/2024/03/1147976.
7. On the US's support to Israel, see the most comprehensive book on this topic by Ilan Pappe, *Lobbying for Zionism on Both Sides of the Atlantic* (Oneworld, 2024). See also Nasim Ahmed, 'MEMO launches Ilan Pappe's book Lobbying for Zionism', *Middle East Monitor*, 11 June 2024, https://www.middleeastmonitor.com/20240611-memo-launches-ilan-pappes-book-lobbying-for-zionism/.
8. See 'Fact Sheet: Meir Kahane The Extremist Kahanist Movement', *Institute for Middle East Understanding*, 17 May 2024, https://imeu.org/article/fact-sheet-meir-kahane-the-extremist-kahanist-movement.
9. Percy Bysshe Shelley, *Prometheus Unbound* [1820] (Cambridge University Press, 2013).

In tune with their time
Nasser Abourahme

> This threatening atmosphere of violence and missiles in no way frightens or disorients the colonized. We have seen that their entire recent history has prepared them to 'understand' the situation. Between colonial violence and the insidious violence in which the modern world is steeped, there is a kind of complicit correlation, a homogeneity. The colonized have adapted to this atmosphere. For once they are in tune with their time.
>
> Frantz Fanon, *The Wretched of the Earth*, 1961[1]

> There will be time to bury the dead. There will be time for weaponry. And there will be time to pass the time as we please, that this heroism may go on. Because now we are the masters of time.
>
> Mahmoud Darwish, *Memory for Forgetfulness*, 1982[2]

Israel is a defeated project. I don't mean this as a moral indictment. I take it to be, at this stage, quite simply a historical fact. An Israel that has normalised its status in the world and region, rules stably over subject populations, ceases to practice apartheid, closes its open frontier, declares borders, no longer relies on extra-legal discretionary settler violence, and transitions out of a permanent war footing will never happen. It is already finished. It is at best a badly frayed, but lethal, fantasy. The kind you hold onto more out of spite than genuine anticipation. In a certain but important sense – one that needs plain stating – we already live in a world *after* this possibility, after Israel. This Israel is already a future-past. The persistence of Palestinian life and its refusal to simply die and disappear has already achieved this. And *any* vision of a noncolonial mode of cohabitation in historic Palestine must begin with this recognition.

What we are living through today is Zionism's endgame. This is not to be sanguine. Colonial endgames can last a long time; they are almost always utterly brutal. But the brutality is as much a sign of their defeated denouement as much as anything else.[3] Colonial endgames are defined by a diminishing range of options and the fact that each move leads exponentially faster toward the end. Zionism's endgame is not born simply of the Israeli project's immanent contradictions rising to the surface. It is born decisively out of the persistence of Palestine's long century of anticolonial struggle that has over the last two decades amounted to the most sustained challenge in a renewed war of national liberation in generations. About this we should be clear and unapologetic: the Palestinian war of national liberation is posing an intractable challenge to the colonial order. Zionism is not failing. Zionism is being defeated.

The headfirst charge into a frenzied genocidal campaign in Gaza can only be understood if parsed in the full historical arc of struggle over Palestine that reaches this current inflection point. That is, this conjuncture can only be understood if it is located in the *foundational impasse* of the Zionist project. Zionism is at an impasse because it is defined by the stunted drive of its conquest. It is a project that when faced with a resilient arc of refusal finds itself temporally stuck, unable to transition beyond its foundational moment, unable to make permanent and finalise dispossession in stable regimes of property and law, unable to move past the past. Political orders that cannot close their moments of foundational conquest and consign that conquest's violence to the political unconscious are vulnerable orders. They are unsettled orders.

Nadine Fraczkowski

Zionism's entire purpose, its *raison d'etre*, has always been the establishment of a racially pure or majoritarian Jewish state in Palestine, and yet it finds itself today, governing and ruling over seven million native Palestinian subjects – over half the population it controls – that it has no intent or ability of ever absorbing as members of its national body politic. This is simply an irreducible contradiction. From the standpoint of the racial state, it is an immunological disaster; one that not only means the state must remain formally or legally defined in racial terms (and can never transition to the devices of liberal democratic formal equality) but also dooms it to a constant reenactment of the violence of conquest. In the long-term historical sense – and it is precisely this temporal sense and horizon that now imposes itself – Zionism only has two options in front of it: equality (and thus self-negation) or genocide. That it opts so clearly for genocide, underlines just how much the elimination of the Palestinians is Zionism's master-desire, the primary object of its drive.

From the standpoint of a stalled project of colonial settlement, genocide is neither irrational nor simply vindictive. For Zionism, it is a corrective return to a blocked pathway. It is clamoured for and *felt* as vitally necessary because it might be a way out of the impasse, beyond the challenge. In truth, genocide is never far from the surface in settler colonial orders. And though it is but one among many instruments of elimination and the negation of indigenous peoplehood (alongside: removal, assimilation, native citizenship), historically speaking, it rises to the surface when the frontier is still open and contested. In Palestine, genocide, understood even within the narrow confines of the UN convention not as the mass killing of individuals (which is the rarer case) but as the intentional destruction of a people's capacity to exist, has always been the condition of possibility for political Zionism – the *Nakba* was in many ways a clear case of genocide, even if it almost still cannot be named as such.[4] But that genocide-as-event returns, that it moves from latent to actualised logic, is an effect of the magnitude of the challenge posed by Palestine's renewed war of liberation to an already stuck settler project.

It is precisely this sense of the moment as both *impasse/frustration* and *exit/freedom* for the colonial regime that explains things like the sheer volume of open genocidal incitement across both Israeli society and state. I mean here the generalised will to discourse in the almost daily calls to flatten, to wipe out, to level, to finish them; or in language that more directly indexes the immunological anxieties of a threatened racial order: to erase (*l'mchok*) or to purify/disinfect (*l'tahir*); or, possibly even more tellingly, in language that codes the incitement in calls for a completion of the foundational conquest: 'Nakba 2.0', 'rolling out the Gaza Nakba', 'the second war of independence'. This dual sense of impasse and exit is also there in the affective discharges so regularly displayed in Israeli social media around images of the death and destruction in Gaza: the glee, the mockery, the rancour, the cruelty, the need to humiliate; it is hard otherwise to explain the entirely excessive amount of circulated images and videos of soldiers looting homes, wasting food, mockingly playing with the toys of dead or displaced kids, or posing with the underwear of dead or displaced women. This generalised collapse of the repressive barrier and inhibition in speech cannot be explained simply by the new permissiveness of tabooed desire; it is also an effect of the deep frustrations of the stunted libidinal drive of this project as it is checked by a people it '*knows*' to be inferior in every possible way, and yet cannot somehow decisively defeat but *can* now humiliate and punish. Frustrations that are marked even now in the ubiquitous retort that this is not really a genocide because, 'if it wanted to Israel could wipe Gaza off the face of the earth'. A retort that, of course, only betrays how much Israel's supporters want precisely that but are unable (for now) to achieve it.

This mixture of frustration and freedom is also the only way to understand the nature of the total, obliterating and frenzied violence that has been meted out to Gaza. Violence that is often called indiscriminate but is actually targeted and intentional and aimed not only at widespread destruction but at the very basis of collective habitable life. Violence that includes the imposition of total siege, the active engineering of conditions of starvation and epidemic disease, and mass summary executions.[5] How else can one understand the obliteration of most of Gaza's housing and the demolition of entire residential blocks by the army's engineering corps *after* fighting? Or the hundreds of two-thousand-pound bombs, some of the largest conventional munitions on earth that kill or destroy everything within hundreds of feet, dropped not just on densely populated neighbourhoods, but on those neighbourhoods designated as 'safe zones'? Or the systematic devastation of the entire public health system in Gaza, with almost every single hospital being besieged, invaded or bombed multiple times, and with two hospitals, including Shifa, the largest in the Strip, effectively turned into death camps?[6] Or the over 80 attacks on aid distribution?[7] Or the wholesale erasure of the universities, municipalities, libraries, and archives? Or the systematic targeting of Gaza's professional classes, its doctors, medical practitioners, journalists, academics and poets and writers? Gaza City, Palestine's last remaining coastal city and the hub of the Strip's life-supporting infrastructure, has been all but destroyed. This active production of the uninhabitable, this will to rubble, cannot be explained simply as momentary 'bloodlust' or vengeance. It has to be understood, historically and affectively, as the release of long pent-up exterminatory energies that in the project's highest moment of vulnerability feel free to pursue the threatening object of their desire.

The time of initiative/*Zaman al-Mubadara*

Yet it would be a mistake to read the conjuncture only from the vantage point of a settler order that feels besieged and senses a way out. A deeper reading has to recognise that at some level this siege – the siege of the fort, the siege of the siege – is real and not just a figment of settler society's narcissistic attachments to fears of injury and reversal. That is, it is not simply that Israel, like any colonial order, is haunted by the prospect of the reversibility of its relations of force, but that this reversal has over the last two decades become increasingly possible, if not likely. The Zionist regime has managed its contradictions over the last two decades (since the collapse of the façade of a forward-moving 'peace process') essentially by biding time, by lethal conflict management in a drawn-out suspended temporality: siege, permanent counter-insurgency, mass arrest and detention, deepening apartheid and segregation, economic pacification and economies of humanitarian aid, and the use of forms of native authority on the Bantustan model. In Gaza, this has been accompanied by regular bombing campaigns and massacres that were tellingly described by the state as 'mowing the lawn', indexing not only the idyllic rot of suburban Americana at the heart of Israel's self-image, or the reduction of Palestinian life to an unruly mute nature, but also the utterly banal and repetitive nature of this violence for its orchestrators – mowing the lawn is something you do routinely and almost unthinkingly.

But the problem with biding time is that forms of resistance don't stay still, they expand and grow in depth, penetration and sophistication with every year. The last two decades have seen the most pronounced growth of the Palestinian liberation movement since the end of the Palestinian Revolution in the siege of Beirut in 1982, and the capture of its main political parties as the effective facilitators of Israeli occupation in the West Bank a decade later. This is clear if we consider the forms of resistance in their full and global gamut: civic activism, the boycott and divestment campaign, sustained forms of direct action, the growth of the Palestinian solidarity movement and the deepened ties with left parties, labour unions and movements for Black and Indigenous liberation globally, and armed struggle in Palestine and the region.

It is the armed struggle and its rootedness in resilient forms of life that remains illegible or unapproachable to so many contemporary observers. And yet there is no chance of grasping this conjuncture without reading it within a historical arc of a renewed war of national liberation that has begun to pose insurmountable challenges to the very logic of settler colonial power in Palestine. An arc that starts with the liberation of South Lebanon in 2000 – an event of singular historical significance, being the only time land was liberated from Israeli occupation without a broader recognition of the Israeli state – and includes the routing of the Israeli army in the 2006 War in Lebanon, and the growing capacities of the Palestinian resistance in Gaza in the 2008/9, 2014 and 2021 wars. These were buttressed by the Great March of Return in 2018, a wave of popular protests that challenged the siege of Gaza but were met with overwhelming lethal violence, and the Unity Intifada in 2021 that saw, for the first time in a generation, simultaneous mobilisation in every part of historic Palestine. The Unity Intifada was also the cue for a renewed organisation of the armed resistance in the West Bank into self-defense zones around the major refugee camps. If the settler colonial project has in this period sought to close time in what a senior Israeli political advisor called in 2004 a formaldehyde solution that would 'freeze the political process',[8] resistance factions have sought to make and open time, to set its rhythms and tempos, in what they call 'the time of initiative'.

Yet there remains, even among those of us dedicated to the liberation of all peoples in historic Palestine, a certain incapacity or unreadiness to read this historical arc, to recognise its historicity. An incapacity that stems from, on the one hand, a misunderstanding or a forgetting of what anticolonial national liberation wars are about, such that we are often told, in ways that internalise a mythology of Israeli military supremacy, that armed struggle here is futile, counterproductive, or at best symbolic. And on the other, an incapacity stemming from the capture of our grammars in liberal politics of respectability and recognition that are fundamentally incapable of processing anticolonial political violence in anything other than flat moral frames that invariably privilege state power and reify the legal categories of colonial history.[9] Here armed struggle is read *only* at the point of its transgression of a moral limit, and we end up with a kind of performative moral disavowal that folds entire anticolonial struggles into the pathologies of sadism and vengeance (only a short step away from the language of 'barbarism' and 'savagery'). This incapacity dogs large sections of a global left seemingly unable to do its own revolutionary histories any justice in the present.

These are both serious mistakes. The power of anticolonial national liberation war is not in any final decisive confrontation. There is rarely a final battle or a storming of the palace. It is about the incremental upending of colonial power's modalities of rule; its temporality is the long durée and it is never simply a question of material arithmetic. It is always about the opening of *political* possibility through overturning relations of force – it is as such a fundamentally different logic of war to genocidal colonial war.[10] But here we need to understand the particularity of colonial power to grasp the stakes. The most primary organising logic in colonial order is separation. This separation is not simply physical or spatial. It is ontological and psycho-affective. It is a separation between subject and object, between the living body and the 'body-things' around it.[11] Colonialism, then, takes the entangled intimacies, the dependencies on native bodies, labour, land, energies and presences, and transforms them into separations and a refusal of mutuality or any kind of commonness.

The exercise of colonial domination in turn is premised most fundamentally on the logic of *non-reciprocity*. It is an ability to wage constant penetrative violence into native society without the core of colonial life being touched, without any kind of response in kind. Its essence is not simply that it is raw and arbitrary, but that it is *untouchable*. This is how it dehumanises, because it refuses any kind of mutuality at the very point of intimacy, precisely where it intrudes deepest into bodily integrity. Essentially, in the tactile terms through which colonial power understands and imposes itself, it is the ability to touch and not be touched in return. In Algeria, it was precisely this logic that connected the systematic torture regime with the push to unveil Algerian women; both were understood as part of counter-insurgent and civilising practices that sought to touch the depth of the intimate interiorities of the indigenous – corporal, psychic, domestic, familial – from a position that foreclosed any touch in return.

Nadine Fraczkowski

In a settler order, this untouchability has to extend to the social body as a whole. The body of the settler and the settler body politic are co-constituted in the violence of immunisation. And what we can think of as the settler social contract is built precisely on this (non)relation: a core of settler good life in the interior that remains untouched even as the elastic colonial frontier is a space of total violence and ruination. Gaza as a concentration camp of dispossessed refugees that can be killed at will is the unsaid condition of Tel Aviv as the laid-back global city of Bauhaus architecture and night life. But the structure only works if the regime of violence is unquestionable and unconditional.

This unconditional non-reciprocity is why for colonial order, every act of resistance, armed or not, is experienced as violent. Because every act of resistance questions this divide between the untouchable super-human and the disposable sub-human (in Fanon's terms, it mutually humanises). Colonial violence, in turn, always has to be entirely excessive. All the wrangling about proportionality by people still invested in international law misses the point entirely. When challenged, colonial power has no choice but to be totally disproportionate. It *has* to carpet bomb neighbourhoods. Not for any military reason, but because it has to constantly strive to re-establish non-reciprocity. This is why the Israeli state understands the restoring of deterrence as an exercise in destruction. It measures its political achievements in scales of rubble. It expresses its political aesthetic in the dissemination of almost sublime images of ruination. 'Gaza' as a lesson in total obliteration has to be mediatised and displayed on every screen. The scale and reach of destruction has to be so severe, so total, and so visible that it reimposes the fact of the untouchability of the colonial sovereign in the very consciousness of the objects of its violence. The declared aim of many of Israel's bombing campaigns in Gaza of 'restoring quiet' is exactly a euphemism for this non-reciprocity – the periods of 'quiet' are when the colonial state can kill, imprison, dispossess and displace at will without riposte, without relations in kind.

The last twenty years of struggle have challenged this logic, even upended it in places. What has been achieved in Gaza alone has been immense. A refugee people driven from their homes, encamped, militarily occupied for decades and entirely besieged in a tiny strip of flat coastal land without a single mountain or valley, without jungle or forest, and pummeled routinely from the air, have been able to puncture the skies and subterranean depths of a nuclear-armed garrison state. In a very real way, Gaza has in moments reversed the logic of the siege. They have taken the very munitions dropped on their homes and turned them into a capacity for indigenous weapons-making and self-defense – when some say that in anticolonial struggle 'every bullet is a bullet returned', in Gaza this is meant quite literally. In other words, they have institutionalised a base of cumulative indigenous knowledge and organisational capacity. When in the early days of the siege, the resistance factions fired rockets that were by all accounts dubbed 'primitive,' people rushed to point out that this did not warrant the intensity of the Israeli bombardment, that the rockets were effectively a kind of 'fireworks' and best understood as 'symbolic'. This missed the point. The colonial regime understood it much more clearly: even the smallest prospect of an indigenous capacity to develop military technology, no matter how 'primitive', is a threat to the logic of non-reciprocity.

These are the capacities defining the terms of battle today. Penned in entirely by an almost total blockade on all sides and without a single inch of territorial depth or rear supply lines, the Palestinian resistance has nonetheless developed an ability to confront and repel the armoured invading columns of one of the most equipped and ruthless armies in the world, over months of warfare. It is hard to find any historical precedent for what the resistance in Gaza has so far withstood and achieved. The Algerians had their supply lines through Bourguiba's Tunisia and the Atlas Mountains of the interior; the Vietnamese had Maoist China and Cambodia and acres of dense jungle. The Palestinians in Gaza have no territorial rear depth at all but their own resilience and ingenuity. Regardless of what happens, it is unquestionable to my mind that the battles waged against this genocide will eventually be recognised historically up there with the great feats of anticolonial history, with the battle at Dien Bien Phu or, for that matter, with the Battle of Bint Jbeil in the 2006 War in Lebanon, even if we still don't quite have the language to talk about it as such.

Yet there is no final battle here. No analogue to the fall of Saigon or the storming of Santa Clara is on the horizon. Palestinians can never muster anywhere near the magnitudes of violence the colonial state has at its disposal. But what they can do is refuse the order of colonial non-reciprocity. They can open and make time in a war of national liberation that denies the settler order its transition beyond the impasse. And here it bears reminding that the bedrock of any war of national liberation is ordinary people's capacity to keep rejecting the terms of defeat and insisting on life at all costs. This insistence is there in the mother who buries her dead child in a mass grave and in the same moment declares that she won't be moving anywhere; it's there in the image of a young man pulled out from the rubble, face barely discernible under the grey cover of dust, taken out on a stretcher, who somehow finds the strength to sit up and throw up a victory sign; it's there in the doctors who refuse to leave their patients even as inevitable death encroaches; it's there in the elderly man who returns to inhabit the ruin of his home in a makeshift tarp tent so that he can search for the bodies of his children and grandchildren beneath the rubble. In the spring of 2024, the Israeli army re-invaded areas in the north of Gaza it had claimed it had cleared *not* because the resistance factions remained standing, but primarily because people insisted on returning to inhabit the ruins. This insistence on habitable life and its ordinary rhythms – that is, the refusal of the wasteland Zionism has always sought to engender in/as Palestine – is the basis of the broader challenge to the settler regime. There's nothing to romanticise in this; the point is not to fold it into some image of sacrificial heroism. We know better than most that images of selfless muscular armed insurgency are deficient. They've let us down before. The grief is immeasurable, and nothing can fold it back onto a symbolic plane. But to remove this grief from the temporality of a war of liberation is to remove it from political meaning entirely, to render it in the only language liberalism will allow: a strictly personal injury. Palestinian political community, by contrast, has always – out of sheer necessity but with political effects – hinged on its capacity to turn grief into defiance.[12]

These are forms of struggle entirely illegible to most of the liberal-left in the west. And yet so much of the contemporary advocacy for Palestine remains premised on the notion that the Palestinian struggle for liberation will succeed if only we appeal to certain conventions of recognition or legitimacy in the west. This misreading should have been the first victim of this genocidal war. The issue is not *how* we make or articulate our demands for freedom; it is that the very demand for Palestinian freedom is fundamentally objectionable.[13] There are no politics of persuasion that will change that. Even in our mass death, our humanity is denied; even as nameless numbers, we are subject to suspicion. This humanity is constitutively exclusive of us and always has been. It is not simply that our life is valued differently, but that it is in fact incommensurate with value entirely. There are no performances of racial innocence, no choruses of condemnation that are going to buy membership into the club. At best, the liberal-left formation in the west might see Palestinians as righteous victims, but never as historical actors capable of and justified in waging a war of national liberation. The allies we have won, we have won not by appealing for recognition, but by refusing to roll over and die, by situating our struggle, and that struggle's principles, within the global histories and inheritances of revolutionary anticolonialism.

None of this is to skirt over the questions of the ethical limits of anticolonial violence. Nor to imply that these limits haven't been breached in the history of Palestinian anticolonialism, or indeed that they weren't breached in the al-Aqsa Flood operation on October 7th. Less still that these breaches should not be reckoned with and criticised. Palestinians have long thought about and grappled with these questions, not as an exercise in publicity, but as part of their own political dialogue. Because nowhere do the colonised owe these limits to their colonisers, or the editors of western journals, or the mythic object that is the international community. The colonised owe it to themselves, and only to themselves; they owe it to the horizons of futurity and cohabitation their struggle will perform, to the world their children will inherit.

Fanon's plea at the end of *The Wretched of the Earth* to '...leave this Europe which never stops talking of man yet massacres him at every one of its street corners, at every corner of the world',[14] has never been more urgent. It has also never been more achievable. Israel is the regional outpost of an imperial order that is reeling. Yemen, one of the poorest countries on earth, moves oceans and defies empires to join the struggle. South Africa turns international law on its head, breaching the unspoken colonial boundaries around the charge of genocide.[15] But more still, millions of people globally are interpellated by the genocidal violence in Gaza; millions are called out by and recognise themselves in it. They look at Gaza and see not just a hundred years of colonisation in Palestine, but the last five hundred years of Euro-American racial colonial domination. The campaign in Gaza is like a condensed restaging of every colonial war in history, bearing every hallmark: the pummeling of dispossessed and besieged peoples by an overwhelming military power in the name of self-defense and 'western civilisation and values;' the demonology and language of savagery, zoology and bestiality; the devaluation of life in racial taxonomies that actively produce disposability as the condition of value elsewhere; the presentism and the refusal of any claims of a historical past or historical injustice. All of these are immediately recognisable to millions of people in the world, not simply as the persistence of a common past and history but also as the ominous sign of an imminent future on a warming planet that we are again being told is 'overpopulated'.

Nadine Fraczkowski

Palestine, in this sense, is the living archive of our future. But it is also the name of a renewed planetary consciousness. It has been the cause for the largest global student movement in generations, the biggest manifestations of left internationalism the west has seen in decades, and probably the largest mobilisations of Jewish anti-Zionist activism America has ever seen. These gains have not been won despite Palestine's war of liberation but *because* of it; without the challenge of Palestine's anticolonialism, without the ability to upend the colonial logic of rule and refuse the entire imperial arrangement, all of this would be a moot point. None of the diplomatic, legal or ideological gains would have been made without the armed struggle ensuring there was still something on the ground worth fighting for.

This too is Zionism's impasse. Its utter dependence on imperial patronage has never been clearer. But so too has its function as both moral-ideological and geopolitical-military pillar of a crumbling US-dominated imperial capitalist order, and the genocidal extent to which that order will go to keep that function operative. The stakes of the conjuncture, then, are global and could not be bigger – Palestine is everywhere because it names a political subject of radical universal emancipation.[16] If Zionism has come to stand in for the 'rights' of settler colonialism and ethnonationalism *everywhere*, that is for the rights to close any kind of reckoning with ongoing colonial injustice and dispossessive violence anywhere in the world, then Palestine's war of liberation today carries the anticolonial idea globally. If Zionism has become one of the points that brings together (and exposes the deep elective affinities between) late liberalism and late fascism, then Palestine carries the task of not just renewing the common heritage of the left's revolutionary history where no one else will, but also bringing it into lived time, into the 'time of initiative'. It is at once an awful and beautiful weight to carry.

Nasser Abourahme is a writer and teacher, and currently Assistant Professor of Middle Eastern and North African Studies at Bowdoin College.

Notes

1. Frantz Fanon, *The Wretched of the Earth*, trans. Richard Philcox (New York: Grove Press, 2004), 40.
2. Mahmoud Darwish, *Memory for Forgetfulness*, trans. Ibrahim Muhawi (Berkeley: UC Press, 1995), 11.
3. Joseph Massad, 'Why Israel's savagery is a sign of its impending defeat', *Middle East Eye*, 16 April 2024.
4. Martin Shaw, 'Palestine in international historical perspective on genocide', *Holy Land Studies* 9:1 (2010): 1–24.
5. *al-Jazeera*, 'Civilians sheltering inside a Gaza school killed execution-style,' 13 Dec 2023, https://www.al-jazeera.com/program/newsfeed/2023/12/13/civilians-sheltering-inside-a-gaza-school-killed-execution.
6. Seraj Assi, 'Israel's horrific massacre at Gaza's largest hospital', *Jacobin*, 3 April 2024.
7. Forensic Architecture, 'Attacks on aid in Gaza: Preliminary findings', 4 April 2024, https://forensic-architecture.org/investigation/attacks-on-aid-in-gaza-preliminary-findings.
8. Mouin Rabbani, 'Israel mows the lawn,' *London Review of Books*, Vol. 36 No. 15, 31 July 2014.
9. Samera Esmeir, 'To say and think a life beyond what settler colonialism has made', *Mada Masr*, 14 October 2023, https://www.madamasr.com/en/2023/10/14/opinion/u/to-say-and-think-a-life-beyond-what-settler-colonialism-has-made/.
10. Bikrum Gill, 'Two logics of war: Liberation against genocide', *Ebb* Issue 1, January 2024.
11. Achille Mbembe, 'The society of enmity', *Radical Philosophy* 200, Nov/Dec 2016, 25.
12. Abdaljawad Omar, 'Can the Palestinian mourn?' *Rusted Radishes*, 14 December 2023, https://www.rustedradishes.com/can-the-palestinian-mourn/.
13. Steven Salaita, 'Down with the Zionist entity; long live the "Zionist entity"', 23 May 2024, https://stevesalaita.com/down-with-the-zionist-entity-long-live-the-zionist-entity/.
14. Fanon, *The Wretched*, 235.
15. Darryl Li, 'The charge of genocide', *Dissent*, 18 January 2024, https://www.dissentmagazine.org/online_articles/the-charge-of-genocide/.
16. Jodi Dean, 'Palestine speaks for everyone', *Verso Blog*, 9 April 2024, https://www.versobooks.com/blogs/news/palestine-speaks-for-everyone.

Against singularity
Palestine as symptom and cause

Sami Khatib

A symptom is usually understood as something indicative of a cause, be it in the realm of medicine or ideology. Unlike in linear causal reasoning, however, a symptom cannot be derived from an assumed cause; rather, a cause needs to be constructed 'backwards' from the significance of 'its' symptom. In the realm of ideology, a symptom designates the point where ideological speech contradicts itself. The underlying hypothesis of this article is that the question of Palestine functions as the 'world community's' symptom: it marks the point where this community reveals itself as exclusive, limited, essentially Western, exposing the hypocrisy and function of its current ideology, the 'Human Rights Discourse' (HRD).[1]

This terminology and acronym (HRD) follows Robert Meister's take in *After Evil: A Politics of Human Rights,* (2011). HRD refers to a set of practices and beliefs that gained ideological traction in a US-led post-Cold War world. Meister holds 'that the present political character of Human Rights Discourse is distinct from the broader concept of human rights associated with 1789, which was the topic of debate and struggle between the revolutionary and counterrevolutionary movements of the nineteenth and twentieth centuries … The post-1989 politics of human rights is not meant to be contested in the same *political* way as its predecessor – rather, it presents itself as an *ethical* transcendence of the politics of revolution and counterrevolution that together produced the horrors of the twentieth century – Nazism and communism … Today the invocation of human rights is often part of a political project fundamentally at odds with the revolutionary struggles based on human rights: it is the war cry of a self-described "international community" led by the victors in the cold war' (2011, 7).

In psychoanalysis, a symptom signals the return of the repressed. However, for the symptom, the return is original, it cannot directly be deduced from that which has been repressed. Rather, the symptom, although temporally posterior, is the starting point to construct what has been repressed 'in the first place'. Repression is an unconscious process, and it is only by virtue of a retroactive logic that the repressed reveals its meaning belatedly through its 'return' in the form of symptoms. In other words, the repressed cannot be properly disentangled from its distorted return and symptoms.[2] To gain a conscious knowledge of symptom formation, a psychoanalytic working-through is necessary.

In discourse and ideology, symptoms are even more difficult to discern. If the 'unconscious is structured like a language',[3] as Lacan famously phrased his take on Freud, language is the site of both unconscious repression and its symptoms. As Žižek argues with Marx and Lacan, a 'symptomatic' reading of ideology 'consists in detecting a point of breakdown *heterogeneous* to a given ideological field and at the same time *necessary* for that field to achieve its closure, its accomplished form.'[4] The task for a critique of HRD is thus twofold: identifying the elements that both *undermine* and *stabilise* the consistency of its ideological field and speech acts.

In its persistence and return, the Palestinian question can be read as such an element. My argument is that the Palestinian question, despite being often articulated in the language of humanitarianism, signals the breaking point of the entire ideological field of humanitarianism and the fantasy of 'conflict management', exceeding the depoliticising language of HRD and introducing an antagonistic *political* dimension heterogeneous to 'humanitarian' crisis responses. Recalling humanitarianism's repressed, the Palestinian question is articulated from a non-identitarian position that remains non-assimilable in the current world order. An answer to the Palestinian question thus necessitates a change of this order.

The attacks of 7 October 2023 happened at a time when Israel, the US and their allies thought they had moved beyond the Palestinian question, relegating it to the status of a necropolitical management of contained space under Israeli sovereignty. This type of conflict management failed. Palestine as a signifier of political struggle and liberation is back on the centre stage of global politics. Conducting a war of annihilation in the Gaza strip and committing unprecedented massacres against its population, Israel is creating a reality that will not allow a return to the status quo ante. In their circulation of ideological content, Israel, the US and their allies acknowledge this reality (there is no way back), yet at the same time, disavow this knowledge when referring to plans for the future administration of the territory (or, what will have been left of it to govern).

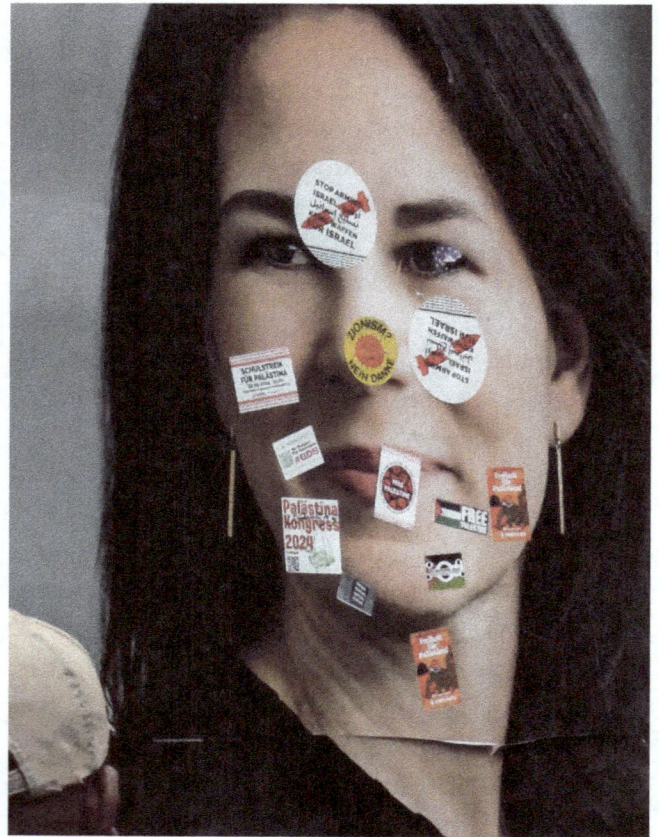

Probably the most indicative utterance of this disavowing knowledge is that of the compulsive pseudo-question: 'Do you condemn Hamas?'[5] Those who act out by repeating this question already know that the addressee does not conform to the questioner's worldview. The rationale of this pseudo-question is thus paradoxical: it only accepts a yes, yet knows that a yes is either a lie or tautological. As a question, it cancels itself out. Instead, it pronounces an ideological interpellation: do you support the Western world order, its ruling ideology (HRD), and do you condemn the entire spectrum of Palestinian resistance, from peaceful boycotts to the Hamas attacks of 7 October? Palestinians should accept their colonial subjugation, should not resist, and should, ideally, disappear and with them the annoyance of the Palestinian question.

Human Rights Discourse as counter-revolution

In *After Evil: A Politics of Human Rights*, Robert Meister formulated a groundbreaking critique of the post-1989 Human Rights Discourse. While HRD consists in declaring a new 'post-ideological' age that 'would repudiate past violence ... by endorsing exceptional violence – that of rescue and occupation', the 'old' Holocaust functions as the foundational crime of this new age.[6] The project and mission of preventing the return of such exceptional violence would necessitate granting the self-declared survivor and victim-state, the state of Israel, impunity and constitutive exemption from international law.

Explaining the blatant mismatch of Israel's human rights abuses against Palestinians and neighbouring populations, and Israel's self-image as an endangered 'victim-state', Meister contends:

> In post-Holocaust debates about human rights the violence that Israel uses to defend itself has become a laboratory for the violence that the 'world community' (and especially the U.S.) would be obliged to use in protecting an Israel that could not defend itself. The post-Holocaust security of Israel thus stands as the constitutive *exception* on which twenty-first-century humanitarianism is based.[7]

The phrase 'constitutive exception' points to the nexus of what is considered 'normal' (systemic) state violence, on the one hand, and its 'exceptional' (sovereign, colonial or otherwise) extreme, on the other. Today, Israel does not only function as a techno-scientific laboratory for exceptional state violence and its 'live' enforcement, but also as the ideological test site for the fabrication of justifications for the latter. In this way, the 'world's most moral army' produces and reproduces the 'ethics' of the 'justified' killing of unprotected civilians. Within this 'humanitarian' battle zone, Palestinians, civilians and fighters alike are not only the physical but also the ideological target.

Walter Benjamin, writing in 1940, stated that in modern states the 'state of emergency' [*Ausnahmezustand*, or 'state of exception'] is not the exception but the rule.'[8] Already in pre-Holocaust Europe there was no excuse for the moralising astonishment that exceptional acts of state violence are 'still' possible in the twentieth century. Rule and exception are internally interrelated in the sense that the exception constitutes, produces and tests out the 'normal' functioning of rule-conforming violence. Following Meister's argument, in the exceptional case of the state of Israel, its victims, although ultimately contingent, also function as the 'necessary exception' to justify the 'normal' legitimised use of Western state violence, be it 'peacekeeping' or 'peacemaking', military invasion, 'war on terror' or suspension of basic human rights in the name of state security. In this way, the 'world community' becomes the beneficiary of its own declared 'humanitarian' mission and 'responsibility to protect potential victims of another Holocaust'.[9]

Following Meister's argument, in the case of systemic state violence, triadic relations of *perpetrators*, *victims* and *beneficiaries* are neither symmetric nor reciprocal. Beneficiaries can enjoy their gains in the spatial absence of perpetrators while condemning their deeds; the victims of structural violence (class, race, gender) can be offered compassion and charity while maintaining structures of injustice, exploitation and submission. The 'world community' (that is, the West) casts its role of an ongoing beneficiary of past 'evil' (colonialism, imperialism, fascism, genocide) as the 'rescuer' of future victims of an imagined new genocide, while denying the existence of a real genocide as it currently unfolds in Gaza. Within the logic of HRD, the question of rescue and moral responsibility is only posed as long as beneficiaries of past evil are not addressed as such, implicated in current injustice, but as compassionate bystanders, acting on behalf of innocent victims, purified of all vengeance and spite.

> A beneficiary who bears witness to the innocence of past victims can thus conceive of himself as a would-have-been rescuer rather than a would-be perpetrator. The question for the human rights convert is always whether it is already too late to rescue, or still too soon. By agonizing over the question of his own potential guilt as a bystander, the witness to human suffering attempts to save his soul without necessarily relinquishing his position of advantage.[10]

Once a victim group is framed as terrorist or as an exponent of past evil (Palestinians as the new antisemites, as the reincarnation of Nazis), the responsibility to protect and rescue is inverted: protection becomes persecution, rescue becomes annihilation.

Meister's multi-layered argument, in consequence, can explain why the historically contingent victims of the state of Israel are necessarily framed as terrorist, barbaric and illegitimate as long as they insist on their fight for justice. Palestinians and their allies, voluntarily or not, by resisting Israel also resist the current world order of Western humanitarianism, which deems the struggle for justice and the age of revolution (roughly speaking 1789-1989) as 'past evil' – a presumably totalitarian cycle of violence and counter-violence that the post 1989 'world community' seeks to leave behind, buried in an 'evil past'. Those who resist HRD, seek violent revolution or fight against structural violence, regardless of their means of struggle, appear as the living anachronism of past evil (therefore 'terrorist'). In the current world order, the Palestinians and their allies are targeted for having failed to give up a presumably outdated, therefore terrorist and antisemitic cause. This is the meaning of 'Do you condemn Hamas?': renounce all forms of resistance, violent or non-violent, Islamist or otherwise. Current Western government policies of 'anti-antisemitism' are thus consistent with HRD.

Germany's Palestine problem

Anti-antisemitism is the ideological name of a discourse that demonises critics of the Israeli state.[11] In Germany this discourse takes shape in chiefly state-sponsored campaigns whose racist implications are particularly extreme.[12] Endorsing a politically motivated redefinition of antisemitism[13] according to which criticism of Israeli state action can be labelled antisemitic, German media and politicians have become one of the key actors in granting Israel impunity. While Germany casts its global role as humanitarian, liberal and cosmopolitan, it maintains its position as ongoing beneficiary of past evil (the Holocaust), economically, politically, culturally and morally. Since official Germany is *past evil*, that is past-antisemitic, the *current* agents of past evil (antisemitism, revolutionary violence, or both) can be condemned in the figure of the Palestinian and Palestine solidarity movements. In this way, current Palestinians become the externalised figure of Germany's antisemitic past – and present.

Coming to terms with this twisted logic, one could speak of a quasi-transcendental anti-Palestinian sentiment in Germany. It presents a key element of what A. Dirk Moses called 'The German Catechism'[14] – a set of beliefs that underpins the German public discourse, embedded in an increasingly state-run 'memory culture' that under the watchword 'Never again' claims to have drawn the correct political, cultural and affective lessons from the Holocaust. The concluding dogma of this catechism holds that antizionism equals antisemitism, avowing unconditional support for the state of Israel.[15] This 'catechism' does not only apply to mainstream political discourse but also structurally organises who can speak and whose voices are heard where and under what conditions in public debates.[16] In a post-migrant society like Germany, this discursive gatekeeping amounts to back-door racial profiling: people from non-German backgrounds are expected to learn and get used to this 'catechism' and its specifically anti-Palestinian sentiment.[17] In effect, this 'catechism' manufactures consent to actions of the Israeli state and frames the construction of Palestinian identity under the premises of 'Israel-related antisemitism'. This can lead to the accusation that the very signifier of 'Palestine' (along with mentioning the word 'occupation') is perceived as antisemitic. A German newspaper even called the slogan 'Free Palestine' a contemporary version of the Nazi salute 'Heil Hitler'.[18] Such bizarre distortions are not accidental; they rely on a specifically German version of HRD that embraces a sort of 'redemptive' Zionism to atone for Germany's Nazi past. Seen through the lens of this redemption narrative, Germany's support of Zionism and an ethnocratically defined Israel ('Israel as a Jewish state') acquires a quasi-religious character. This critique chimes with Meister's critique of HRD as an essentially Christian or post-Christian belief system, derived from a Pauline logic of conversion.[19]

The credo of the anti-Palestinian sentiment in Germany is thus simple: the state that claims to speak in the name of those murdered in Germany's name cannot itself be a state of injustice. For if it were so, the calculation of moral reparation by the descendants of Germans from 1933 to 1945 would not add up. From the perspective of German *Staatsräson*[20] (reason of state), the unconditional support of the state of Israel, regardless of the mode of its existence, proves Germany's success in moral redemption and material reparation for the Holocaust. In this way, Israel's existence becomes the external embodiment of Germany's post-Holocaust moral goodness. Within this imaginary universe, Israel is not a real place but the narcissistic mirror image of Germany's goodness, which after the Cold War takes centre stage in the German version of HRD.[21] For such a mindset, it is inconceivable (both cognitively and emotionally) to imagine the state of Israel as a state actor of war crimes, systematic human rights abuses, apartheid policies or genocide.

Against such a *desired reality* one has to insist on a *historical reality* in which victims can become perpetrators and vice versa; at times they are both victim and perpetrator within one and the same space of history.[22] However, there is no symmetry, neither historical nor moral, between the two. The idea of pure victim and perpetrator identities and the grouping of people and their deeds into abstract collective identities, is among the most problematic legacies of the age of nation states. A common talking point of Israel's apologists is the forced emigration and violent expulsion of Jewish populations of Arab states after Israel's establishment in 1948. Heterogeneous groups of people are lumped together under abstract notions of 'Jew' and 'Arab' in order to be put into an equation with another group of people, that is non-Jewish Palestinians who lived in the land of Palestine prior to modern nation states. By way of *abstract equation*, the violent expulsion of around 750,000 Palestinians (*Nakba*) is not only rationalised but ex post legitimised – as if the violence against one abstractly defined group of people could somehow equalise the violence against the other. Such abstractions are an integral part of the violent rationale of modern 'nation-building'; it inherently creates, as Hannah Arendt already foresaw in 1951, the group of 'stateless people'.[23] Within this rationale of nation building, genocide becomes a thinkable reality, despite (or precisely because) of the Genocide Convention of

1948.[24] Once an ethno-national state project succeeds in defining itself as the representative and successor of an *exceptional* victim group, the acts of resistance against this state can be framed as illegitimate, terrorist or, in the case of Palestine, antisemitic.

The German discourse might be an extreme case; however, it is in tune with a general (post)historical shift. Enzo Traverso, echoing Meister, remarks that after 1989 the age of memory culture places the figure of the victim in the centre of its political imaginary:

> In the age of the victims, the Holocaust becomes the paradigm of Western memory, the foundation upon which the remembrance of other ancient or recent forms of violence and crimes should be built. Thus, the propensity emerges to reduce history to a binary confrontation between executors and victims.[25]

Such a binary, however, reduces the question of revolution and defeat to a depoliticised sequence of violence and counter-violence; it does not account for beneficiaries, structural injustice and failed revolutionary attempts at changing history. Past executors can thus be condemned as perpetrators while the current beneficiaries of past violence can enjoy their gains in an 'ethical' way. As depoliticised victims, the defeated of past revolutions can be memorialised without remembering the lost causes and dreams they fought for. As Traverso puts it, 'the memory of the Gulag erased that of revolution, the memory of the Holocaust replaced that of antifascism, and the memory of slavery eclipsed that of anticolonialism.'[26] In short, post-1989 memory culture comes down to a project of rethinking history without the negative dimension of antagonistic struggle. As a posthistorical ideology, it thus culminates in the self-congratulatory formula of today's HRD: the past is evil, but the evil is past.[27]

This project, however, only functions once memory culture is organised by the state or a quasi-state actor and politically linked to an officially assumed 'historical responsibility' that can speak *on behalf* of a historical victim group. In the case of the German state, this logic is particularly evident: German state actors, almost completely non-Jewish, speak on behalf of 'Jews'. Such ventriloquism only works once real Jewish people in their concrete difference and diversity are abstracted and transposed into an imaginary group of 'the Jews' who become the *object* of German state protection and assumed responsibility.[28]

The singularity-effect of Holocaust memory culture

This dehistoricised version of the past relies on a transformation of Holocaust memory culture in which historical specificity is substituted by ahistorical singularity. In Holocaust studies, the widely accepted criterion of historical singularity is 'uniqueness' and 'unprecedentedness'.[29] 'Unprecedentedness', however, is not a sufficient criterion for uniqueness as it leaves open which historical event can become a precedent for another.[30] And likewise, uniqueness is not singular; all historical events are unique as they are relational. In historical terms, singularity can hardly refer to the spatio-temporal singularity of the mere fact, but must aim at grasping the contexts and conditions of the constitution of these facts.[31]

As soon as we enter the realm of history, there are only mixed relations, mediations, combinations of new and old factors, whose historically singular constellation is not immune to structural repetition. Thus, the historical notion of singularity only comparatively makes sense, discriminating between more or less 'singular' historical events. As has been pointed out in Holocaust and Genocide Studies, historical scholarship thrives on its comparative capacity, on comparing historical events, structures and motivations. The work of comparing is not the one of equating; it preserves the status of the historical as context and does not level the individual event to the general concept. The qualitatively new, therefore singular, aspect of the Holocaust as a state-organised extermination programme consisted in a new combination of factors that, in retrospect, had their precursors in other, colonial, racist contexts of violence of capitalist modernity.[32] The current debate on the singularity of the Holocaust, however, seems to have moved beyond this historical meaning of singularity, lapsing into the misty realm of metaphysics and theology.[33]

Proponents of the singularity thesis usually bring forward the ideological self-referentiality of exterminatory antisemitism. The Nazis intended to kill the Jews *as* Jews, not for some profane gains; annihilation was perceived as an end in itself. The Nazis, while intentionally 'coining' the term in its racialised arbitrariness,[34] killed real people in the abstract name of the 'Jew', enacting a monstrous transformation of human to number, concrete life to abstract death, a 'multitude of "unpronounceable names"' into a 'master signifier'.[35] This is one of the specificities of the Holocaust as historical complex that exceeds the explanatory framework of genocide, if the latter is reduced to a positivist account of mass killings of victims in relation to an assumed intent of perpetrators. However, if one modifies the notion of genocide and acknowledges that psychopathological fantasies, conscious or not, are integral to the genocidal mindset and actions of perpetrators, the explanatory framework of genocide can be extended beyond the legalistic terminology of the Genocide Convention of 1948. A. Dirk Moses argues that genocidal end goals are often driven by the paranoid fantasy of 'permanent security'.[36] Perpetrators pre-emptively kill entire groups of people in the present in order to achieve guaranteed security in the future. The paranoid intention of 'self-defence' can yield similar effects as genocidal intent. Moses' criticism implicitly puts into question whether the assumed (ir)rationality of political ends provides a supra-historical standard of judgment for historical events. The discrimination of means and ends is itself a relational one, it does not designate an absolute separation.

Once the Holocaust is understood as an assumed end in itself – a self-referential hate crime, devoid of any further political or historical purposiveness – it can be singularised and separated from other 'generic' genocides like modern slavery during colonialism or the Rwandan genocide. The question, whether violent means (from 'accidental' genocide to 'collateral damage') can be clearly distinguished from their colonial or imperial ends, makes sense only for those who regard these ends, be their names power, profit, 'progress', or 'civilisation', as rational, at least in theory. However, even the basic dogma of bourgeois theories of violence according to which 'just ends can be attained by justified means, justified means used for just ends'[37] is not universally accepted. Therefore, for the victims of these teleologies of violence, the conceivability of an absolute distinction between violent means (colonial genocide) and violent end (Holocaust) cannot be assumed. If reason and unreason, rationality and irrationality, civilisation and barbarism, contain each other dialectically, the *Zivilisationsbruch,* 'rupture in civilization'[38] of the Holocaust appears as a rupture only from the *particular* perspective of the *false universality* of bourgeois commodity economy.[39] As argued by Horkheimer and Adorno, the 'dialectic of enlightenment' inherent in rational purposiveness indicates that Western rationality and irrationality, civilisation and barbarism, violence and peacefulness, are not external opposites. 'With the spread of the bourgeois commodity economy the dark horizon of myth is illuminated by the sun of calculating reason, beneath whose icy rays the seeds of the new barbarism are germinating.'[40]

Regardless of these objections, the singularity thesis has already created a political epistemology and reality. These consequences drive a general logic that Fredric Jameson, although in a different context, calls the 'singularity-effect'.[41] Without getting into the details of his intricate argument,[42] one could summarise it as a late postmodern strategy of dehistoricisation and decontexualisation. Jameson warns that 'the concept of singularity is itself a singular one, for it can have no general content, and is merely a designation for what resists all subsumption under abstract or universal categories'.[43] Jameson's term proves instructive when read with and against posthistorical tendencies within contemporary discourses on antisemitism and Holocaust memory culture.

It is consistent with the logic of the singularity-effect, if modern antisemitism is no longer understood as a *specific* form of racism in general, but as the name of a hate crime *sui generis* that, at least in principle, can be detached from its history in Christian anti-Judaism. For such a singularising theory of modern antisemitism, the historical relationship of antisemitism as *abstract worldview* and antisemitism as *concrete history*, ranging from hate crimes to genocide, appears, in the last instance, contingent.[44] The historical difference between religious and modern antisemitism, however, cannot be explained without the pseudo-scientific concept of race and modern racism since the nineteenth century. With the singularisation of antisemitism, these relations become reified and dehistoricised. As a result, the analytical difference between antisemitism and racism is transformed into an absolute one. While in singular antisemitism the abstract concept seems to coincide with its own concretion (the antisemitic phantasma of the Jew is abstract and, in its abstractness, still addressed to concrete people), in 'non-singular' racism only the merely conceptual abstraction remains. In this way, any concept of racism that does not also include antisemitism disintegrates into the abstract concept of its own theory on the one hand, and the concrete experience of its historical phenomena on the other. In contrast to racism and its conceptual challenges to account for *particularity* and *universality*, antisemitism becomes the theory of its own *singularity* and, accordingly, the singular source of its own definition. Conversely, as soon as racism as *really existing concept* can no longer be addressed in reality, only particular anti-X-racisms remain (anti-black, anti-Arab, anti-Muslim), which tend to get singularised and ontologised.[45] As a consequence, the general term of racism enters into competition with antisemitism and is increasingly addressed as an abstract particularity devoid of universal meaning and concrete reality. Against this singularising tendency, one should insist with Etienne Balibar that

> a general category of racism is not an abstraction which runs the risk of losing in historical precision and pertinence what it gains in universality; it is, rather, a more concrete notion of taking into account the necessary polymorphism of racism, its overarching function, its connections with the whole set of practices of social normalization and exclusion...[46]

Such a concept of racism, in which concreteness is mediated with universality, could counteract the singularity-effect of competing definitions of antisemitism and also refrain from making its 'irrationality becoming its own cause'. How then to avoid, as Balibar puts it, 'the exceptional character of Nazi anti-Semitism turning into a sacred mystery, into a speculative vision of history which represents history precisely as the history of Evil'?[47] If one only changes its preferred victim group, historical event or main protagonist, one is certainly doomed to repeat the logic of this singularity-effect.

In terms of Holocaust memory culture, the singularity-effect has a retroactive direction, originating in more recent and contemporary debates rather than in the historical aftermath of the event. As a historical event, the extermination of the European Jews during the Second World War was the paradigmatic case that led to the Genocide Convention in 1948, although the concept dates back to the genocide of the Armenians in the Ottoman Empire during the First World War. In both cases, their historical singularity and universal significance as crime against humanity for world politics were intrinsically connected. In the case of the Holocaust memory culture, however, particularly since the advent of HRD in post-1989 Europe and North America, universal significance and historical singularity parted ways. As a result, it is possible today to speak of genocides in the plural – regardless of their status under international law – and *the* Holocaust as genocide sui generis in the sense of a singular 'radical evil'.[48] Accordingly, the universal significance of the Holocaust for human history can appear only in an ahistorical horizon of singularity as supra-historical or metaphysical uniqueness.

The subsequent stages of this singularity-effect are well known: the singularisation of the victim collective of the Holocaust was followed by the singularisation of the state that claims to speak in its name. At the end of this chain, we arrive at a singular situation: blatant violations of international law, which otherwise other state actors are blamed for, are not only *not* sanctioned, but appear as the necessary consequence of the unique morality of the state of Israel and its 'most moral army'. The morality of these violent relations is grounded here in the singular security needs of a singular state that claims to speak on behalf of a singular group of victims and their descendants. The latest edition of this singularity-effect even frames the Hamas attacks of October 7th as Holocaust-like pogroms, expressions of a singular antisemitic mindset, as leading Israeli politicians and their Western allies keep telling the world. In a bizarre moment during his speech at the UN Security Council in late October 2023, Israel's UN ambassador, Gilad Erdan, wore a badge shaped like a yellow star on his suit, referring to the notorious yellow star that German authorities forced Jewish people to wear during the Holocaust. Eventually, the singularity-effect comes full circle: tautology meets obscenity.

Palestine as universal cause

I have argued that the question of Palestine is a symptom that marks the breaking point of the ideological edifice of HRD and its supplementing discourses of anti-antisemitism, memory culture and singularisation. The Palestinian struggle does not seek the world community's recognition as a singular, higher-ranked victim group, singularised by the ontological valence of their actual or inherited experience of violence. Rather, it exposes the hypocrisy of a moralised version of realpolitik in which Western beneficiaries can enjoy their gains in an 'ethical' way by reaching out to depoliticised 'innocent' victims and persecuting victims that keep on fighting for their rights. From a Palestinian perspective of struggle, international humanitarianism, its major players, perpetrators and beneficiaries, reveal themselves as the 'ethical' successor of the old evil, the counter-revolutionary project that fights those who fight for their own and their neighbour's justice.

While exposing the 'exceptional' violence of rescue and occupation, the Palestinian struggle exceeds the imaginary of humanitarian politics in post-humanitarian times. It cannot be given a proper place within the ideological fantasy of the non-existing 'two state solution' and conflict management plans that the beneficiaries of HRD have drafted. Of course, the Palestinian cause can be defeated militarily. Pankaj Mishra might be right that '[p]erhaps Israel, with its survivalist psychosis, is not the "bitter relic" George Steiner called it – rather, it is the portent of the future of a bankrupt and exhausted world.'[49] However, while 'Israel today is dynamiting the edifice of global norms built after 1945',[50] the Palestinian cause is not the agent of edifying a new system of international relation within global 'too late capitalism'.[51] As a universal cause, understood and supported globally, the Palestinian struggle reaches beyond the imaginary of institutionalised forms of global injustice and undermines the singularity-effect that grants Israel and its policies impunity.

Calling out anti-Palestinian racism and the atrocities of the genocidal war in Gaza is thus not simply a demand for ending the hypocrisy of HRD; rather, it is part of the critical project of *exposing* and *undoing* global capitalism's teleologies of violence. The Palestinian struggle has shown that ultimately the singularised teleology of Zionism (the creation of a 'Jewish state') is not so different from 'generic' colonial or imperialist teleologies of power, profit, 'progress', or 'civilisation'. As a symptom, the Palestinian question has opened a rift between Zionist means and ends, exposing a fragility at the heart of Zionist goal setting.

Although Israel is the only sovereign state actor in the area of former Mandate Palestine ('from the river to the sea'), Zionism is not a sovereign project of its own.

It relies on Palestinian-ness as oppressed and repressed. The disavowal and implicit affirmation of this dependency is spelled out in the Zionist claim that 'there are no Palestinians'. While the last horizon of the Zionist imaginary is a life without the neighbour, 'the last sky' of that neighbour escapes this horizon: Palestinians have always belonged and will belong to the land (rather than claiming that the land is theirs as property).[52] This Israeli fragility might express itself in paranoid extinction fantasies and biblical tropes. For as long as Palestinians are existing and resisting, Israel faces the impossibility of its Zionist project.[53] In this way, the question of Palestine marks the symptom in the sense defined above: while it spoils the spoils of Zionist land theft, its removal would threaten all of its so far achieved, yet unaccomplished goals. This conjuncture, however, does not imply its reverse: Palestinian-ness does not rely on Zionism. Rather, Palestinian-ness and the Palestinian struggle introduce an element of asymmetry and unsublatable negativity into the logic of the return of the repressed (genocidal violence) and its symptom (the Palestinian question). The answer to the Palestinian question is thus not to be found in the compulsive repetition of worn-out answers of HRD but in changing the question: What are the universal conditions of possibility for the particular, Palestinian, emancipation? Unlike bourgeois teleologies of violence, the Palestinian revolution is not a goal of capitalist 'progress' but the latter's frequently miscarried, ultimately achieved, interruption.

Sami Khatib is a founding member of the Beirut Institute for Critical Analysis and Research (BICAR). He is author of Teleologie ohne Endzweck: Walter Benjamins Ent-stellung des Messianischen *(2013).*

Notes

1. The author would like to thank Salma Shamel, Lilly Markaki and members of the *Radical Philosophy* editorial collective for their comments on an earlier draft of this article.
2. Cf. Jean Laplanche and Jean-Bertrand Pontalis, *The Language of Psychoanalysis* (London: Hogarth, 1973; Karnac, 1988), 398–99 and 446.
3. Jacques Lacan, 'Television', trans. Denis Hollier, Rosalind Krauss and Annette Michelson, *October* 40 (1987): 7–50, 24.
4. Slavoj Žižek, *Sublime Object of Ideology* (London: Verso, 1989), 16. Regarding Žižek's own, probably disavowed, belief in Western liberalism, as demonstrated in his incoherent remarks on Palestine and Israel after October 7, 2023, see Jamil Khader's opinion piece in Al Jazeera, 17 Dec 2023, 'Do you condemn Žižek?', https://www.aljazeera.com/opinions/2023/12/17/do-you-condemn-zizek . Khader's critique is right to insist that 'Despite his ambivalent position on the Palestinian genocide, Žižek should not be dismissed as an irrelevant thinker. After all, the core truths of many philosophies exist beyond the biographies of their authors.'
5. Questions of this kind are not new but testify to the persistence of an Orientalist, racist framing of Palestinians as terrorists. In academic discourse, even Edward Said was asked such questions, cf. Edward Said, Peter Osborne and Anne Beezer, 'Edward Said: Orientalism and After', *Radical Philosophy* 63 (1993), 22–32: 'The first question to me … was: "When are the Palestinians going to stop terrorism?"' A more recent example can be found in the *CBS* interview with Husam Zomlot, Palestinian Ambassador to the United Kingdom, aired on 5 November 2023, https://www.cbsnews.com/news/husam-zomlot-palestinian-ambassador-to-the-united-kingdom-face-the-nation-transcript-11-05-2023/.
6. Meister, *After Evil*, IX.
7. Meister, *After Evil*, IX.
8. Walter Benjamin, 'On the Concept of History', in *Selected Writings*, ed. Marcus Bollock and Michael W. Jennings, Vol. 4 (Cambridge: Belknap Press of Harvard University Press, 2003), 392.
9. Meister, *After Evil*, IX.
10. Meister, *After Evil*, VIII.
11. For the global dimensions of this project see Gil Anidjar, 'When Killers Become Victims: Anti-Semitism and Its Critics',*Cosmopolis: A Review of Cosmopolitics* 3 (2007), 1–24. Its political epistemology is further explored in Elad Lapidot, *Jews Out of the Question: A Critique of anti-anti-Semitism* (Albany: State University of New York Press, 2020).
12. The 'Federal Government Commissioner for Jewish Life in Germany and the Fight against Antisemitism', Felix Klein, who has no legislative function, defines his mission as 'to raise awareness among the public and to encourage them to get involved in combating antisemitism, while also encouraging those who have so far remained silent to speak up when that is called for.' According to his definition of antisemitism and perception of political reality, '[a]ntisemitism today has returned with renewed strength. In Germany, Jews and people thought to be Jews are insulted, spit on and threatened in public, on social media, they face an absolute barrage of abuse. Antisemitism has become so obvious and visible that we need new strategies

to fight it', https://www.antisemitismusbeauftragter.de/Webs/BAS/EN/home/_documents/beauftragter.html. The results of such campaigning are already felt in the domains of culture, politics, education and the arts, overwhelmingly targeting non-German persons and projects. The website 'Archive of Silence', a crowdsourced archive documenting silenced voices in Germany, lists at least 157 cases since 7 October 2023 (as of 28 June, 2024) in which events were cancelled or persons disinvited under the pretext of 'fighting antisemitism'. The cancellations were enforced by state-sponsored as well as privately-run institutions. See: https://docs.google.com/spreadsheets/d/1Vq2tm-nopUy-xYZjkG-T9FyMC7ZqkAQG9S3mPWAYwHw/edit?gid=1227867224#gid=1227867224 and https://www.instagram.com/archive_of_silence/.

13. The widely used, yet scholarly disputed 'working definition' of the International Holocaust Remembrance Alliance (IHRA) relates the examples of application of its definition primarily to so-called 'Israel-related anti-Semitism' and therefore lends itself – intentionally or not – to delegitimising political criticism of Israeli state action as anti-Semitic, https://www.holocaustremembrance.com/de/resources/working-definitions-charters/arbeitsdefinition-von-antisemitismus.

14. A. Dirk Moses, 'The German Catechism', *Geschichte der Gegenwart*, 23 Mai 2021, https://geschichtedergegenwart.ch/the-german-catechism/print/.

15. The latest iteration of this policy manifests itself in a new legislation for migrants seeking German citizenship: applicants for naturalisation must declare 'Israel's right to exist' as part of a mandatory loyalty test for new citizens, cf. Haaretz, 26 June 2024, https://www.haaretz.com/world-news/2024-06-26/ty-article/report-new-german-citizenship-law-requires-applicants-to-declare-israel-right-to-exist/00000190-54ef-d31c-afb9-dcff82b40000.

16. The firing of the German-Palestinian journalist Nemi El-Hassan, who had worked for the German public TV station, demonstrated the limits of these conditions, cf. Hanno Hauenstein, 'Triumph of the BILD: Nemi El-Hassan's firing was just plain wrong', *Berliner Zeitung*, 4 October 2021, https://www.berliner-zeitung.de/en/triumph-of-the-bild-nemi-el-hassans-firing-was-just-plain-wrong-li.186770.

17. Esra Özyürek notes in *Subcontractors of Guilt: Holocaust Memory and Muslim Minority Belonging in Post-War Germany* (Stanford: Stanford University Press, 2023), that '[d]espite its commitment to antinationalism and antiracism, German memory culture failed to include members of society who are not ethnically German ... As a result, Muslim-background Germans could not be included in the postwar German social contract, through which a new and free (West) German society was allowed by the Allies to emerge on condition of having learned the correct lessons from the Holocaust.'

18. *Die Welt* podcast, 'Free Palestine ist das neue Heil Hitler', https://www.welt.de/podcasts/welt-talks/article248996436/Rapper-Ben-Salomo-Free-Palestine-ist-das-neue-Heil-Hitler.html?wtrid=socialmedia.socialflow....socialflow_twitter.

19. Meister, *After Evil*, 41–42: 'For those who claim to be *converted* by the events of Auschwitz or Hiroshima or both, new ways to save the innocent from a return to twentieth-century violence are not more of the same; instead, they are a way of bearing witness to the cyclicity of that violence so as to end it.' For German politicians, the claim that the Holocaust marks a biographical motivation to enter politics is a common trope. A well-known example is the former German foreign minister Heiko Maas ('I entered politics because of Auschwitz'), cf. Federal Foreign Office, 20 August 2018, https://www.auswaertiges-amt.de/de/service/laender/polen-node/maas-polen-auschwitz/2128686.

20. Cf. the speech of the former German Chancellor Angela Merkel to the Israeli Parliament on March 18, 2008, https://www.bundesregierung.de/breg-de/service/bulletin/rede-von-bundeskanzlerin-dr-angela-merkel-796170.

21. The psycho-political implications and underlying structure of desire of this imaginary relation to Israel have been explored further in Hannah C. Tzuberi, '"The Sun Does Not Shine, It Radiates": On National(ist) Mergings in German Philosemitic Imagery of Tel Aviv', in *The Future of the German-Jewish Past: Memory and the Question of Antisemitism*, ed. Gideon Reuveni and Diana Franklin (West Lafayette: Purdue University Press, 2020), 179–192.

22. Cf. Mahmood Mamdani, *When Victims Become Killers: Colonialism, Nativism, and the Genocide in Rwanda* (Princeton: Princeton University Press, 2001).

23. Hannah Arendt, *The Origins of Totalitarianism* (San Diego: Harvest and HBJ, 1951, 1973), 290: 'After the war it turned out that the Jewish question, which was considered the only insoluble one, was indeed solved – namely, by means of a colonized and then conquered territory – but this solved neither the problem of the minorities nor the stateless. On the contrary, like virtually all other events of our century, the solution of the Jewish question merely produced a new category of refugees, the Arabs, thereby increasing the number of the stateless and rightless by another 700,000 to 800,000 people. And what happened in Palestine within the smallest territory and in terms of hundreds of thousands was then repeated in India on a large scale involving many millions of people. Since the Peace Treaties of 1919 and 1920 the refugees and the stateless have attached themselves like a curse to all the newly established states on earth which were created in the image of the nation-state.'

24. The limitations and problems of this convention are discussed in detail in A. Dirk Moses, *The Problems of Genocide: Permanent Security and the Language of Transgression* (Cambridge: Cambridge University Press, 2021).

25. Enzo Traverso, *Left-Wing Melancholia: Marxism, History, and Memory* (New York: Columbia University Press 2016), 16.

26. Traverso, *Left-Wing Melancholia*, 10.

27. Cf. Meister, *After Evil*, 69.

28. In this context, it worth rereading the official denomination of Germany's commissioner for the fight against antisemtism: 'Federal Government Commissioner for Jewish Life in Germany and the Fight against Antisemitism.' The federal government commissioner is joined by local official antisemitism commissioners in 14 of Germany's 16 federal states, as Peter Kuras writes in his comprehensive report 'The Strange Logic of Germany's Antisemitism Bureaucrats', *Jewish Currents* (Spring 2023), https://jewishcurrents.org/the-strange-logic-of-germanys-antisemitism-bureaucrats. Kuras's report highlights the fact that 'some of the antisemitism commissioners have sought to burnish their authority by associating themselves with Jewishness', although most (if not all) are non-Jewish Germans. Such acts of patronising travesty can go as far as attempting to discipline Jewish Israelis to tone down their voices. In this vein, as Kuras reports, Federal Government Commissioner Felix Klein 'told the *Berliner Zeitung* in a January 2021 interview that "tendentially left-leaning Israelis in Berlin" should "be sensitive to Germany's special historical responsibility" when they criticize Israel.'

29. Cf. Steffen Klävers, *Decolonizing Auschwitz? Komparativ-postkoloniale Ansätze in der Holocaustforschung* (Berlin: de Gruyter, 2019), 17.

30. Yehuda Bauer, *Rethinking the Holocaust* (New Haven: Yale University Press, 2001), 20.

31. The differentiation into 'ordinary uniqueness', 'unique uniqueness' and 'transcending uniqueness' that Eckardt and Eckardt propose can be read as a symptomatic attempt at turning a tautology into a paradox. See Alice L. Eckardt and A. Roy Eckardt, 'The Holocaust and the Enigma of Uniqueness: A Philosophical Effort at Practical Clarification', *The Annals of the American Academy*, 450 (July 1980), 165–178). If one accepted this terminology, historically speaking only 'unique uniqueness' as a historical singularity makes sense; otherwise, one merely signifies the spatio-temporal uniqueness of all historical events, or slides into the metaphysical-theological language of a mystery that defies scientific investigation.

32. Cf. A. Dirk Moses, 'Colonialism' in *The Oxford Handbook of Holocaust Studies*, ed. Peter Hayes and John K. Roth (Oxford: Oxford University Press, 2010), 68–80.

33. An overview of current debates is provided by Klävers, *Decolonizing Auschwitz?* and the volume *Historiker Streiten*, eds. Susan Neiman and Michael Wildt (Berlin: Ullstein, Propyläen, 2022).

34. Recall the infamous dictum 'I determine who is a Jew', attributed to Nazi Reich Marshall Hermann Göring.

35. Cecile Winter, 'The Master-Signifier of the New Aryans: What Made the Word "Jew" into an Arm Brandished Against the Multitude of "Unpronounceable Names"', in Alain Badiou, *Polemics* (Verso, 2014).

36. Moses, *The Problems of Genocide*.

37. Walter Benjamin, 'Critique of Violence', *Selected Writings*, eds. Marcus Bullock and Michael W. Jennings. Vol. 1 (Cambridge, MA: Belknap Press of Harvard University Press), 236–252, 237. I have commented on this passage in 'Chapter 37: Society and Violence', *Sage Handbook of Frankfurt School Critical Theory*, Vol. 2, eds. Werner Bonefeld, Beverley Best, Chris O'Kane (Newbury Park: Sage, 2018), 607–624.

38. This is the title of Dan Diner's edited volume *Zivilisationsbruch: Denken nach Ausschwitz* (Frankfurt: Fischer, 1988).

39. Diner remarks: 'Only against the background of a largely secularized world view are the contours significant to the events of the Holocaust able to be depicted; in view of the Enlightenment permeating the Western worlds of life, including the forms of thought of Enlightenment philosophy, the Holocaust emerges as what it also was in view of such an advanced disenchantment: a breaking through of all levels of reason, a rupture of civilization.' See Diner, *Countering Memories: On the validity and impact of the Holocaust* (Göttingen: Vandenhoeck & Ruprecht, 2007), 104–105.

40. Max Horkheimer and Theodor W. Adorno, *Dialectic of Enlightenment: Philosophical Fragments*, trans. Edmund Jephcott (Stanford: Stanford University Press, 2002).

41. Fredric Jameson, 'The Aesthetics of Singularity', *New Left Review* 92 (March/April 2015), 122.

42. Cf. Sami Khatib, 'Singularitätseffekte', *Historiker Streiten*, eds. Susan Neiman and Michael Wildt (Berlin: Ullstein, Propyläen, 2022), 59–74.

43. Jameson, 'Aesthetics', 126.

44. The aporia of the missing link between practical and theoretical antisemitism was taken to its logical conclusion by Moishe Postone in his influential article 'Anti-Semitism and National Socialism', first published in *New German Critique* 19 (Winter 1980), *Special Issue 1: Germans and Jews*, 97–115, subsequently reworked and translated into German. The explanatory framework of how *antisemitism as abstract ideology*, rooted in the naturalising mindset of capitalist 'commodity fetishism' (Marx), relates to the *concrete history of modern antisemtism* relapses into a truism. In capitalist modernity, the 'fetishized form' of thought structurally underpins all kinds of worldviews. Hence the isomorphism of capitalist value and characteristics that Nazi antisemitism attributed to Jews (i.e. abstraction, invisibility, automation, impersonal domination) applies to all forms of thought that (mis)take a concrete form of appearance for a naturalised, personified, concretised essence. Postone cannot sufficiently explain why the Nazis actually 'naturalized and biologized' the 'abstract dimension of capital' in the figure of the Jew and not in a different figure. For such a theory, one would need to study the actual history of modern European and global antisemitism. Implicitly acknowledging this aporia, disciples of Postone have coined the term 'structural antisemitism', which applies to all critiques of modernity and capitalism that do not limit themselves to the critique of abstract relations of domination. See Lars Rensmann and Samuel Salzborn, 'Modern Antisemitism as Fetishized Anti-Capitalism: Moishe Postone's Theory and its Historical and Contemporary Relevance', *Antisemitism Studies* 5:1 (Spring 2021), 44–99, 81). Conveniently, the term can be mobilised to label any strand of anti-capitalism as 'antisemitic' once relations of capitalist domination are addressed in a concrete manner, pointing at real persons, companies or institutions. It is worth mentioning that one co-author of the cited reference, Samuel Salzborn, currently serves as the Berlin commissioner of antisemitism (see e.g. https://www.antisemitismusbeauftragter.de/Webs/BAS/DE/service/laenderbeauftragte/laenderbeauftragte.html).

45. An example might be the discourse of Afropessimism, which singularises anti-Blackness as derived from 'the singular structure of anti-Black violence'. Frank B. Wilderson III, *Afropessimism* (New York: W. W. Norton, 2020), 216. The crucial political question is whether anti-Blackness is a form of racism 'incommensurable with all other forms of social domination'. See Salma Shamel, with Gary Wilder, 'From Image to Flesh in a World Seen from the South: A Conversation with Gary Wilder', *Social Text* 158 (March 2024), 119.

46. Etienne Balibar, 'Racism and Nationalism', in Balibar and Immanuel Wallerstein, *Race, Nation, Class: Ambiguous Identities* [(London: Verso, 2011)], 49.

47. Balibar, 'Racism and Nationalism', 51.

48. Cf. Alain Badiou, *Ethics: An Essay on the Understanding of Evil*, trans. Peter Hallward (London: Verso, 2001), 62.

49. Pankaj Mishra, 'The Shoah after Gaza', *London Review of Books* 46:6 (21 March 2024), https://www.lrb.co.uk/the-paper/v46/n06/pankaj-mishra/the-shoah-after-gaza.

50. Mishra, 'The Shoah after Gaza'.

51. I borrow this apt term from Anna Kornbluh's title *Immediacy, or The Style of Too Late Capitalism* (London: Verso, 2024).

52. Cf. Peter Linebaugh, 'Palestine and the Commons: Or, Marx and the Musha'a', *CounterPunch*, 1 March 2024, https://www.counterpunch.org/2024/03/01/palestine-the-commons-or-marx-the-mushaa/. I owe this reference to Marwa Arsanios.

53. Jacqueline Rose notes that 'Herzl's projects for the creation of a Jewish state all crumbled on their own diplomatically fueled grandeur (kaiser, sultan, one imbroglio after another). But Herzl may also, in his magisterial failure, have been wise to something. Like the unconscious, Zionism had to be staged (as only a playwright might understand). Zionism was a conjuring act.' See Jacqueline Rose, *The Question of Zion* (Princeton: Princeton University Press, 2005), 67. Such a conjuring act first has to remove the traces of Palestinian-ness to feel 'safe' and become thinkable, at least on stage or in literature. For the latter see also Ghassan Kanafani, *On Zionist Literature*, trans. Mahmoud Najib (Oxford: Ebb Books, 2022), particularly chapter 7.

The urgency of anti-imperialist feminism
Lessons from Palestine
Walaa Alqaisiya

This war is a war that is not only between Israel and Hamas. It's a war that is intended, really, truly, to save the values of Western civilization [...] because we are here to defend the values of liberal societies, of LGBTQ which Hamas fights endlessly ...[1]

The Hamas rapist machine bears full moral responsibility for all the casualties in this war that it launched on October 7 and is waging inside and under schools, mosques, homes and UN facilities.[2]

Throughout its genocidal war on the occupied Gaza strip, Israel and its allies in the Western imperialist core have justified their actions by weaponising the plight of women and girls who have been 'systematically' violated by Hamas.[3] While Israel continues to deny access to independent investigators, making it impossible to verify these allegations,[4] 'October 7' has become a marker for unspeakable sexual violence, which the US President Joe Biden,[5] and Secretary of State Antony Blinken,[6] have respectively described as appalling and beyond belief. Israeli official representatives, such as Isaac Herzog and Eylon Levy quoted above, insist that Israel stands the ground of 'sav[ing] values of western civilisation,' while the 'Hamas rapist machine' is held entirely culpable ('bear[ing] full moral responsibility') for the slaughter waged on Gaza for the past several months. At the core of this moral value system defining Israel's right to fight those 'human animals'[7] and 'eliminate everything in Gaza,'[8] stands the protective duty towards women and LGBTQ people (encompassing the 'values of liberal societies'). In the context of addressing women's organisations and 'civilised nations,' the Israeli Prime Minister, Benjamin Netanyahu, urges them to fight uncompromisingly 'the barbarism that threatens to wash over the world'.[9]

When LGBTQ and feminist-liberal values end up playing a central role in enabling a genocidal war, it is imperative to revisit and interrogate the meanings and nature of feminism in a more radical philosophical manner. In this regard, the philosophical traditions of feminist decoloniality and Third World Marxism serve a twofold aim. First, they help to historicise the functionality of gender-/sex to the onto-epistemic foundations of Zionist settler colonialism, what I call the occupation of gender by genocidal means. Second, they advance an understanding of gender/sex in relation to the mode of social reproduction that Zionism requires and serves under US-led imperialism. During these times of wasting of Palestinian life, anti-imperialist feminism becomes a subject of intellectual and political urgency, gesturing towards alternative epistemes that have been buried beneath the social and conceptual categories abstracting away from the materiality of history. What are the limitations of a poststructuralist reading of sex/gender, when dealing (or not) with the question of national liberation and counterviolence of the oppressed in contexts such as Palestine, and the Arab region at large? The centring of the national question redefines the moral and political parameters shaping feminist and queer mobilisation and alludes to the value of historical inventiveness incarnated through revolutionary consciousness.

The occupation of gender by genocidal means

Western modernity draws a boundary between human versus non-human that concurs with the gendering processes under colonial capitalism. The work of decolonial feminist scholars, such as Sylvia Wynter and Maria Lugones,[10] historicises the emergence of 'gender' to substantiate the ideological and material cognates of European imperialism and capitalism. By identifying how European gender categories and values were imposed in the context of the Americas and the Caribbean, Lugones and Wynter[11] show how gender underscores the racialising logics of bourgeois 'Man' and thus cannot be isolated from the racial and class constituents of colonial capitalism. The to-be emancipated 'women' of the colonies have been embroiled within a political strategy of gendered recognition[12] that reproduces their material and historical proximity to bourgeois Men,[13] thereby reifying the onto-epistemic violence of colonial modernity. Such violence stems from conceptual terrains – for Lugones, 'the coloniality of being',[14] and for Wynter, 'colonial difference'[15] – that incarnate the social institution of capitalist modernity throughout the sixteenth century's racial longue-durée. Wynter examines the ontological distinction between 'natural masters' and 'natural slaves' that mandated the socio-economic and political order of Spaniards' 'expropriation of the indigenous peoples' lands and the enserfment of their lives/labour.'[16] Lugones identifies 'the process of active reduction of people, the dehumanisation that fits them for the classification, the process of subjectification, the attempt to turn the colonised into less than human beings.'[17]

Looking at the events that have been unfolding since the Zionist regime began its brutal onslaught on the Palestinian people in the Gaza strip, we see yet again how gender is used to draw the contours of settler colonial encroachment.[18] Gender as the property of colonial capitalism manifests in how Israeli settlers come to *occupy* the gendered/sexed subjectivities that bestow upon them the right to plant LGBT flags on scorched Indigenous land (see Figure 1). Their backers in the imperialist core mobilise the discourse of protecting 'our' (meaning: Israeli) women and girls from the perverse monstrosities of Muslim terrorist men,[19] their gendered vulnerability supposedly encapsulating the plight of humanity at large.[20] This is best captured in the declarations made by followers of the Hillary Clinton-style feminist personality cult, including the likes of Sheryl Sandberg who has claimed that the core concern at hand is 'not what is happening in the Middle East, but what is happening to our humanity'.[21] Sandberg means to convey that humanity itself is at stake and its restoration the task of those endowed with the natural right to act against Palestinian-waged terror. Such discourse on humanity generates and follows a conception of the human animated by a material and moral value system that benefits, in a Wynterian sense, the White Bourgeois Man. The defining principle of this moral system is the distinction it sets between the human and non-human animal (in the words of Israeli general, Yoav Gallant),[22] as well as new definitions of Nature, separating 'the garden' from 'the jungle' as Vice-President of the European Commission, Josep Borell, describes.[23] Both the 'animal' and the 'jungle' capture racialised projections of self and other construed in the very process of humanisation. The Native American, the African, the Arab and the Muslim need to be humanised (become 'Man') through colonialism's civilising mission.

In *The Birth of a Jungle*, Michael Lundblad develops a cultural analysis of the 'discourse of the jungle',[24] revealing how racialisation of animality imbricates classed, gendered and sexualised processes in the US at the turn of the twentieth century. Examining *Tarzan of the Apes* by Edgar Rice Burroughs, published in 1914, Lundblad shows that bourgeois white men are constructed as innately able to restrain their animality with reason and rationality.[25] Situating his analysis on the 'discourse of the humane' in relation to animals within the context of widespread lynching of black Americans, Lundblad reveals how 'animality is essentially elevated over blackness,' 'enabling white men to torture and vivisect black men, thus treating them worse than animals at the turn of the century.'[26] A Darwinist-Freudian conception of 'the savage' underlines the rewriting of blackness as wildness of Africans, conceiving of them as innately amoral and savage as opposed to white men who can take a stroll on the wild side, yet maintain their 'inherited instinct for chivalry.'[27] The Darwinist and Freudian analytical combination suggests that savagery of the black African in the jungle manifests in two main and interrelated aspects: first, the delight in cannibalism/torture and killing in the most hysterical manner;[28] and second, the delight in the rape of white women, which derives from the 'essentially instinctual nature of savages and the resulting inability, supposedly, to repress sexual instincts.'[29]

The mobilisation of a taxonomy analogous to the 'discourse of the jungle' has been at the core of this Zionist genocidal campaign, in which the category of the Arab-

Figure 1; https://twitter.com/Israel/status/1723971340825186754?lang=en.

Terrorist-Savage has been relied upon and reproduced to both trigger and enable the ongoing genocide. Israeli media describes a nation that remains 'shocked at the unrestrained murderous savagery that thousands of our neighbours unleashed upon us', the civilised garden.[30] While the alleged Hamas rapes classify as 'crimes against humanity',[31] they also mobilise a 'no moral equivalence' discourse in the face of those, including within the US political establishment (such as Representative Pramila Jayapal), who call for a more balanced approach to the conflict:

> There is no 'balanced approach' to a group that commits this type of barbarity. The only approach is their total elimination.[32]

Rape and sexual violence against Israeli women call for nothing less than unequivocal condemnation. Israel did not invade Palestinian homes and rape and sexually violate Palestinian women. Hamas did invade Israeli homes and did rape and sexually violate Israeli women. There is no 'balance' or 'both sides' or 'moral equivalence' here. Period.[33]

The 'no balance' approach reveals the active role of the US in providing ideological and material cover for the Zionist regime as it commits genocide. When a journalist asked US State Department Spokesperson, Matthew Miller, about the double standards implied in US actions, as it continues to fund an army that is plausibly believed to be committing genocide, Miller responded:

There is a false equivalency embedded in that question. There is a difference between members of a terrorist organisation who went out and intentionally killed innocent civilians [...] that is different than a military campaign conducted in an environment where that terrorist organisation hides behind civilians.[34]

Such a statement not only draws a boundary between a legitimate 'Israeli military campaign' versus terrorism, but also activates a moral and political compass towards the only identifiable raped/invaded/innocent civilians of that equation (Israel).[35] While the civilian presence in Gaza is seemingly acknowledged in Miller's statement, it is quickly overshadowed by asserting their proximity to the terrorists/jungle realm. This effectively captures the moralising grounds of the continuous slaughter in Gaza, perceived as nothing but a hub of pure terror. As the Israeli President affirms, there are 'no innocent civilians in Gaza',[36] and the projected beastliness manifests in IDF daily videos documenting their civilising strolls in the jungle. In some videos, where IDF soldiers pose next to animals found alive in Gaza (see Figure 2), we see how animality is elevated above the beastliness of the Indigenous Palestinians.

Figure 2; https://twitter.com/ytirawi/status/1746322932643610798.

In other videos, documenting soldiers rummaging through Palestinian women's lingerie (see Figure 3), the savagery of the jungle emerges through sexualised projections, where unchecked 'sluttiness' lurks beneath 'externally enforced taboos,' as per Freud's description of savages.[37] In the performance of triumphal intimacy with the possessions of killed and displaced Palestinian women, we see a graphic and almost literal illustration of what I have been calling the occupation of gender.

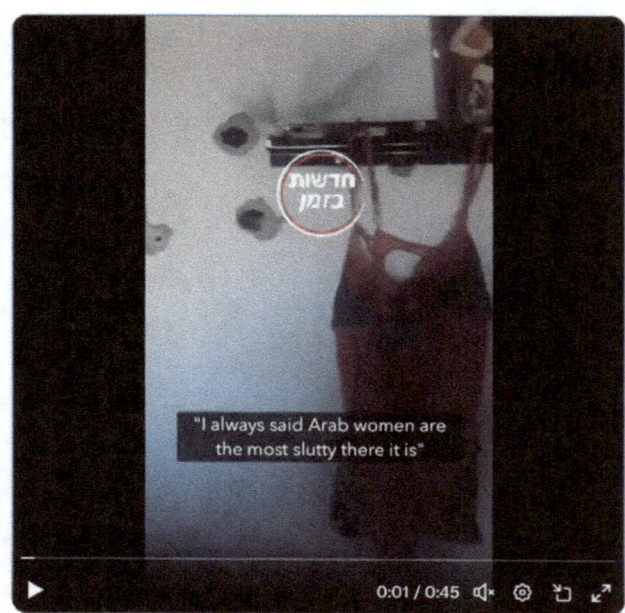

Figure 3; https://twitter.com/ASE/status/1732507774066520162?lang=en.

Wasting as (un)gendering

The delineation of the boundary between humans and beasts is not merely an ideological construction that colonialists advance within a civilisational discourse that pits itself against 'the jungle.' Rather, such (de)humanising projections are an extension of an ideological apparatus that sustains the capitalist mode of social reproduction under US-led imperialism, where the Arab region has been playing a key role for decades.[38] We need turn no further than the work of Third World Arab Marxists to unpick the layers of what we mean by US-led imperialism, including the functionality of the Zionist settler colonial outpost to the project of American hegemony.[39]

In these analyses, imperialism refers to the process of capital accumulation on a world scale, where development is apportioned unequally along racial and class lines.[40] Established on a relation of unequal development, imperialism requires the overexploitation of labour and perennial extraction of resources from peripheral countries, including through the use of monetary and financial warfare. In such a process, the global South loses national autonomy over its economic policies, while being prevented from harnessing resources for popular developmental goals and instead forced to cater to imperialist diktats. Overall, the social reproduction of imperialism occurs through the consumption of the developing world, thus economising the living conditions of workers and nature. Building on this philosophical tradition, Ali Kadri introduces the concept of *accumulation by waste*. For Kadri, the political economy of dollarised financial imperialism is predicated on a specific logic of waste, which has always annihilated the lives of the working masses of the South. Yet, as per the requisites of financialisaton, it does so at higher turnover rates. In such a context, wars, militarism and repression play a unique role because they respond almost instantaneously – via killing – to the needs of financial capital. In other words, killing and wasting are 'intrinsic characteristics' of the domain of production under US-led imperialism.

This logic of waste has a twofold implication for the Arab region, and especially Palestine. First, US-led imperialism violates state sovereignty through wars of encroachment, waged through concrete practices of arms factories, counterinsurgency, surveillance and the physical land bases and attendant stability needed for those processes.[41] Since 9/11, US-led wars have killed around 5 million people,[42] and this domination of the region wastes Arab human potential. To kill Arab life is to shorten its labour longevity, thus it is the ultimate form of cheapening labour power under capital, and doing so is not some sort of unwanted by-product or collateral damage. Rather, the purposeful wasting of human life is a sphere of production and an end in itself.[43] To say that it is a sphere of production is to reveal that wasted life through imperialist and colonial encroachment are *outputs* as well as *inputs* into surplus value making.[44]

Second, this explains the eliminatory logic of Zionist settler-colonialism, which has a fundamental role to play within the waste industry of US global capital industry.[45] Palestinian resistance movements in the 1960s understood this very well when they told us that Zionism is a spearhead of imperialism.[46] Being a European settler colonial formation, much like the US, the Zionist regime incubates a mode of social reproduction that promotes imperialist values and secures US interests in the Arab region and on a world scale.[47] By acquiring nuclear weapons and through its numerous military attacks on and invasions of other countries in the region – such as Iraq, Lebanon and Syria – Israel has been the major force behind imperialist capital accumulation and its corollary, Arab de-development.[48] Historically, what binds them together is a racist capitalist regime of 'hetero-conquest'[49] needed for the continued domination of the Indigenous, poor, and racialised peoples of the world. Israel is a material investment for the US in militarism, a reality that has emerged clearly during this latest genocidal war. Every aspect of the Zionist regime – from its liberal-progressive ideological values to its military capacity and economic strength – engrosses its sub-imperial or functionary role within the entire Middle East region. As Theodore Herzl proposed to his then British Imperial allies, the to-be Jewish state would serve as 'the portion of the rampart of Europe against Asia, an outpost of civilization as opposed to barbarism'.[50]

Expectedly, in the aftermath of October 7, Western ruling classes rushed to support uncompromisingly (in moral, political and economic terms) the Herzlian state. The Zionists, together with the reactionary regimes in the region – the Gulf monarchies, Jordan and to some extent Egypt – are a fundamental cog in the continuity of the waste industry assigned by US-led imperialism. The genocidal war that has been unfolding for the past eleven months is an intensified form of the waste industry. Whereas before the genocidal onslaught, Gazans were facing a slow genocide, their caloric intake controlled entirely by the occupiers besieging them by air, sea and land,[51] the recent intensification of the killing perfectly encapsulates the waste marketplace of imperialism.

In such a context, it is important to understand how the 'body' becomes wrapped up in the myth-making medium of Western-invested genocide. A whole panoply of bodies: disfigured, tortured, mutilated, burnt, decomposed, crushed, bulldozed, thieved, even as they lay restless and nameless in gruesome mass graves. Numbers and bodies collide to produce a percentage of conferred collateral damage. When Joe Biden is told that 70 per cent are women and children, he responds that there is no truth in these figures.[52] The only truth imperialists know and propagate is that 'a worthy Indian is a scalped Indian', 'a worthy African is a blackened enslaved African', and 'a worthy Arab is a Joint Direct Attack Munition (JDAM) decimated terrorist.'[53] Wasting is the logic through which US-led imperialism reduces life in its expansive capacity, to bits of flesh among wreckage and rubble, chunks of dead meat for Gaza's hungry dogs to chew on. In doing so, it materialises what I call, borrowing from Hortense Spillers,[54] a scene of unprotected flesh, of terrorist wasted flesh *(un)gendered*.

(Un)gendering operates on two intertwined levels. First, it relies on the ideological and material reduction of the Other to terrorist subspecies. The casting of racialised Others outside of humanity, and by extension of sexed/gendered scripts, is central to the domain of accumulation by waste under Zionism and US-led imperialism. This is best seen in how Palestinians of all genders have been systematically painted by Zionists and their allies, feminist and otherwise, in the imperialist core as legitimate killing targets. The 'usual' protections accorded to 'women and children' do not apply to Palestinians.[55] Second, (un)gendering sustains a symbiotic relationship with the *gendering* scripts that reify the epistemological structures of settler colonialism and imperialism. This is where racialised Others can turn from being undifferentiated terrorist-subspecies to various modified versions of sexed/gendered identifications, concurring with the shifting calibrations of Western bourgeois ideology. We can think, for example, of how Western narratives about vulnerable gays and women of the Arab world encapsulate the ideological terrain of colonial saviourism, rescuing these poor souls from 'the timeless homogeneous mythical place called Islamland'.[56] These gendered/sexed representations demonstrate what Palestinian queer organisers and their allies identify as pinkwashing[57] to explain Zionist and Western hegemonic mobilisation of the 'oppressed veiled woman' and the 'in-need-of-saving LGBT Arab'.

Such colonial projections have a functional role to play in the waste industry. That is, the conceptual production of victimised gendered/sexed Arab bodies activate *accumulation by waste* on two levels. First, the ideological production of sexed/gendered victims underscores the violence of abstraction imposed on bodies and objects commodified 'in total separation from their specificity and materiality.'[58] In challenging the false propagandisation of Israel as a haven for oppressed gay Arabs, queer Palestinians reply: 'there are *no* pink doors in the apartheid wall'.[59] Second, these ideological abstractions not only hide the social reality of ungendering ('the apartheid wall has *no* pink doors') of the Zionist regime, but also advance the material reproduction of the same *accumulation by waste* regime harboured under US-led imperialism. Feminists like Clinton are amongst the benefactors of this class regime that abstracts and wastes Arab human potential. Their feminism equates to 'saving the gays and the women of Iraq' by levelling Iraq to the ground,[60] and greenlighting the genocide of the Palestinians to save the world from Hamas male savagery. The question then becomes, is historical abstraction all we are left with, or might there still be room to defy the imperialist and settler colonial canons of (un)gendering?

Ruptures: anti-imperialist upheavals

> The duality of the US, the West, and the civilised friends of gay people is being used against the Iraqi people and government, who are instead homophobic. This gives the Americans the right not to respect the will of the Iraqi people or of the Iraqi gay community to determine their own paths of struggle. Instead, they imposed the love of gayness and democracy on them, in a ready-made package, sent from America with love. Similarly, Israel uses this discourse in its attempt to whitewash its crimes in front of the whole world.[61]

When Palestinian organisers in the group *alQaws for sexual and gender diversity in Palestinian society*[62] explain their firm rejection of the single-issue approach to sexuality, they do so by historicising the journey that got them to mobilise queerness as a 'radical approach to political mobilisation and decolonisation'.[63] That is, Zionist settler-colonisation of Palestinian Indigenous bodies and lands has animated activists' political reconstitution by virtue of growing away from Zionist and western LGBT frameworks. They instead have become more attuned to the material reality embedding Palestinian Indigenous struggle for humanity. In that process, we see a definition of Palestinian queer affiliation that is Palestinian first and foremost and identifies itself within the terrains of Palestinian national struggle for freedom and liberation. At the same time, anti-pinkwashing activists reveal to us the violence within the identity-based affiliations that Zionists and their Western allies seek to impose onto the Palestinian context, which require Palestinians to emerge as victims of their homophobic pride-negating society and seek the freedom that their coloniser is supposedly going to extend to them.[64] This, in effect, corresponds to the dependent nature of social development to which the colonised are forced to subscribe in the process of their peripheralisation and so integration within the 'progressive' market of the imperialist core.

Palestinian mobilising against pinkwashing is not, however, simply an act of unveiling colonial investment in women's and gay rights. Rather, and more crucially, these anti-pinkwashing mobilisations demand that we seek the alternative epistemes that have been buried beneath the social and conceptual categories abstracting away from the materiality of history.[65] Making international calls for boycott, while being active contributors on the ground in political mobilisation, anti-pinkwashers/pinkwatchers show the power that Palestinian queers have, contrary to Zionist and western saviour projections. Most importantly, these actions gesture towards anti-colonial/anti-capitalist forms of struggle. In their political activism, for example, alQaws activists state that rather than seeking pride they seek Dignity;[66] instead of the liberatory façade of capitalism's possessive individual they seek to be rooted in communities.[67] They also explain that instead of seeking the occupier's supposed 'pink doors',[68] they stand by the right of the occupied to wage their uprising for self-determination;[69] and rather than singling out a struggle based on sexuality they refuse the very premise of bourgeois ideology as it abstracts sexuality from the violent structures (settler colonialism and imperialism) maintaining bourgeois dominance.[70]

This emphasis on the structures of oppression – which the imperialists and settler colonialists always seek to hide in their bourgeois projections of what queerness or womanhood ought to signify for Indigenous Palestinians – reveals the grave limitations of post-structuralist queer-feminist critiques, which manifest on three intertwined fronts. First, the dilution of class and structural analysis that followed from French-influenced post-structuralism has led to the production of idealist and dehistoricised conceptions of identities, heavily invested in a deconstructionist paradigm.[71] As Gabriel Rockhill argues, even anti-essentialist versions of this strand of thought, such as those articulated by Judith Butler, continue to approach gender and sexual relations discursively, without providing 'a materialist analysis of capitalist social relations that have produced these categories of gender and sexuality, their existence as major sites of collective class struggle is occluded'.[72] 'At best', they remain 'oriented toward a liberal pluralism in which class struggle is replaced by interest-group advocacy'. Second, we see the occlusion of US-led imperialism and, consequently, the centrality of the national question for those who remain under settler colonial and imperialist aggression.[73] This is accompanied by an analysis that undermines feminist/queer nationalist anti-colonial politics, characterising them as unproductively stuck within a politics of essentialism and puritanism.[74] These critiques instead glorify sexed/gendered configurations that are conceived within a hybrid anti-essentialist idiom for the sake of activating abstract notions of co-existence: 'Palestine/Israel.'[75] Third, we see approaches that push the deconstructionist approach to such an extent that advocating queerness in its subjectless capacity or the zone of death drive becomes possible.[76] Queerness is conceived against the logic of reproductive and heteronormative futurism, supposedly imposed everywhere, while forgetting that racialised working class people are already confined to the realm of wasting and shortening of their lives.

Butler's initial response to October 7 and Israel's launching of its genocidal war - 'The Compass of Mourning'[77] – provides an instructive illustration of such limitations. Beginning with a recognition of the problematic liberal imperative to 'condemn or approve', Butler effectively reinforces this imperative with their unequivocal condemnation of the 'terrifying and revolting Hamas massacre.'[78] The essay moves on to reiterate the value of nonviolence as a moral compass for both Israelis and Palestinians under what Butler named in a previous work a 'cohabitation' paradigm.[79] Acknowledging the colonial context in Israel/Palestine, Butler nonetheless challenges the putatively dubious moral stance of some pro-Palestine activists, referencing the Harvard Palestine Solidarity Committee (HPSC). For Butler, in this essay, the group's contextualisation of the Israeli apartheid regime as the only one to blame for the escalation of violence serves to 'exonerate' Hamas's 'hideous killings':

> I deplore the violence unequivocally at the same time as I, like so many others, want to be part of imagining and struggling for true equality and justice in the region, the kind that would compel groups like Hamas to disappear, the occupation to end, and new forms of political

freedom and justice to flourish.[80]

At times, Butler acknowledges the necessity of historical contextualisation regarding the existence of groups like Hamas, as when they say that 'we have to know the history of the situation, the growth of Hamas as a militant group in the devastation of the post-Oslo moment'.[81] However, this momentary engagement with history recedes in the face of overwhelming theoretical abstraction dictated by an idealist vision of non-violence, as Butler tells us that alternative political and moral possibilities lie in a 'struggle for a free Palestine in which Hamas would be dissolved or superseded by groups with non-violent aspirations for cohabitation'.[82] The notion of cohabitation or coming together of Israeli Jews and Palestinians, which Butler proposes as the most productive political and moral trajectory, is emblematic of the very identarian base of their theorisation, even though they would strongly claim otherwise. As Lisa Bhungalia and I argued in 2014, 'cohabitation' emerges from and follows dehistoricised, depoliticised, Weberian notions of 'hate', 'religious conflict', and 'ethnic war'.[83] It ignores the material structures that maintain one group's exclusive domination over another, effectively eliding the mode of social reproduction that Zionism requires, that is, the wasting and killing of Palestinians. Consequently, it divorces Zionism from its functionary role within US-led imperialism. Moreover, the abstract notion of Palestinians and Israeli Jews 'coming together' fails to engage productively with the deep history of existing anti-colonial and anti-imperialist struggles (and strategies) deployed to imagine liberation beyond academic-sanctioned versions of 'decolonisation'.

In contrast, anti-imperialist feminism gestures towards a new moral praxis to be found within the revolutionary will of those who, following so many years of dehumanisation and besiegement, have the full right, in the words of the late Popular Front for the Liberation of Palestine (PFLP)[84] leader George Habash, to 'protect our revolution. Our code of morals is our revolution.'[85] This emerges further in two interviews conducted three weeks after the joint military operation,[86] Al Aqsa Flood, with the revolutionary PFLP figure Leila Khaled. In one of the interviews, she reflects on the the cumulative and intergenerational nature of resistance,[87] focused on the return of Palestinian refugees to their lands and Palestinian national liberation. Considering the current situation in Gaza, she remarks that there is only one option for Palestinians – resistance – and notes that even amongst the families being bombed by Israel, there is 'nobody speaking out and saying they're against resistance.' She observes, reflecting on how Palestinians in Gaza have reacted to the loss of their families and loved ones, that their reactions show 'that the people's culture is a culture of resistance, not of surrender.'

In a related interview, she reflects on armed struggle:

> the only choice we have is to fight and to liberate our land including through armed resistance... people have the right to resist with all means, including armed struggle. This is in the Charter of the United Nations... it's a fundamental law. Where there is repression, there is resistance... history taught us that people resist to keep their dignity and land.[88]

In the same inteview, Khaled recalls the hijacking operations that she was part of in the late 1960s, which have seen her branded a terrorist by Zionists and imperialists to this day. Khaled explains that hijacking was a tactic intended to get the world to pay attention to the Palestinian question 'because they didn't listen to us when we were in the camps'. Recounting details of the operations of which she was part, Khaled describes how she took control of the cockpit while invoking the name of Shadia Abu Ghazaleh, the first Palestinian martyred woman in the wake of the 1967 Naksa.[89] She then reflects on how upon encountering Western media, all she was asked by an American journalist was: 'How many hours do you stand in front of the mirror?'[90] Such a question, for Khaled, sits within wider Western projections about Arab women as passive and domesticated, incapable of political thought and action.[91] These gendering scripts of imperialism operate alongside the ungendering processes that relegate Khaled, like many other Palestinian resistance figures, to the dehumanising realm of the terrorist, nonsensical, amoral savage. A recent cancellation of her seminar at a US-based university was propelled by anti-terrorism laws that led the president of the university to affirm:

> terrorist violence conflicts with academic freedom... it is at odds with the values that universities hold dear: reason, dispassion, freedom of speech and inquiry, respect for individuals and individual liberties.[92]

However, lying beneath these (un)gendering scripts of empire are the words of Khaled when she asserts: 'We are ready to pay blood and flesh to liberate this land.'[93] If, borrowing from Spillers, we read Palestine as a scene of unprotected flesh, then Khaled's words promise a defiance arising out of that very abjection.

Khaled gestures towards an anti-imperialist feminism, where Indigenous counterviolence is the site of inventiveness of the colonised flesh, once it emerges beyond the socio-political taxonomies dictating colonised non-being.[94] In the face of the ongoing genocide waged against the Palestinian people, Khaled and her comrades in the Palestinian resistance movement point us to the significance of standing firmly with the plight of the oppressed to fight against the usurpation of their right to claim their own history. The fight itself activates a process of social transformation propelled by 'the ability to determine the mode of production most appropriate to the evolution of the liberated people.'[95] This – the quest for autonomous development of national productive forces – 'opens new prospects for the cultural development of the society in question, by returning to that society all its capacity to create progress.'[96] In other words, the waste-driven economy of the imperialists is put into crisis when the colonised rise to declare the rightfulness of their Intifada. Palestinian Intifada stands as a living example of a 'class struggle' where *homo politicus* replaces *homo economicus* in the process of materialising revolutionary consciousness.[97] Claiming their place within the revolution, women and the rural poor become crucial pillars of a national productive force that could activate *insihab* (delinking)[98] from the material imperatives of the US-led global waste industry. In so doing, the struggle for national liberation proves its capacity to reconfigure the social sphere. In the face of dispossession, there is ongoing *sumud* (steadfastness, staying put on one's land). In the face of genocidal killing, there is an aspiration for *shahada* (living martyrdom) by resisting Indigenous subjects. They not only refuse to die[99] but are also aware of the role they play in History: facing up to Zionism and US imperialism.[100]

Walaa Alqaisiya is a Marie Curie Global Fellow based at Ca' Foscari University of Venice, Italy. She is the author of Decolonial Queering in Palestine *(Routledge, 2022) and Associate Editor with the journal* Middle East Critique. *The work in this article was supported by the European Commission (Grant number 101024045).*

Notes

1. MSNBC, 'Israeli president: War against Hamas intended "to save the values of Western civilization"', *YouTube*, 5 December 2023, https://www.youtube.com/watch?v=v64TVMo2vKw&t=286s.

2. Patrick Wintour, 'Stakes High As South Africa Brings Claims of Genocidal Intent Against Israel', *Guardian*, 4 January 2024, https://www.theguardian.contentsm/world/2024/jan/04/stakes-high-as-south-africa-brings-claim-of-genocidal-intent-against-israel.

3. Jeffrey Gettleman, Anat Schwartz and Adam Sella, '"Scream without Words": How Hamas Weaponised Sexual Violence on Oct. 7', *New York Times*, 28 December 2023.

4. CNN reporting on sexual violence and the New York Times Hamas rape story have been exposed as relying on non-credible witnesses (see e.g. 'CNN report claiming sexual violence on October 7 relied on non-credible witnesses, some with undisclosed ties to Israeli govt', *Mondoweiss*, 1 December 2023, https://mondoweiss.net/2023/12/cnn-report-claiming-sexual-violence-on-october-7-relied-on-non-credible-witnesses-some-with-undisclosed-ties-to-israeli-govt/; Jeremy Schill and Ryan Grim, 'Kibbutz Be'eri Rejects Story in New York Times October 7 Exposé: "They Were Not Sexually Abused"', *The Intercept*, 4 March 2024, https://theintercept.com/2024/03/04/nyt-october-7-sexual-violence-kibbutz-beeri/). Investigative journalists also reveal that ZAKA, the Israeli non-governmental organisation, provided testimonies on sexual violence along with the commission led by Cochav Elkayam-Levy that were non-reliable and fraudulent (see e.g. 'ZAKA is not a trustworthy source for allegations of sexual violence on October 7', *Mondoweiss*, 30 December 2023, https://mondoweiss.net/2023/12/zaka-is-not-a-trustworthy-source-for-allegations-of-sexual-violence-on-october-7/; Ali Abunimah, 'Israeli "commission" on 7 October rape claims exposed as fraud', *The Electronic Intifada*, 25 March 2024, https://electronicintifada.net/content/israeli-commission-7-october-rape-claims-exposed-fraud/45401). Further, doubts over reliability and credence were cast over the UN report issued in the follow up to Pramila Patten's visit to Israel. It is important to note that the report concludes that the UN team 'was unable to establish the prevalence of sexual violence and concludes that the overall magnitude, scope, and specific attribution of these violations would require a fully-fledged investigation', Office of the Special Representative of the Secretary General on Sexual Violence in Conflict, 'Official visit of the Office of the SRSG-SVC to Israel and the occupied West Bank', 4 March 2024, https://www.un.org/sexualviolenceinconflict/wp-content/uploads/2024/03/report/mission-report-official-visit-of-the-office-of-the-srsg-svc-to-israel-and-the-occupied-west-bank-29-january-14-february-2024/20240304-Israel-oWB-CRSV-report.pdf. Finally, a recent UN OHCHR report, released in May 2024, confirms that the Investigating Commission was not able to independently verify allegations of rapes by Hamas due to 'a lack of access to victims, witnesses, and crime sites as well as obstruction of its investigations by the Israeli authorities'. Also, the report states that 'the Commission found some specific allegations to be false, inaccurate or contradictory with other evidence or statements and discounted these from its assessment'. See A/HRC/56/26, 'Report of the Independent International Commission of Inquiry on the Occupied Palestinian Territory, including East Jerusalem, and Israel', 27 May 2024, https://www.ohchr.org/en/press-releases/2024/06/israeli-authorities-palestinian-armed-groups-are-responsible-war-crimes.

5. Libby Cathey, 'Biden calls reports of Hamas' sexual violence against Israeli women "appalling"', ABC News, 6 December 2023, http://abcnews.go.com/International/biden-calls-reports-hamas-sexual-violence-israeli-women/story?id=105401641/.

6. Antony Blinken described the sexual violence as 'beyond anything I've seen'. Paul Becker and Joel Poznansky, 'Hamas weaponized sexual assault to deliver a message to its enemies', *The Hill*, 8 March 2024, https://thehill.com/opinion/international/4517306-hamas-weaponized-sexual-assault-to-deliver-a-message-to-its-enemies/.

7. Emanuel Fabian, 'Defense Minister announces "complete siege" of Gaza: No power, food or fuel', *The Times of Israel*, 9 October 2023, https://www.timesofisrael.com/liveblog_entry/defense-minister-announces-complete-siege-of-gaza-no-power-food-or-fuel/.

8. Al Arabiya English, 'We will eliminate everything in Gaza', *YouTube*, 11 October 2023, https://www.youtube.com/watch?v=LkCo1UXbvOc.

9. NBC News, '"Where the h--- are you?": Netanyahu

demands more international support', *YouTube*, 6 December 2023, https://www.youtube.com/watch?v=OCGiW2hYsmA.

10. Maria Lugones, 'Toward a Decolonial Feminism', *Hypatia* 25:4 (2010), 742–759; Sylvia Wynter, 'Unsettling the Coloniality of Being/Power/Truth/Freedom: Towards the Human, After Man, Its Overrepresentation – An Argument', *CR: The New Centennial Review* 3:3 (2003), 257–337.

11. Lugones, 'Decolonial Feminism', 743; Wynter, 'Unsettling', 257.

12. Lugones, 'Decolonial Feminism', 755.

13. Wynter, 'Unsettling', 317.

14. Lugones, 'Decolonial Feminism', 745.

15. Wynter, 'Unsettling', 260.

16. Wynter, 'Unsettling', 298.

17. Lugones, 'Decolonial Feminism', 745.

18. Walaa Alqaisiya, 'Beyond the Contours of Zionist Sovereignty: Decolonisation in Palestine's Unity Intifada', *Political Geography* 103 (2023), 1–11.

19. Jennifer Cunningham, 'Sheryl Sandberg, Hillary Clinton, Senator Kirsten Gillibrand and others issue a global call to action to denounce sexual violence at UN summit', *Business Insider*, 5 December 2023, https://www.businessinsider.com/sheryl-sandberg-urge-world-to-denounce-hamas-for-sexual-violence-october-7-attack-2023-12.

20. Jack Brile, 'Hillary Clinton slams progressives ignoring Hamas horrors: "no excuses"', *Washington Examiner*, 5 December 2023, https://www.washingtonexaminer.com/news/2627532/hillary-clinton-slams-progressives-ignoring-hamas-horrors-no-excuses/.

21. Cunningham, 'Sheryl Sandberg'.

22. Fabian, 'Defense Minister'.

23. Middle East Eye, 'EU's foreign policy chief Josep Borrell calls Europe "a garden" and the rest of the world "a jungle"', *YouTube*, 17 October 2022, https://www.youtube.com/watch?v=-MncHLS51uM.

24. Michael Lundblad, *The Birth of A Jungle* (Oxford: Oxford University Press, 2013), 2.

25. Lundblad, *Birth*, 145.

26. Lundblad, *Birth*, 27.

27. Lundblad, *Birth*, 144.

28. Lundblad, *Birth*, 153.

29. Lundblad, *Birth*, 49.

30. David Horovitz, 'Shock at the October 7 catastrophe gives way to horror and fury at global immorality', *The Times of Israel*, 29 October 2023, https://www.timesofisrael.com/shock-at-the-october-7-catastrophe-gives-way-to-horror-and-fury-at-global-immorality/.

31. Brile, 'Hillary Clinton slams'.

32. Congressman Jeff Van Drew on *X*, 4 December 2023, reported in the *Washington Examiner*, https://www.washingtonexaminer.com/news/2450813/-white-house-calls-hamas-rapes-reprehensible-in-wake-of-jayapal-controversy/.

33. Ritchie Torres, 'Rape and sexual violence against Israeli women calls for nothing less than unequivocal condemnation', *X*, 3 December 2023, https://twitter.com/RitchieTorres/status/1731439939902992708.

34. Prem Thakker, 'Republicans and Democrats have made a deal that they will cut UNRWA funding through next year', *X*, 18 March 2024, https://twitter.com/prem_thakker/status/1769717253732171912?t=0oSmemBdg5RAgjLNTUfV4Q&s=08.

35. Sexual and gender-based violence that Zionists have perpetrated for decades against Palestinian men (see e.g. Daniel J. N. Weishut, 'Sexual torture of Palestinian men by Israeli authorities', *Reproductive Health Matters* 23:46 (2015), 71–84); women (see e.g. Kathryn Median, 'Israeli Settler colonialism, "Humanitarian Warfare", and Sexual Violence in Palestine', *International Feminist Journal of Politics* 23:5 (2021), 698–719; Nadera Shalhoub-Kevorkian, 'The Politics of Birth and the Intimacies of Violence against Palestinian Women in Occupied East Jerusalem', *British Journal of Criminology* 55:6 (2015), 1187–1206); and children (see e.g. Claire Nicoll, 'Defenceless: the Impact of Israeli Military Detentions on Palestinian Children', Save the Children Report (2020), https://resourcecentre.savethechildren.net/document/defenceless-impact-israeli-military-detention-palestinian-children/) has received a fraction of the outrage and condemnation directed against the alleged Hamas rapes on October 7 by western politicians.

36. The Wire, '"No Innocent Civilians in Gaza", Israel President Says as Northern Gaza Struggles to Flee Israeli bombs', 14 October 2023, https://thewire.in/world/northern-gaza-israel-palestine-conflict.

37. Mary Turfah, 'Running Amok', *The Baffler*, 18 June 2024, https://thebaffler.com/latest/running-amok-turfah.

38. Ali Kadri, *Arab Development Denied: Dynamics of Accumulation by Wars of Encroachment* (London: Anthem Press, 2015).

39. Anour Abdel-Malek, *Social Dialectics: Nation and Revolution* (Albany: SUNY Press,1981); Ali Kadri, *Arab Development Denied* (London Anthem Press, 2015); Samir Amin, 'U.S. Imperialism, Europe, and the Middle East', *Monthly Review*, 1 November 2004, https://monthlyreview.org/2004/11/01/u-s-imperialism-europe-and-the-middle-east/.

40. Samir Amin, *Unequal Development* (New York: Monthly Review Press, 1976).

41. Matteo Capasso and Ali Kadri, 'The Imperialist Ques-

tion: A Sociological Approach', *Middle East Critique*, 32:2 (2023), 149–166.

42. Stephanie Savell, 'How Death Outlives War: The Reverberating Impact of Post 9/11 Wars on Human Health', Watson Institute for International and Public Affairs, 2024, https://watson.brown.edu/costsofwar/papers/2023/IndirectDeaths.

43. Ali Kadri, *The Accumulation of Waste: A Political Economy of Systematic Destruction* (Leiden: Brill, 2023).

44. War is a primary and direct form of killing. Yet, sanctions, IMF-led SAPs, and the entire neoliberal assault on the masses of the global South should also be considered as part of the process of *accumulation by waste*.

45. Max Ajl, 'Palestine's Great Flood: Part 1', *Agrarian South: Journal of Political Economy*, 13:1 (2024), 62–88.

46. George Habash, *Revolutionaries Never Die* (Lebanon: Saqi Books, 2009). Source in Arabic.

47. To frame Zionism as a spearhead of US-led imperialism is to depart from some of the theoretical limitations of settler colonial theory, highlighting its failure to engage with dynamics of class and capitalism as they shape colonialism and racism. Zionist elimination of Indigenous Palestinians is a mode of social reproduction under settler colonialism that tallies (does not contradict) with the functionality of US-led imperialism in the region and on a world scale. In other words, the elimination of Palestinian life for Zionist settler colonial encroachment should not be abstracted from the material processes dictating: first, a class regime (including with internal class contradictions/profits for comprador elites) working in the interests of US imperialism in the region via direct wars, coup d'etat operations, IMF and World Bank policies; and second, a labour regime from which a politics of national resistance is borne out to challenge the class positionality of Palestinians and wider working Arab masses who form part of Palestine's strategic depth and war against Zionism, reactionism and imperialism. For more on this debate, see Max Ajl, 'Logics of Elimination and Settler Colonialism: Decolonization or National Liberation?', *Middle East Critique* 32:1 (2023), 1–25.

48. Hassan Harb, 'Imperialism, Zionism and Reactionism in the 21st Century', *Ebb Magazine*, 15 October 2023, https://www.ebb-magazine.com/essays/al-aqsa-flood.

49. See Walaa Alqaisiya, 'Palestine and the Will to Theorise Decolonial Queering', *Middle East Critique* 29:1 (2020), 87–113.

50. Oxford Learning Link, 'Document-Excerpts from Theodor Herzl, The Jewish State (1895)', Oxford University Press, 2024, https://learninglink.oup.com/access/content/von-sivers-3e-dashboard-resources/document-excerpts-from-theodor-herzl-the-jewish-state-1895.

51. Reuters, 'Israel Gaza blockade study calculated Palestinians' calories', 17 October 2012, https://www.reuters.com/article/idUSBRE89G0NM/.

52. PBS NewsHour, 'Biden casts doubt on Hamas reported death toll', *YouTube*, 26 October 2023, https://www.youtube.com/watch?v=h42Nm05zF-w.

53. This is US-made weaponry. Since its deployment, it has been used in all US wars including Iraq, Afghanistan, Syria and Yemen. See: https://www.middleeasteye.net/opinion/okinawa-palestine-how-us-military-machine-connects-occupied-territories.

54. Hortense Spillers, 'Mama's Baby, Papa's Maybe: An American Grammar Book', *Diacritics* 17:2 (1987), 68.

55. On the concept of 'unchilding' in relation to Palestinian children see Nadera Shalhoub-Kevorkian, *Incarcerated Childhood and the Politics of Unchilding* (Cambridge: Cambridge University Press, 2019).

56. Lila Abu Lughod, 'Do Mulism Women Need Saving?' *Time*, 1 November 2023, https://ideas.time.com/2013/11/01/do-muslim-women-need-saving/.

57. Walaa Alqaisya, Ghaith Hilal and Haneen Maikey, 'Dismantling the Image of the Palestinian Homosexual: Exploring the Role of AlQaws', in *Decolonizing Sexualities*, ed, Sandeep Bakshi, Suhraiya Jivraj and Silvia Posocco (Oxford: Counterpress, 2016), 125–140.

58. Ewa Płonowska Ziarek, *Feminist Aesthetics and the Politics of Modernism* (New York: Columbia University press 2012), 130.

59. Haneen Maikey, 'Liberation in Palestine: A Queer Issue', presentation at SOAS University of London, 28 February 2014.

60. See Nadje Al-Ali and Nicola Pratt, *What Kind of Liberation? Women and the Occupation of Iraq* (Berkeley: University of California Press, 2009).

61. Haneen Maikey and Sami Samali, 'International Day Against Homophobia: Between the Western Experience and the Reality of Gay Communities', alQaws, 23 May 2011, https://www.alqaws.org/siteEn/print?id=26&type=1.

62. alQaws is a queer Palestinian civil society organisation founded in grassroots activism. See: https://alqaws.org/about-us.

63. Walaa Alqaisiya, *Decolonial Queering in Palestine* (London: Routledge, 2022), 67.

64. Alqaisiya, *Decolonial Queering*, 117.

65. Walaa Alqaisiya, 'The Decolonial Wor(l)ds of indigenous Women', *Social & Cultural Geography* (2023), 1–19.

66. Alqaisiya, 'Beyond the Contours', 7.

67. Alqaisiya, *Decolonial Queering*, 117.

68. Alqaisiya, *Decolonial Queering*, 58.

69. Alqaisiya, *Decolonial Queering*, 139.

70. Alqaisiya, *Decolonial Queering*, 59.

71. Domenico Losurdo, *Il Marxismo Occidentale Come nacque, come morì, come può rinascere* (Bari: Laterza, 2017).
72. Gabriel Rockhill and Zhao Dingqi, 'Imperialist Propaganda and the Ideology of the Western Left Intelligentsia: From Anticommunism and Identity Politics to Democratic Illusions and Fascism', *Monthly Review*, 1 December 2023, https://monthlyreview.org/2023/12/01/imperialist-propaganda-and-the-ideology-of-the-western-left-intelligentsia/. As a counterpoint, for a historical materialist account of gender and sexuality see Gary Kinsman, *The Regulation of Desire: Queer Histories, Queer Struggles* (Vancouver: University of British Columbia Press, 2024).
73. Jasbir Puar's homonationalism framework has been extended, albeit uncritically, to contexts of Indigenous and other Global South contexts, including Palestine. See Puar, *Terrorist Assemblages: Homonationalism in Queer Times* (Durham, NC: Duke University Press, 2007). Contrary to many feminist and queer politics in the Western imperialist core, nationalism continues to be a relevant framework for third-world activism (e.g. Ranjoo Seodu Herr, 2003, and other Indigenous feminist/queer movements across both global South and North contexts). See e.g. Alqaisiya, *Decolonial Queering*, 2022; Qwo-Li Driskill, Chris Finley, Brian Joseph Gilley and Scott Lauria Morgensen eds., *Queer Indigenous Studies: Critical Interventions in Theory, Politics and Literature* (Arizona: Arizona University Press, 2011).
74. Sa'ed Atshan, *Queer Palestine and the Empire of Critique* (California: Stanford University Press, 2020).
75. Gill Hochberg, 'Introduction: Israelis, Palestinians, Queers: Points of Departure', *Journal of Gay and Lesbian Studies* 16:4 (2010) 493–516.
76. Lee Edelman, *No Future: Queer Theory and the Death Drive* (Durham: Duke University Press, 2004).
77. Judith Butler, 'The Compass of Mourning', *London Review of Books*, 19 October 2023, https://www.lrb.co.uk/the-paper/v45/n20/judith-butler/the-compass-of-mourning.
78. Butler, 'The Compass'.
79. Butler, *Parting Ways: Jewishness and the Critique of Zionism* (New York: Columbia University Press, 2012). A few months after the *LRB* piece, short clips circulated online where Butler appears to claim that Hamas is part of 'Palestinian armed resistance'. However in a lengthy interview following these claims, (available at PoliticsJOE, 'The west knows nothing about the Palestinian struggle', *YouTube*, 25 March 2024, https://www.youtube.com/watch?v=XU5Ao50uog8), Butler clarifies that the Israeli far right had a vested interest in the making and circulation of these clips, and that her position towards the 'mass atrocities committed by Hamas remains unchanged'. I must also emphasise that my critique engages with the corpus of Butler's work regarding nonviolence and cohabitation in Palestine and is not based on a few scattered statements.
80. Butler, 'The Compass'.
81. Butler, 'The Compass'.
82. Butler, 'The Compass'.
83. Mary Thomas, 'On the Civilian in Gaza: Walaa Alqaisiya and Lisa Bhungalia interviewed by Mat Coleman and Mary Thomas', *Society and Space*, 16 September 2014, https://www.societyandspace.org/articles/on-the-civilian-in-gaza.
84. Popular Front for the Liberation of Palestine: a Marxist Leninist party founded by George Habash in 1967.
85. *Ebb* magazine, 'George Habash on morality and the Palestinian Revolution', 10 October 2023, https://www.ebb-magazine.com/essays/our-code-of-morals-is-our-revolution,.
86. It is crucial to challenge the common assumption, particularly within Western media and political discourse, that Hamas was the only group that participated in the launching of this military operation. Other Palestinian political factions, including the PFLP and Islamic Jihad, were involved.
87. She states that 'the process of accumulation [of acts of resistance] lead to qualitative change'. See Leila Khaled: Journey of a Palestinian Icon, https://www.youtube.com/watch?v=PUN64QJTToY, accessed 16 August 2024.
88. *Break Through News*, 'Leila Khaled Interview: Palestine is an International Liberation Struggle', *YouTube*, 27 October 2023, https://www.youtube.com/watch?v=6BBvzyKL-G4&t=208s. Editors' note: International humanitarian law recognises a right to armed resistance in the context of occupation. See Marco Longobardo, *The Use of Armed Force in Occupied Territory* (Cambridge: Cambridge University Press, 2018), 147–164.
89. *Break Through News*, 'Leila Khaled'.
90. *Break Through News*, 'Leila Khaled'.
91. *Break Through News*, 'Leila Khaled'.
92. Alice Speri and Sam Briddle, 'Zoom Censorship of Palestine Seminar Sparks Fight Over Academic Freedom', *The Intercept*, 14 November 2020, https://theintercept.com/2020/11/14/zoom-censorship-leila-khaled-palestine/.
93. *Break Through News*, 'Leila Khaled'.
94. Frantz Fanon, *Black Skin, White Masks* (London: Pluto Press, 1967).
95. Amilcar Cabral, '1970, Amilcar Cabral, "National liberation and culture"', BLACKPAST, 10 August 2009,

https://www.blackpast.org/global-african-history/1970-amilcar-cabral-national-liberation-and-culture/.

96. Amilcar Cabral, '1970'.

97. Adel Samara, *Beyond De-linking: Development by Popular Protection vs. Development by State* (Glendale, CA: Palestine Research and Publishing Foundation, 2005), 133.

98. Samara, *Beyond De-linking*, 134, explains how by building their own cooperatives and reviving a land-based economy, women and peasants advance the formation of a resistance economy, what he identifies as 'delinking by popular protection'.

99. Both in the metaphysical sense of the word as well as in reference to the material continuity of the struggle captured in Palestinian common belief that resisting subjects can be killed but the idea/cause for which they die lives on.

100. Encapsulated in the words of a recent Gaza survivor: 'They have killed everyone in the house! Congratulations to this free world! Congratulations to the European Union and the US for showing off your strength by killing off women and children. If they think that the Palestinian people will be broken down into surrendering, I swear to God we won't accept humiliation or breaking down and we will not leave this land. Tonight, I will sleep in my demolished house, and I will not leave! We will never leave from here! Look I came out from underneath the rubble. Look Biden, all your rockets and missiles, your aircraft carriers, which came to kill us, and I came out from under the rubble standing defiant.' *Middle East Eye*, 'Palestinian man sends a message to Israel that Palestinians will never surrender', *YouTube*, 12 October 2023, https://www.youtube.com/watch?v=xnUqAAzn0oY.

Shock without awe
Zionism and its horror
Abdaljawad Omar

On 27 June 1976, the Popular Front for the Liberation of Palestine, in conjunction with their German allies from the Red Army Faction, orchestrated a daring operation that seized, in mid-flight, an Airbus A300 en route from Tel Aviv to Paris. They redirected the plane towards Libya and then guided it to its final stage in Uganda, finding sanctuary at Entebbe Airport. A mere week later, the commandos of the Israeli elite unit Sayeret Matkal undertook a still more daring extraction operation. It involved a radar-evading flight spanning over 2000 miles, camouflage, swift and decisive action, pre-prepared escape routes and minimal casualties.[1] The meticulously executed manoeuvre culminated in a resounding triumph for the Israeli special forces.

Entebbe does not stand alone as an isolated instance within the archive of Israel's special military operations. It figures instead as an exemplary case of a more general strategy, a use of force that fully succeeded in evoking a mix of awe and terror.[2] Such operations simultaneously elicit horror at the spectacle of violence together with admiration for their meticulous execution and, ultimately, also for their instrumental success. The aesthetics of such military operations play a crucial role in evoking these powerful emotions. The symbolic substance they help to convey – heroics in the face of adversity, overcoming resistance, eventual triumph – have played a foundational role in the formation of Israeli identity around military power and its exercise. They have also helped turn its aesthetic effects into mythological narratives, narratives that have been well used to attract new settlers, entrench and reinforce the support from imperial centres, and solidify its primary social base. These operations also induce a sense of awe and terror among the Arab and Palestinian masses and contribute to the conception of an Israeli military that is undefeatable. This conception is reinforced with every new battle, operation and war.

These 'splendid' spectacles, mediated through the apparatus of military operations and large-scale battles, appear also as retrospective evidence of the 'righteousness' of Israel's settler-colonial project. Such retrospective legitimation finds support not only in the notion that 'might is right' but also in the aesthetic effects that Israeli military power can evoke – both within its own society, against its enemies, and in the impression it leaves on distant observers, both friend and enemy alike. Here, the technology and operational dimensions of military power transcend mere instrumentality or tactical outcomes. The capacity to reach, strike, generate or extract targets, to enact violence with precision and rapidity, to win wars spectacularly, operates not only as a demonstration of power but as a performative act of demobilisation, fracturing Palestinian and Arab resistance and eroding their will to resist. It has also built a cult of victory that sees in perpetual war not only the means to fend off enemies or deter them but a recurrent testing of Israeli power and its ability to overcome all forms of resistance, confirmed through endless streams of battles, special operations and large-scale wars.[3]

Military aesthetics

The nexus between aesthetics and war is a domain fraught with profound philosophical contention,[4] not least in responses to the rise of fascism in the early twentieth century. Walter Benjamin traces the phenomenon of German fascism to a distinct effacement of the inherent cruelty and stark reality of war, elevating it instead to a glorified pursuit that ultimately finds its purpose within itself, in a celebration of 'war for war's sake'.[5] Such erasure of war's cruelty, its bloody and bone-breaking reality, is necessary for the propagation of war as an honourable national pursuit. For Benjamin, such pursuit not only remains blind to the abject horrors of war, and not only serves to perpetuate property relations within fascist regimes; it fundamentally ignores the pivotal role of technology in mediating the raw experiences of war and ideological claims to heroism. For Benjamin, the glorification of war within many German intellectual circles belies the loss of heroics that new technologies and mechanical weapons systems effaced.[6] It also redirects the struggle from internal civil conflicts (conflicts regarding social and economic emancipation) towards an external enemy, while ignoring the growing reliance on technology in its celebration of heroics invested in machinery and munitions. This diversion permits the true fight for social and political emancipation to be squandered on a false battlefield.[7]

What emerges as most significant in Benjamin's analysis is the way intellectual circles, even those directly scarred by war, grappled with the experience of their encounter with combat. He unveils a disturbing aestheticisation within German intellectual discourse about the First World War, whereby the sting of defeat was not only disregarded but subtly transmuted into a catalyst for future wars. It is within this nexus between interpretations of defeat and glorification of war that the seeds for renewed war were sown, a sombre testament to the perilous interplay between reification of war and the relentless drive towards another encounter with vast devastation. The aestheticisation of war in works by Ernst Jünger and others, its mystification, emerges as a peculiar response from a nation marked by defeat that now internalises this defeat as part of its very essence. Yet, this glorification is not merely a retrospective veneer or mystification, as Benjamin contends; it also springs directly from the raw experience of war itself. This is an element that Benjamin overlooks. Within the chaos and the abyss of war, there lurks an element of the sublime.[8]

In his book *The Warriors: Reflections on Men in Battle* (1959), J. Glenn Gray evokes a feeling of the sublime in war that possesses an 'ecstatic character', where ecstasy is understood in its original Greek meaning as 'a state of being outside the self.'[9] Even amidst the mundane curiosities of battle there is a momentary suppression of the ego, a slight dissolution of the self's barriers. However, this pales in comparison to the more rarefied states of awe that soldiers sometimes experience. These moments of ecstasy bring a deep satisfaction, stemming from the consciousness of 'a power outside us with which we can merge in the relation of parts to whole.'[10] As Gray emphasises, in this state the soldier's feelings of triumph or depression are suspended, replaced by a pervasive sense of wonder.[11] This wonder satisfies because it reassures the individual of their place within the larger world, mitigating the isolation and insufficiency of the ego. What especially intrigues Gray is the way it also enables the idea of brotherhood to attain its highest articulation. Unlike Jünger and his cohort, Gray was not a war enthusiast. As Hannah Arendt writes in her foreword to the book, quoting Gray himself, his reflection 'makes opposition to war forceful', and it does so 'by not just warning us, but making us understand "why there is in many today as great a fear of a sterile and unexciting peace as of a great war".'[12]

Recognising the ecstatic feeling and sublime moments prompted by war does not necessarily negate its horrors. For Gray, it also highlights certain aspects of war that make it an alluring object. This acknowledgment addresses the allure that war holds for soldiers, commanders and those who identify with the war effort, who view and perceive its effects as spectators. This pull towards war finds parallels in various liberal, democratic, settler-colonial and other political formations. In Israel, the pull is central to the formation of 'Israeli-ness', to the constitution of Israeli identity and its perpetuation as a state, society and economy made and remade by war. In other words, at the heart of my discussion here lies the notion of 'Israeli-ness', a construct forged through the phenomenological and aesthetic resonances of its military praxis.

The choreographed movements of soldiers and armoured vehicles, the interwoven technology, the valour displayed by its forces, the capacity to inscribe its power through its aesthetic effects and performance, the assassinations of Palestinian leaders and activists, the covert operations by undercover units in the labyrinthine spaces of refugee camps and dense urban area, all the grand military engagements against Arab armies, culminating in spectacular victories, function not just as displays of dominance, they also open a narrative space in which the state's very identity might be reinscribed. These triumphs, alongside the systematic exclusionary measures and regular recourse to lethal force that structure everyday life for Palestinians, underscore the aesthetic nature of Israeli military operations and its perpetual yearning for spectacular victories. It is an intricate interweaving of force and finesse. In this performance, the Israeli military not only seeks to overcome resistance, but also to inspire awe and wonder, and to reinforce a unified sense of self-identity that spans whirlwind encounters in operations, battles and wars.

The allure of war for Israel, and more precisely for Israeli-ness, lies in the ability to elicit a moment of exaltation, of ecstasy – what Amos Oz called, commenting on the 1967 war, 'the orgy of victory.'[13] What is at issue are moments when a nation facing a perceived and overhyped abyss is instead lifted by the power to surprise, kill and win.[14] This pursuit of a military sublime, and consequently victory, is central to Israel's historical constitution and to its continual aspiration for war – an elusive and perpetual search for total victory marked by creative, innovative and daring military operations. Here, the destructiveness of war is paradoxically coupled with a drive for an artistic, almost divine, form of realisation, where the horrors of war are transmuted into a narrative of sublime self-assertion.

Since the beginning of Israel's onslaught on Gaza, however, Israel has lost its once-potent ability to deliver 'awe-inspiring' operations. Gone is the capacity to land a decisive, silencing blow upon its enemies, rendering them mute and incapable of further resistance. Instead, Israel has pivoted to a different regime of the sublime – one marked by an obscene enjoyment of death and destruction pure and simple. This shift involves a brazenly unapologetic, shameless transgression of established norms, laws and the codes of war. The spectacle of power is now mediated through advanced AI and representational media, operationalised primarily through an utterly dominant air force.

The recent failure to 'awe' is certainly not total, since Israel retains the ability to induce forms of pure affective negativity, such as fear, disgust, anger and feelings of hopelessness and insignificance in the presence of an overwhelming display of firepower. But it now fails to inspire enjoyment in its own operational design, its creative use of military power, its intelligence and precision and rapid dominance. It is a form of militarism that simply unleashes force without constraints, or that only acknowledges such constraints by announcing that it intends to transgress them – as in the case of Shifa Hospital, or the destruction of universities, or the targeting of sanctuaries, and the near destruction of Gaza as a whole.

This obscene enjoyment now centres on Israel's ability to transgress all apparent limits, to both declare *and* desecrate sanctuaries, and to violate the law of sanctuary itself. No longer does the regime seek to inspire awe; instead, it simply shocks without the accompanying reverence, indulging in a grotesque display of unrestrained brutality. The public consumption of these massacres marks a troubling turning point, as the aesthetics of military operations feed into a dark pleasure, stripping away the former veneer of heroics and replacing it with a brutal, unvarnished lust for domination. This is a military performance that relishes in the act of transgression itself, a spectacle that sows pure fear and horror, at the expense of its historic cultivation of disciplined and awe-inspiring militarism.

Sublime domination

A decade before Operation Entebbe, back in October 1967, the dynamics of Middle Eastern geopolitics were indelibly altered. The Israeli military, employing a combination of airpower, strategic surprise and audacious rapid manoeuvring, succeeded in decimating the Arab armies within six days. This swift and decisive war, known as the Six-Day War, became etched in the collective memory of Israelis as a miraculous event – an almost divine vindication of their historical claims over Palestine. As Tom Segev points out in his book *1967*, the triumph in the war reversed an ambient mood of hopelessness, a pervading feeling of doom among Israelis that had preceded it. It was declared as evidence of the 'hand of god' by Israel's newspaper *Yediot Ahronoth*.[15]

The air campaign decimated the Egyptian air force, gaining air superiority that would prove to be the key to Israel's tactical and operational advantage. On the ground, the Israeli forces executed a blitzkrieg across the Sinai Peninsula that left the Egyptian army in disarray.[16] In the north, the formidable Syrian tanks posed

Israeli attack on Egyptian air force base, June 1967; source: Wikimedia Commons

a significant threat from the high grounds of the Golan Heights. Yet here too, the Israeli forces managed to fend off the Syrian incursions, securing a buffer zone in a place that had long been a source of hostility, a buffer zone in which Israel could then build settlements and later officially annex as part of its territory.[17] And in the east, the rapid takeover of the West Bank underscored the agility and the sheer momentum with which Israel operated by weaponising surprise and superior firepower. The territorial gains made during those six days were staggering, expanding the settler colony's borders and reshaping the regional map in ways that continue to have far-reaching implications.

As Palestinian accounts of the 1967 war confirm, when tanks came rolling from the east into Nablus, Palestinians went to greet them, believing they must be Jordanian and Iraqi tanks – only to discover that they were Israeli tanks that had manoeuvred behind Jordanian lines.[18] The rapidity, surprise and impact of this victory on cultural representations and understandings of collective identity, both for Israelis and Palestinians, cannot be underestimated. Although the Nakba saw harrowing massacres combined with fierce Palestinian resistance and an extensive ethnic cleansing campaign, the Naksa can be seen as more of a Nakba than the Nakba itself, precisely on account of the sublime character of the victory. The only difference that rendered it more tolerable for Palestinians was the emergence of a new revolutionary project embodied by the *fida'i* – a figure of self-sacrifice that emerged to take centre stage in the fight against Zionist colonisation at the very moment the Arab armies themselves faltered.[19] But also, the collective lessons of the Nakba played a crucial role in limiting the mass expulsion of Palestinians from their homeland, as many insisted on staying put, in exactly the same way that hundreds of thousands of people have also refused to leave North Gaza in this current phase of the war.

For many Israelis, the 1967 war transcended mere military triumph. It was perceived as a providential event, one that made war and victory synonymous, encouraging a widespread intoxication with power. Unlike other mythologisations that have been woven into Israeli identity, such as Tel-Hai, the fall of Masada, or even the Warsaw Ghetto uprising, this was not an ethical or moral victory (a celebration of the power of rebellion even if miscarried, or an exploration of the heroism of tragic heroes, along with their ethical implications) – it was instead a purely military victory, a sublime moment that left Israelis in awe of their own technological and military prowess, the ingenuity of their military design and their sheer operational supremacy.[20] It was an Event that retroactively affirmed the right to the land, mediated through the spectacle of victory and its breathtaking speed. It also included within its very invocation of the miraculous and providential that sublime element which remained in essence unrepresentable, excessive and uncapturable.[21]

These narratives of national survival and the possibility of their mythologisation born from sublime victories attempt to depict the undepictable. They strive to articulate the experience of standing outside oneself, and to celebrate an agential sublimity produced by Israel's military prowess and its effects. Lyotard, in his exploration of the Kantian sublime, elucidates how this overwhelming emotion, which he describes as 'strong and equivocal', encompasses both pleasure and pain.[22] This emotion disrupts the basic reality and physical materiality of what was known before the encounter, and is triggered by an experience of the immensity of nature, or by a grand concept, or by a striking scene or image. In such moments, when the imagination is unable to fully grasp what lays before it, a feeling of bewilderment or wonder arises, a suspension of the ability to understand and comprehend. This failure to grasp the vastness of the object was central to the Romantic rendition of the sublime, for instance in the work of Edmund Burke.[23]

Kant expanded the reach of the sublime, however, when he situated it not only in what lies outside the subject, but also in the inward movement of the mind performed by the subject in relation to the supersensible.[24] And what changes if the encounter with the supersensible is itself the product of an agent? What if it retains the character of an unexpected encounter, one that fulfils the ecstatic suspension of the ego, yet retains an agential source?

Israel's militarism embodies a paradoxical suspension, whereby the imagination's capacity to apprehend is simultaneously arrested and inscribed as an artefact of its own creative force and agency. This militarism entwines the roles of artist and spectator, where the artist both creates yet stands in awe of his own creation. Mythologisation emerges as a secondary effect of this encounter with the supersensible, through which textual, artistic and other expressive forms are deployed to extricate events from their historical specificity.[25] This in turn enables a national identity to oscillate between a propensity for war and an underlying dread of peace or political engagement with its adversaries. This in turn reinforces a permanent quest for victory, where victory is not only 'sufficient' or pragmatic, but also an affirmation of a creative agency at play.[26]

Early Zionists, epitomised by Ze'ev Jabotinsky's articulation of the 'Iron Wall' (1923), construed war as an exigency borne from Palestinian resistance and their refusal to relinquish their land. This militaristic mode of thinking has since evolved into an active operational strategy vis-à-vis the Palestinians. It finds expression in quotidian colonial terror, in advanced technologies of surveillance and assault, and now in a genocidal war in Gaza. The Iron Wall has historically anchored itself in deterrence and territorial expansion, underscoring the fundamental conflict between Israeli territorial claims and Palestinian indigeneity. It is a wall that in principle seeks to engrave the Arab and Palestinian consciousness with the permanence of Israel's existence, an indelible fact resistant to negation. However, it is also more than simply a wall facing the Palestinians or Arabs. The Iron Wall is not solely a defensive structure; it transcends the simplistic function of a barrier and divider. It embodies the potential to surpass its own present pinnacle, to rise above its current state.[27]

The logic of this wall also helps to secure the otherwise circular argument defended in Jabotinsky's treatise on the 'ethics of the Iron Wall.' Here Jabotinsky boldly asserts that 'if Zionism is just, then justice must be realised without taking into consideration anyone's consent or lack of consent.'[28] The aestheticisation of military operations, the meticulous choreography of power, and the ongoing reification of the Iron Wall all serve to reinforce a form of ethical reassurance or solace that is deeply entwined with Zionist ideology, and grounded in Israelis' capacity to emerge victorious, and to silence or punish those who do not consent. This solace is derived from the ability to impose a self-referential and self-sustaining justice, perpetuating a vision of sovereignty that is unchallenged by the realities and voices of those on the other side of the wall.

Yet the wall, like any wall, has two sides. Military power not only sears the consciousness of Palestinians and the larger Arab world but also serves to both constitute Israeli-ness and resolve the ethical contradictions and implications inherent in Zionism, i.e. fundamentally and dramatically to re-orient the consciousness of Israelis. As Talal Asad points out in his recent reflections on the genocide in Gaza, the new Jew or the new 'Hebrew' that Israel constituted was attractive to the diasporic Jew not only on account of their 'eternal victim status', or on account of the history of antisemitism in Europe, as a Jewish solidarity that arose out of the experience of the Holocaust and was channelled through a yearning for the national home embodied in Israel. The new state was attractive precisely for the *power* that it was capable of mustering, the sublime nature of its military and the spectacular nature of its victories. As Asad makes clear, 'Israel's many political, cultural and technological achievements merely reinforce its transnational standing, and contribute to the desire of Jews to identify strongly with Israel.'[29]

Conversely, when Walid Daqqa endeavoured to delineate the methodologies that transformed the practices of Israeli torture during the Second Intifada, he sought to encapsulate the intersection of shock and what he termed the 'searing of consciousness' of Palestinians.[30] For Daqqa, the incursions into Palestinian cities, camps and villages transcended the mere material and direct objective of arresting or killing resistance fighters. These operations, driven by the formidable force of airpower, armoured vehicles and D9 bulldozers, unfolded as a form of 'extreme horror' intended to shock the Palestinians. The goal was to deliver the sort of overwhelming shock that might render Palestinians malleable, soft and impressionable. Disenchanted with their capacity to resist, Palestinians could then be expected to give up, and to initiate a process of healing in accordance with terms, discourses and politics defined broadly by the Israeli colonial apparatus.

Daqqa challenged a more widespread interpretation among many Palestinian analysts at that historical juncture (Second Intifada), who tended to assume that Israel had gone mad. In Daqqa's view, this presumed madness did not signify a loss of reason but rather represented a calculated deployment, aimed not only at dismantling the resistance but also at eroding its spiritual foundations – the virtues and political conceptions underpinning resistance. The primary battleground for Daqqa was the Palestinian faculty of representation and perception of the world, the way they try to make the world intelligible. He saw that Israel's (perfectly rational) objective was to shock the Palestinians and render them docile by attacking the inward movement of the subject. The 'shattering experience' of facing the shock of unconstrained military force would enable Israel to saturate the Palestinians with its own interpretation and expressions of its victory. This 'searing of consciousness' sought to induce a state of acquiescence among Palestinians, leading to a gradual self-effacement.[31]

Warring perceptions

'There is no war ... without representation', Paul Virilio asserted in his exploration of cinematic techniques in warfare. He emphasised that 'no sophisticated weaponry exists without psychological mystification.'[32] For Virilio, weapons, and by extension military operations and tactics, are not merely tools of destruction but also instruments of perception. He showed how these objects of war are also 'stimulants that affect the human sensory and neurological systems, influencing reactions and even the perceptual processes involved in the identification and differentiation of objects.'[33]

In particular, from the initial use of missiles in World War Two to the catastrophic flash of Hiroshima, Virilio illustrates a paradigm shift where the 'theatre weapon' supplants the traditional 'theatre of operations.'[34] This shift marks a significant change in the history of warfare, emphasising the evolution of perceptual fields over tangible territorial or political gains. Virilio's concept of the theatre weapon underscores how warfare has increasingly relied on the manipulation and control of perception. The term itself reveals the essence of modern combat: an ongoing use of military power not merely for physical territory or economic resources but for the dominance of immaterial perceptual realms. The manipulation of perceptions becomes a strategic objective in and of itself.

The Shock and Awe doctrine of the 1990s stands as a

testament to the aesthetic and perceptual designs of military strategy and its attempt to dominate on the lever of perceptions. This doctrine emerged in the twilight of the Cold War, aspiring to display a sanitised, swift, economical and formidable use of superior firepower in newly one-sided or asymmetrical imperial conflicts.[35] It was intended to overcome the bloody and failed history of engagements like Vietnam, where the combination of an indomitable Vietnamese will to resist coupled with high American casualties and a large and growing anti-war movement in the United States forced the empire to withdraw and cut its losses. The impact of Vietnam on the ways the United States would reconceptualise its war machine was and remains tremendous.[36] The new priorities would be avoidance of long intractable battles, clear definition of strategic objectives, rapidness and speed, and the tendency to rely more emphatically on airpower and other forms of remote firepower.

These new doctrines also took their cue from a long history of military manoeuvres, surprise attacks and other ways of using overwhelming force to secure victory. The rapid fall of France under the surprise of the German Blitzkrieg, the dropping of nuclear weapons on Hiroshima and Nagasaki, or even the Tet offensive launched by the North Vietnamese army would all serve as examples of operations where the use of devastating weapons or rapid operations ultimately eroded the enemy's will to fight. Shock and Awe would be thought of as a solution to the various challenges facing further deployment of Western militaries, for instance as a way of warding off domestic opposition while serving and preserving the economic interests that depended on the persistence of war.[37]

The doctrine explicitly sought to recreate through military power a sublime experience and spectacle.[38] The nexus between aesthetic effects and war has become central, investing the aesthetic dimension with practical and even ethical consequences. These shifts were also intimately tied to media and control of information, or management of this flow. The shock and awe would presumably take place on the battlefield, but its effects could be amplified by introducing cinematic techniques whereby images and narratives of wars were curated and reframed, and reinforced through media representations. The concept of a mediated sublime involves creating an awe-inspiring perception of power by simultaneously downplaying the horrors of war and emphasising sanitised, grandiose images of might and grandeur. This strategy aims to efface the atrocities while magnifying the war's evocative and majestic aspects.

Intrinsic to both effects-based operations and shock and awe campaigns was the appearance of a suitably sanitised, ordered, precise and rapid war. The new military logic reflects Kant's rendition of the sublime in war, which he also insisted must be ordered and fall within rules and norms.[39] This notion itself harbours a profound contradiction, for the sublime, in its essence, lies outside form. Lyotard elucidates this paradox in his discussion of the sublime, asserting that the sublime indeed involves a sacrifice of the aesthetic. This aporia between the sublime being contingent on an ordered war and the sublime as a sacrifice of the aesthetic is central to contemporary discourse on technology, aesthetics and war. It gestures towards another dimension of sublimity in war: the potential for destruction must encompass elements beyond the mere capacity to kill, maim or reduce cities to rubble. This applies particularly when this capacity for destruction is associated with a military machine that engages in expressly 'calculative' thinking – a mode of thought that estranges the human from the battlefield and, to evoke Heideggerian terms, renders the battlefield as *Enframing (Gestell)* and as 'standing reserve' or *Bestand*.[40]

In one sense, the doctrine of Shock and Awe promised the impossible. It was characterised by a profound mismatch between its conceptual foundation and the grim reality of war, a discrepancy that was apparent in the actual operation and representation of American and British forces in the First Gulf War. Here, war was transfigured into a media spectacle, where the curating and editing of war's brutal consequences on its victims were obfuscated and removed from the public's gaze. Within this curated media spectacle, American and British forces would indeed follow 'the rules of war', but the vast destruction on the ground, and the thousands of Iraqis killed and injured, would remain firmly out of view. The wide-scale bombings were broadcast without the visceral imagery of the suffering bodies, sanitising the horrors of war for the global audience and ensuring that no significant resistance would arise. The theatre of weapons is a theatre that insists on showcasing the grandeur of explosions while suppressing the actual experience of those suffering the consequences of its fire. The mystification of airpower, the capacity to fight wars from a distance, the reliance on cinematic media techniques, and so on, led Jean Baudrillard famously to propose that the First Gulf War 'never took place': it was less a war than an attempt by the American empire to perpetuate its logic of deterrence through the use of shock and awe, targeted not so much at the Iraqi regime as at the spectators watching the unfolding images play out on TV.[41] This simulacrum of war, or 'non-war' as Baudrillard calls it, would reassure those identifying with the empire, and shelter them in the safety of military supremacy – but it was also a war that weaponised images to create a *spectacle* of awe, representing the Iraqis killed as little more than extras hovering on the edges of the show.

Such artifice, however, becomes increasingly untenable in an era of ubiquitous cell phones and the consequently immediate, unfiltered dissemination of raw images following each bombing or attack. This problem is particularly evident in the context of Israel's current assault on Gaza. The unmediated display of devastation now confronts the spectator with the inescapable reality of human suffering.

In response to this grim reality and the failure to conduct military operations that can evoke awe in a way that is both sufficiently overwhelming *and* sufficiently sanitised, the ongoing war in Gaza has instead taken a shape that openly affirms the devastation it is causing. It binds two logics together, a logic of deterrence premised on the capacity to evoke horror and celebrate its effects, and a logic of punishment adapted from the familiar image of the Iron Wall. These logics are applied through various devices, including the appropriation of representational media, the *Matrix*-like capabilities embedded in command-and-control centres in Israel, the deliberate maintenance of distance from the battlefield, and the utilisation of AI both to generate endless lists of targets and to direct drones and fighter jets towards them.[42] Each of these simulacra highlight the fact that Israel's familiar sense of itself as defined by a heroic engagement with sacrifice and as exemplified through daring, bold and creative operations, now belongs mainly to the past. In the phantasmagoric realms of warfare, these simulated codifications perform a disavowal, recasting the sublime not as an encounter with self-loss (whether agonising or ecstatic) but as a manifestation of imaginary omnipotence – an omnipotence that fully embraces the notion that war is indeed hell, and affirms it repeatedly.

The current spectacle of war in Gaza, therefore, elicits either an obscene enjoyment in the spectacle of asymmetric punishment or silent complicity in its occurrence and unfolding among Israeli society writ large. October 7th marked a pivotal moment when the symbolic and imaginary fabric underlying a core tenet of Israeli identity – the sublime object of its ideology embodied in the Iron Wall and its own invincibility – was shattered. Israel's 'operational art', to borrow a term from military studies, is now being reframed away from a sacrificial and heroic sublime into a regime of sublime horror that lacks any sort of grandeur or magnificence. Virilio's observation rings true: the theatre of weapons unleashed on Gaza combines with the generative capacity of AI to articulate a coldly mechanical code of targeting centred on widescale bombardment and the mass killing of Palestinians. Israel no longer seeks to curate its war, rather it has chosen to overflow the senses with endless streams of visceral imagery, confirming its readiness and capacity to engage in an obscene and shameless genocide.

Israel's operational artlessness

After October 7th, Israel embarked on strategies of annihilation in Gaza, viewing them as essential responses to breaches in both its physical and ideological fortifications, and to the erosion of its existential certainty.[43] This turn towards mere obliteration of the enemy starkly contradicted Israel's carefully cultivated image of 'military excellence.' In the 1990s, amidst apprehensions about peace and confronting unconventional challenges from groups like Hezbollah, Hamas and Islamic Jihad, the Israeli military elevated the quality and tone of its intellectual inquiry, delving deeply into the operational complexities of warfare, appropriating elements from systems theory and post-structural theories of space. Among the prominent figures to emerge as a pivotal intellectual synthesiser and innovator in operational theory was Shimon Naveh, founder and former director of Israel's Operational Theory Research Institute (OTRI), which was itself part of its National Defence College.[44]

The definition of political objectives remains primary; operational inquiry then focuses on the method by which these objectives can be achieved, the 'how' of warfare. The intricate selection of ends and means encompasses institutional actors, geopolitical conditions, political factions and internal strife, socio-economic limitations or catalysts, and crucially, the availability of weapons and technology. The fundamental role of operational art is to enable an analytical inventory of these various components so as to provide solutions that overcome the various challenges faced by commanders. To this end, Naveh and his colleagues at OTRI sought to rejuvenate aspects of Soviet operational theory, in particular its emphasis on conducting analysis that examines parts in relation to the whole.[45] The fervour surrounding the operational dimension coincided both with Israel's newly vehement refusal of the political compromises that would be required to end its protracted occupation, and with the emergence of irregular, asymmetric adversaries that began steadily to undermine its capacity for definitive victories.[46]

The fixation on 'military excellence' in Israeli military discourse reveals a broader sentiment permeating the armed forces – a sense of diminishing prowess. This sentiment arises from a complex interplay of factors: a lowering of existential anxiety following peace treaties with Egypt and Jordan, the tumultuous Oslo peace process juxtaposed with the brutal crackdowns during the First Intifada (when the Israeli military infamously 'broke the bones' of Palestinian protesters and employed deadly violence against unarmed protestors), and the rise of adept guerrilla forces in Lebanon and Palestine.[47] The Israeli military, grappling with the need to reclaim its self-fashioned mantle of excellence, embarked on a quest for new operational modes, solutions and technologies. Naveh and his cohort emerged as an influential current within the Israeli army, advocating for innovative approaches to warfare and operations. Eyal Weizman, in his book *Hollow Land*, shows how Naveh's vision for OTRI offered a framework for 'operational architects' within the Israeli military.[48] However, the initial enthusiasm that surrounded OTRI proved to be overblown, and for a time Naveh and his followers were blamed for the Israeli military's setbacks in Lebanon in 2006.[49]

Seeking to grasp, appropriate, synthesise and develop new modes of operation that would set benchmarks for other armies and secure military objectives in any conflict, Israel now found itself thoroughly ensnared in the operational dimension of warfare – a space wedged between political ambitions and tactical manoeuvres. This commitment to operational 'engagement' also reflected a broader malaise within Israel, and reflected a retreat away from diplomacy, negotiations and the delineation of clear political goals (beyond the perpetuation of a status quo based on expanding illegal settlements and quelling Palestinian resistance). The military assumed primary responsibility for maintaining order and advocated purely military solutions that obscured the necessity for political engagement. The operational dimension was therefore taken to be a silver bullet, the means through which Israel could avoid any compromises, while solidifying its permanent hold on historic Palestine.

Under the pressure of fierce resistance, Israel was confronted by the need to make unilateral withdrawals from Lebanon in 2000 and Gaza in 2006. At the same time, it sought to hobble Palestinian resistance in the West Bank and ensure the rise of a collaborative regime, institutionalised in the Palestinian National Authority.[50] It would now concentrate on colonising the West Bank, besieging Gaza and keeping Lebanon at arm's length through a policy of deterrence. Meanwhile OTRI and the soldiers and commanders influenced by them were busy exploring the reinterpretations of space proposed by their operational architects, exemplified by new capacities for 'walking through walls', and new forms of systems analysis and dialectical cognition.[51]

By contrast, other currents within the Israeli military would insist on simplicity, and doubling-down on Israeli strength, its sheer firepower. Following its war in Lebanon in 2006, Israel introduced the infamous Dahiya Doctrine. This doctrine targeted civilians and civilian infrastructure as crucial nodes in any war effort. The new campaigns did not seek to target the resistance-fighters specifically so much as the society from which their resistance arose. The doctrine sanctioned recourse to calibrated massacres and to levels of destruction that can be quickly relaxed and intensified, depending on the evolving balance of deterrence. A sufficiently punishing and deadly campaign against civilians would compel resistance forces to give up or surrender, thereby ending conflicts without having to address the underlying political grievances.

Within the Israeli military, a debate raged for some years, especially after the 2006 Lebanon war, between these two contrasting yet equally lethal ideologies: the simplistic yet deadly approach embodied by the Dahiya doctrine, and the complex lexicon of operational art that was led by those close to OTRI. The former was rooted in older doctrines of airpower that had emerged in Europe in the early twentieth century, as a means of by-passing the obstacles posed by trench warfare. Airpower and longer-distance firepower strategies aimed to exploit their new spatial dimensions, allowing forces to fly above and across battlefields, and to target civilian spaces deep within enemy territory. Warfare was no longer conceived merely as a clash between military forces but as a totalising conflict enveloping the entire socio-economic fabric of the warring nations.[52] Clustered around OTRI, the second and more future-oriented current within Israel's military employed systems theory, post-structural theory and architectural theory to rethink military operations. Naveh would soon emphasise the importance and relevance of both systems theory and dialectical thinking in conceiving operational art, and its acceptance of continuous change.[53]

The debate between these two currents was, in many ways, also aesthetic – a clash between strategies of sheer horror and brutality on the one hand, embodied in the pursuit of annihilation through conception of calibrated and intensifying destruction, and on the other, approaches that aimed to integrate elements of warfare capable of inducing operational shock and awe, thereby restoring Israel's reputation for military excellence. The intellectual dimensions of the debate began to fade as Israel turned its focus to developing new technologies such as AI targeting and missile defence systems, along with innovative networked systems concepts aimed at optimising their military efficacy, especially in ground manoeuvres – for instance, the Israeli military's concept of 'Land Ahead.'[54] Aviv Kochavi, a promising young commander during the Second Intifada and a key proponent of Naveh's 'operational architects', rose to become Israel's chief of staff by 2019 (through to 2023). In addition to cultivating a charismatic presence and some impressive rhetorical skills, Kochavi has long emphasised the need to foreground change and evolution within Israel's armed forces. He has prioritised the pursuit of decisive victories and highlighted the pivotal roles of intelligence, technological innovation and systemic investigations. The language of OTRI, systems theory and post-structuralism had returned to Israeli military discourse, albeit in a somewhat simplified form.

In the years following the 2006 Lebanon War Israel revelled in its means of annihilation, which it perceived as the only winning strategies to have emerged from its conflict with Hezbollah. This approach maintained a constant deterrent capacity, generally sufficient to keep Hezbollah at bay. In Gaza, a similar stance led to repeated military engagements, operations that Israel came to dub 'mowing the grass.' The goal was to maintain a purely military equilibrium, indefinitely. Punitive firepower campaigns and small operations targeting tunnels ensured that Palestinian resistance could neither challenge the status quo nor push the conflict from military terrain (where Israel remained strong) back onto political terrain (where Israel could still be challenged). In this context, Israel doubled down on various defensive technologies, surrounding itself with new layers of protection – security walls and fences, sensors, radars and missile defence systems such as the Iron Dome. In his role as chief of *Aman* (Israel's Military Intelligence), Kochavi played a crucial role in enhancing cyber capabilities, representational media, intelligence gathering and militarised AI.[55] Politically, this military stance was not aimed at disrupting the status quo but rather at maintaining Israel's ability to colonise the West Bank at minimal cost, without having to face significant political engagement or resistance.

However, once Kochavi assumed command of Israel's military in 2019, he began to argue that Israel should no longer be content with merely maintaining this equilibrium. It was time to go back on the offensive. This again required developing a lethal army that is both innovative and awe-inspiring, while also centralising the role of the commander in directing the components of a highly technological and integrated force.

Kochavi draws a compelling parallel between the role of a military commander and the work of an artist, illustrating how both require a blend of creativity and critical reflection. In his observations, Kochavi highlights how an artist experiences a peak moment of identification with their creation upon its completion, only to later engage in a process of self-criticism and distancing. This reflective process, which prompts the artist to revisit and critically evaluate their past work, encourages continuous learning and improvement. Similarly, Kochavi suggests that military commanders should embrace this artistic mindset, recognising that their strategic decisions and operational plans are not static but subject to ongoing critique and adaptation. Just as artists question their past creations, commanders must constantly reassess their actions and the changing dynamics within their organisations. Of the ideal commander, Kochavi writes: 'any person who creates is familiar with the tendencies of artists who reach the peak of their identification with their work at the moment of its completion ... Then comes the process of "distancing" from the work ... Years later, the artist may find themselves critically asking, "I created that?" This is a good quality that promotes learning.'[56] In other words, the ideal commander is one who is aware of the system they lead, and who is able to devise the most effective operations from out of the various components of the systems available.

In 2021, Israel sought to confound Palestinian resistance in Gaza through its so-called 'Metro Operation.' The strategy was deceptively straightforward: leak intentions of a ground invasion of Gaza to the foreign press, thereby compelling Palestinian fighters to seek refuge in an already compromised tunnel network, which Israel then planned to obliterate with its airpower. This operation exemplified the convergence of Israel's advanced technological capabilities – geo-location, surveillance, sensory technologies, 'matrix capability', intelligence and airpower – and the precision required for subterranean targeting.[57] The operation maintained a safe distance from the battlefield and did not risk the lives of Israeli soldiers. It was built on past intelligence of Palestinian fighter movements, who could be expected to take refuge in tunnels. By turning the tunnel network into a death trap, the goal was to allow Israel to shake the foundations of Palestinian defensive strategies. Instead of the tunnels serving as a refuge, they would become graveyards. Nonetheless, after the smoke cleared, Israel was obliged to admit that few 'combatants' had been killed in its operation.

For figures such as Kochavi and much of the Israeli high command, the notion of operational art is inscribed within a technical framework but it also requires the infusion of creative imagination.[58] This creative imagination becomes the locus for the emergence of new ideas and representations, central to the conception of a military force that operates not merely as an efficient machine but as an entity capable of spectacular, deceptive, creative and exalting operations.[59] The military force operates here as both machine and more-than-machine, or as Kochavi emphasises, echoing Naveh, a 'system'. The essence of victory is neither fully technical nor wholly imaginative but oscillates between these two poles, continuously redefined by the exigencies of warfare and the imperatives of innovation. It transforms the battlefield into a space of poetic engagement, in which the lines between reality and representation blur, and where the performative enactment of power becomes the ultimate testament to military prowess.

However, this artistic and adaptive vision is today starkly belied by Israel's actual practice in the current phase of its war in Gaza. The military *machine* has now wholly overshadowed the commander-*artist*, thereby limiting any role for operational art. The conflict has highlighted a reliance on sheer destructive power over strategic ingenuity and creativity. Although it remains in constant flux, the military system now functions in ways more akin to Heidegger's concept of 'standing reserve', and it figures mainly as a mere stockpile of resources and capacities on standby for instrumental use, lacking intrinsic purpose and no longer able to induce an experience of the sublime or enable true creativity. In Gaza, the army's alignment with advanced technology and 'calculative thinking' has led to an operational mode in which humans have to adjust to machines rather than vice-versa. Rather than draw on a dynamic interplay of imagination and machinery, military operations are becoming more and more mechanical, a mere exercise of force.

The bombardment of sanctuaries in Rafah, the destruction of universities, mosques and churches, even the breach of diplomatic norms through attacks on embassies – all these acts of wanton destruction epitomise the chaotic nature of the strategy currently being pursued by the Israeli military. It reflects a new dominance of calculative thinking, guided by algorithmic and instrumental rationality. This approach strips away an essential legitimising mechanism in the eyes of observers and supporters, it eliminates that 'aesthetic' impact of military operations that was so essential to the older aspiration to military excellence. Instead of fostering a creative, innovative and awe-inspiring militarism, it just invokes sheer horror.

Rather than daring heroism, Israel now resorts to the

banality and imbecility of pushing a button and unleashing force. The Dahiya doctrine first triumphed inside Israel in 2006, but its further consolidation in 2023-24 exposes the truth of the Israeli military for all to see. To the world and to itself, Israel now appears as it has always appeared to us Palestinians: as a regime of pure terror.

Shock without awe

In one of the rare moments of the current campaign that sought to reaffirm a clear sense of Israeli-ness, on 8 June 2024, Israeli special forces launched a daring mission within the dense confines of the Nuseirat refugee camp to rescue four Israeli captives. This operation, which the Israeli media hailed as a resounding success, was swiftly compared to the Entebbe raid or 'Operation Thunderbolt' of 1976, igniting a wave of national exaltation and widespread celebration among the many Israelis desperate for some sign that might confirm their nation's ongoing militarist ingenuity and creativity. The Israeli minister of defence called it 'one of the most extraordinary operations' that he has witnessed in more than 50 years.[60] To extricate their forces and the captives, however, Israel had to carpet-bomb the camp itself, resulting in the killing of more than 270 Palestinian civilians.[61] One of the commandos involved in the operation was also killed. Despite the hype, the actual mechanics of the operation confirmed that Israel now has only one strategy for victory in Gaza: a recurrent and daily recourse to massacres.[62]

Israeli-ness is now being redefined, and this is happening in ways that tacitly acknowledge Palestinian perspectives. For us, who have endured and continue to endure the horrors of Zionism and its systematic policies of exclusion, murder, ethnic cleansing, humiliation, revulsion and various forms of erasure, Zionism has always been a form of horror, an ongoing nightmare or Nakba. An emphatically *horrifying* conception of Israeli-ness is now also being redefined for both Israelis and their supporters. This new or emerging regime of the sublime, unfolding through extensive firepower and the removal of battle from war, conducted via heavily armoured machinery and aimed at rendering Gaza mute, represents a continuation of Israel's longstanding policy of ethnic cleansing – but it now does away with attempts to operationalise aesthetics in ways that might inspire wonder or exaltation. It consequently fails to inspire narratives of heroism and creativity. Israel is now confined to the anti-heroics of pure elimination and genocide. This shift is already having a dramatic impact on Israel's ability to elicit political legitimation and support for its colonial enterprise.

It is important to reiterate that, although its reliance on pure horror has recently become more emphatic, Israel's self-cultivated image of military excellence has always coexisted with its recourse to massacres, ethnic cleansing and other forms of brute force. Israel's creation was enabled by the material effect of such massacres, more than by a performative display of awe-inspiring operations. However much the symbolic cultivation of Israeli-ness might centre itself on the sublime assertion of power, in reality the massacres and systematic ethnic cleansing were the primary means of its creation. The long history of the bloody killing of Palestinians predates the Nakba, it intensified during the Nakba, and it has continued all through the subsequent confrontation with Israeli settler colonialism. This history is punctuated by the Kufr Qasem Massacre, the Qibya massacre, the infamous Sabra and Shatila massacre in Lebanon and numerous other atrocities.[63] Though these episodes are or should be well-known, and played an essential role in the assertion of Israeli dominance and control, within Israel itself they were also kept largely hidden from public scrutiny.

By contrast, the current and overt display of Israeli military horror in Gaza serves as a deterrent not only to Gaza but also to Lebanon and the broader region. Israeli propaganda on social media juxtaposes images of 'Beirut Before' with suggestions of a 'Beirut After', evoking the spectre of a devastated city in the event of a large-scale war. This Shock *without* Awe paradigm continues to serve Israel, as it flirts with dangerous fascist ideologies and takes a festive and unapologetic pleasure in its power to punish, kill, maim and destroy.

Today, Israel's hope is not that the world will soon forget this current phase of the conflict. Nor does Israel seek to encourage the world to recognise itself in its carefully cultivated image as a lone liberal democracy holding back a sea of Arab and Muslim barbarians. Instead, it now hopes that the world will soon catch up with its stark monstrosity, and cement its collusion in all the horrors that 'total victory' might require.

Abdaljawad Omar is a part-time Lecturer in the Philosophy and Cultural Studies Department at Birzeit University and has contributed to a number of different outlets, including Mondoweiss *and* Electronic Intifada.

Notes

1. Saleh Abdel Jawad argues in his review of Bassem Sharif's book on Wadie Haddad, the Arab Nationalist leader assassinated by Mossad in 1978, that Israeli successes in extraction operations were largely due to the hijackers' orders not to harm passengers and their ethical commitments, which enabled Israel to stage these spectacular triumphs without risking much resistance from the hijackers themselves. See Saleh Abdeljawad, 'Abu Sharif on Wadie Haddad: Towards a Critical Review of External Operations', *Al-Akhbar*, 2014, https://www.al-akhbar.com/Opinion/2648.

2. A large corpus of mainstream books, alongside many dramatised takes on Israeli militarism, such as *Fauda* on Netflix, attest to this self-cultivated image of an embattled liberal state facing monstrous enemies. See for instance: Michael Bar-Zohar and Nissim Mishal, *Mossad: The Greatest Missions of the Israeli Secret Service* (New York: Ecco, 2012); Ronen Bergman, *Rise and Kill First: The Secret History of Israel's Targeted Assassinations* (New York: Random House, 2018); Yaakov Katz and Amir Bohbot, *The Weapon Wizards: How Israel Became a High-Tech Military Superpower* (New York: St. Martin's Press, 2017); Yossi Melman and Dan Raviv, *Spies Against Armageddon: Inside Israel's Secret Wars* (New York: Levant Books, 2012).

3. For an overview of the cultural and intellectual responses to this defeat in the Arab World, see Elizabeth Suzanne Kassab, *Contemporary Arab Thought: Cultural Critique in Comparative Perspective* (New York: Columbia University Press, 2009), 48–115.

4. Cf. Jens Bjering et al., eds., *War and Aesthetics: Art, Technology, and the Futures of Warfare* (Cambridge, MA: MIT Press, 2024).

5. Walter Benjamin, 'Theories of German Fascism: On the Collection of Essays *War and Warrior*, Edited by Ernst Jünger', *New German Critique* 17 (1979), 122.

6. Benjamin points out how the technologies and materials of warfare, particularly gas warfare, make the desire for war an empty gesture. This is because it eliminates the 'outdated symbols of heroism' that Jünger and others celebrate (Benjamin, 'Theories of German Fascism', 121).

7. Benjamin, 'Theories of German Fascism', 127–8.

8. Barbee-Sue Rodman, 'War and Aesthetic Sensibility: An Essay in Cultural History', *Soundings: An Interdisciplinary Journal* 51:3 (1968), 308.

9. J. Glenn Gray, *The Warriors: Reflections on Men in Battle* [1959] (Lincoln: Bison Books, 1970), 36.

10. Gray, *The Warriors*, 36.

11. Gray, *The Warriors*, 36.

12. Gray, *The Warriors*, xii.

13. Quoted in Joshua Leifer, 'What Amos Oz Couldn't See', *Dissent Magazine* (Spring 2019), https://www.dissentmagazine.org/article/what-amos-oz-couldnt-see/.

14. Tom Segev, *1967: Israel, the War, and the Year that Transformed the Middle East*, trans. Jessica Cohen (New York: Metropolitan Books, 2007), 247.

15. Segev, *1967*, 15.

16. Segev, *1967*, 676.

17. Amnesty International, 'Israel/OPT: 10 Things You Need to Know About Annexation', 2 July 2020, https://www.amnesty.org/en/latest/news/2020/07/israelopt-10-things-you-need-to-know-about-annexation/.

18. Mu'in al-Taher and Tabgh wa-Zaytoun, 'Hikayat wa-Suwar min Zaman Muqawim [Tobacco and Olives: Stories and Pictures from a Time of Resistance]' (Doha: Arab Centre for Research and Policy Studies, 2017), 19.

19. Rosemary Sayigh, *Palestinians: From Peasants to Revolutionaries* (London: Zed Books, 1979).

20. Dalia Gavrieli-Nuri, 'Saying "War", Thinking "Victory" – The Mythmaking Surrounding Israel's 1967 Victory', *Israel Studies* 15:1 (2010), 96.

21. For a discussion on war, the excessive and the relationship to the sublime, see Vivienne Jabri, 'Shock and Awe: Power and the Resistance of Art', *Millennium* 34:3 (2006), 821–4.

22. Jean-François Lyotard, *The Postmodern Condition: A Report on Knowledge* (Minneapolis: University of Minnesota Press, 1984), 77.

23. Edmund Burke, *A Philosophical Enquiry into the Origin of Our Ideas of the Sublime and Beautiful* [1757] (Oxford: Oxford University Press, 1990).

24. For Kant this confrontation with the suprasensible produces pain, it instigates a process within the faculty of mind. See Immanuel Kant, *Critique of Judgement*, trans. J. H. Bernard (New York: MacMillan, 1951), 84.

25. Roland Barthes writes about how myths transform history into nature, and thereby extract events from their historical context. See in particular Roland Barthes, *Mythologies*, trans. Annette Lavers (New York: Farrar, Straus and Giroux, 1972), 142–5.

26. For more on Israeli militarism and the fear of peace, see Uri Ben-Eliezer, *War over Peace: One Hundred Years of Israel's Militaristic Nationalism*, trans. Shaul Vardi (Oakland: University of California Press, 2019).

27. For a detailed exploration of Nietzsche and Zionism and the influence of Nietzsche on early Zionist thinking, centring notions such as self-overcoming, mastery, longing for an authentic self and sublime missions, see Jacob

Golomb, *Nietzsche and Zion* (Ithaca, NY: Cornell University Press, 1997).

28. Ze'ev Jabotinsky, 'The Ethics of the Iron Wall', *Razsviet*, 11 November 1923, https://en.jabotinsky.org/archive/search-archive/item/?itemId=114767.

29. Talal Asad, 'Reflections on the Israeli-Palestinian Conflict', *Humanity Journal*, 21 March 2024, https://humanityjournal.org/blog/reflections-on-the-israeli-palestinian-conflict/.

30. Walid Daqqa, 'Sihr al-Wa'i aw l'adat Ta'rif al-Ta'dhib [Searing Consciousness or Redefining Torture]' (Beirut: Centre for Studies and Arab Scientific Publishers, with Al-Jazeera, 2010), 27–33.

31. Daqqa, 'Sihr al-Wa'i aw l'adat Ta'rif al-Ta'dhib.'

32. Paul Virilio, *War and Cinema: The Logistics of Perception*, trans. Patrick Camiller (London: Verso, 1989), 10.

33. Virilio, *War and Cinema*, 13.

34. Virilio, *War and Cinema*, 13.

35. Harlan K. Ullman and James P. Wade, *Shock and Awe: Achieving Rapid Dominance* (Washington, DC: National Defense University, 1996), http://www.dodccrp.org/files/Ullman_Shock.pdf.

36. See for instance Nadia Abu El-Haj, *Combat Trauma: Imaginaries of War and Citizenship in Post-9/11 America* (London: Verso, 2022).

37. For a critical take on Shock and Awe and its relationship to the Vietnam War, see H. R. McMaster, 'This Familiar Battleground', *World Affairs*, 9 October 2009, https://www.hoover.org/research/familiar-battleground.

38. Ullman and Wade, *Shock and Awe*.

39. Lucian Staiano-Daniels, 'Taste and the Claims of War: The Kantian Sublime and the Function of War in Public Aesthetic Judgement', *History of European Ideas* 49:5 (2022), 824.

40. Martin Heidegger, 'The Question Concerning Technology', in *The Question Concerning Technology and Other Essays*, trans. William Lovitt (New York: Harper & Row, 1977), 3–35. For Heidegger, the essence of technology is not technological; rather, it lies in technology as a mode of revelation which he calls 'enframing' [*Gestell*]. Enframing 'is the gathering together that belongs to that setting-upon which sets upon man and puts him in position to reveal the real, in the mode of ordering, as standing-reserve' (24). By enhancing the military and its perceptive capacities through the employment of a wide range of complex tools – sensors, radars, satellites, algorithmic deductions, artificial intelligence, cyber capabilities, representational media, aerial surveillance, among others – both those operating the military system and those targeted by it are reduced to mere data points in a web of calculations. They now come to be seen as resources to be either used or annihilated. Enframing also conceals what it reveals in the context of modern technology. As Heidegger puts it, enframing 'does not simply endanger man in his relationship to himself and to everything that is.' In addition, the enframed resources or inventory of tools at man's disposal 'no longer even let their own fundamental characteristic appear, namely, this revealing as such' (27). Instead of disclosing the truth of being, modern technology distorts it. This has deep implications for the impact of technology in warfare, and for the ways the battlefield comes to be ordered, including human and non-human actants and targets.

41. Jean Baudrillard, *The Gulf War Did Not Take Place*, trans. Paul Patton (Bloomington: Indiana University Press, 1991).

42. A series of articles were published by the Israeli magazine *+972* that discuss the generative targeting power of AI and its use in the war in Gaza. See in particular Yuval Abraham, '"A Mass Assassination Factory": Inside Israel's Calculated Bombing of Gaza', *+972 Magazine*, 30 November 2023, https://www.972mag.com/mass-assassination-factory-israel-calculated-bombing-gaza/; Yuval Abraham, '"Lavender": The AI Machine Directing Israel's Bombing Spree in Gaza', *+972 Magazine*, 3 April 2024, https://www.972mag.com/lavender-ai-israeli-army-gaza/.

43. Although Israeli society speaks of an existential anxiety, this generally remains a productive confession of vulnerability in the face of possible demise. This form of public acknowledgement of precarity hides a deeper sense of security that is paradoxically produced by speaking of vulnerabilities. A large literature exists on existential anxiety of Israeli society – see for instance Gad Yair, 'Israeli Existential Anxiety: Cultural Trauma and the Constitution of National Character', *Social Identities* 20:4–5 (2014), 346–62; Gilad Hirschberger, Tom Pyszczynski and Tsachi Ein-Dor, 'An Ever-Dying People: The Existential Underpinnings of Israelis' Perceptions of War and Conflict', *Les Cahiers Internationaux de Psychologie Sociale* 87:3 (2010), 443–57.

44. The DADO Centre for Interdisciplinary Military Studies was established in 2007 as a reconfiguration of the older Operational Theory Research Institute (OTRI), which was directed by Shimon Naveh. This change occurred as a result of the 2006 Lebanon War, during which Israel's military faced significant criticism for its failures in ground manoeuvres in South Lebanon. The Winograd Commission, set up to investigate these failures, placed some of the responsibility on the language and operative concepts developed by OTRI and the work of Naveh and his team. DADO thus emerged as an updated version of the Institute, one intended to retain what was valuable in OTRI's work while learning from its excesses and mis-

takes.

45. Naveh's 1997 book, *In Pursuit of Military Excellence: The Evolution of Operational Theory*, is replete with various examples of systems analysis and historical experiences of operational art, including the Napoleonic Wars, Blitzkrieg and the 1967 war, among others. He provides analyses of these operations by approaching them through systems analysis, emphasising the capacity to integrate various components into a single operation that successfully achieves its military objectives. The book also includes analyses of how these operations can induce a systems shock in the enemy forces.

46. When Aviv Kochavi came to lead Israel's military in 2019, he redrew its conceptual apparatus around the pursuit of decisive victory. See Yaakov Lappin, 'The IDF's Momentum Plan Aims to Create a New Type of War Machine', *BESA Center Perspectives Paper*, no. 1, 497, 22 March 2020, https://besacenter.org/idf-momentum-plan/.

47. Sergio Catignani, *Israeli Counter-Insurgency and the Intifadas: Dilemmas of a Conventional Army* (London: Routledge, 2008).

48. Eyal Weizman, *Hollow Land: Israel's Architecture of Occupation* (London: Verso Books, 2012), 187–219.

49. Łukasz Przybyło, 'Systemic Operational Design – a Study in Failed Concept', *Security and Defence Quarterly* 42:2 (2023), 35–54.

50. For a critical reading on the Palestinian Authority in the wake of the Second Intifada, see Dana El Kurd, *Polarized and Demobilized: Legacies of Authoritarianism in Palestine* (London: Hurst Publishers, 2019).

51. See in particular Eyal Weizman, 'Walking through Walls: Soldiers as Architects in the Israeli–Palestinian Conflict', *Radical Philosophy* 136 (March 2006), https://www.radicalphilosophy.com/article/walking-through-walls.

52. For an early discussion of airpower and its efficacy and possibilities, see Giulio Douhet, *The Command of the Air*, trans. Dino Ferrari (New York; Coward-McMann, 1942).

53. Shimon Naveh, *In Pursuit of Military Excellence: The Evolution of Operational Theory* (London: Routledge, 1997).

54. Colonel Eran Ortal, 'We're Confused, Too: A Historical Perspective for Discussion of "Land Ahead",' *Military Review* (March-April 2019), https://www.armyupress.army.mil/Journals/Military-Review/English-Edition-Archives/Mar-Apr-2019/82-Confused/.

55. Aviv Kochavi and Eran Ortal, 'Ma'asei Aman: Permanent Change in a Changing Reality', DADO Center, 2 July 2014, https://www.idf.il/en/mini-sites/dado-center/vol-2-change-and-transformation/ma-asei-aman/.

56. Major General Aviv Kochavi, 'To Be a Military Leader: Major General Kochavi', Dado Center, Israel Defense Forces (22 June 2022), https://www.idf.il/en/mini-sites/dado-center/research/to-be-a-military-leader-major-general-kochavi/.

57. David M. Halbfinger, 'A Press Corps Deceived, and the Gaza Invasion That Wasn't', *New York Times*, 14 May 2021, https://www.nytimes.com/2021/05/14/world/middleeast/israel-gaza-disinformation.html.

58. Kochavi, 'To Be a Military Leader.'

59. The metaphoric reference to matrix capability is meant to highlight the representational media available for Israeli commanders. The matrix is designed to integrate vast amounts of intelligence, imagery and other information, displaying this consolidated data on one or multiple screens for commanders and operational leaders. This integration allows for real-time situational awareness and informed decision-making, and is presumed to enhance operational effectiveness on the battlefield. See Ron Leshem, 'IDF Possesses Matrix-like Capabilities, Ex-Israeli Army Chief Says', *Ynetnews*, 30 June 2023, https://www.ynetnews.com/magazine/article/ry0uzlhu3.

60. Al Jazeera staff, 'Nuseirat: Anatomy of Israel's Massacre in Gaza', *Al Jazeera*, 11 June 2024, https://www.aljazeera.com/news/2024/6/11/nuseirat-anatomy-of-israels-massacre-in-gaza.

61. Al Jazeera staff, 'Nuseirat.'

62. Shrouq Aila, 'Nuseirat Massacre: Inside Israel's Failed Hostage Rescue in Gaza', *The Intercept*, 10 June 2024, https://theintercept.com/2024/06/10/nuseirat-massacre-israel-hostage-rescue-gaza/.

63. Much is made of Israeli protests against the 1982 Sabra Shatila Massacres. A confluence of factors encouraged these protests to emerge in Israel at the time, including concerns that Israel might get bogged down in an unnecessary war in Lebanon, More fundamentally, the massacres drew particular condemnation because they were committed by allies of the Israeli military, the Phalange, rather than by the military itself.

Reviews

How settler colonialism ends

Hagar Kotef, *The Colonizing Self: Or, Home and Homelessness in Israel/Palestine* (Durham: Duke University Press, 2020). 300pp., $28.95 pb., 978 1 47801 133 0

Adam Shatz, *The Rebel's Clinic: The Revolutionary Lives of Frantz Fanon* (London: Head of Zeus, 2024). 451pp., £22.50 hb., 978 1 03590 004 6

Mahmood Mamdani, *Neither Settler Nor Native: The Making and Unmaking of Permanent Minorities* (Cambridge and London: Belknap Press, 2020). 401pp., £24.95 hb., 978 0 67498 732 6

Jonny Steinberg, *Winnie & Nelson: Portrait of a Marriage* (London: William Collins, 2023). 550pp., £12.99 pb., 978 0 00835 381 0

In her book *The Colonizing Self*, Israeli political theorist Hagar Kotef recalls overhearing a conversation at a café in a bourgeois left-leaning neighbourhood of northern Tel Aviv in 2012. The Israeli army had been engaged in a war on Gaza at the time that killed over 150 Palestinians and displaced hundreds of families. She describes two people sitting at separate tables who end up sharing a newspaper and a conversation. At some point they conclude, in her paraphrase, that 'if the world blames us for committing crimes against humanity in Gaza we might as well commit genocide and get it all over with' (182). Kotef notes that they did not seem to know one another until their chance encounter in the café, as if to underscore the banality of Israeli genocidal intent vis-à-vis Palestinians such that it could furnish the shared ground for imagined community between strangers.

The anecdote is almost emblematic of a book that is devoted to demonstrating how the settler-colonising self, and specifically the Israeli self, is forged through an attachment to violence and structures of injury. Kotef distances herself from theoretical approaches that seek to account for mass violence in the reproduction of political community through recourse to notions of coercion, cruelty and disassociation. Instead she places her bets on desire, arguing that the settler is attached to violence in the way that Lauren Berlant accounts for attachment to 'bad objects': 'as part of an almost tragic effort to stabilize identity – the meaning of who we are' (48). Much of the book is devoted to substantiating this argument with reference to the quest for home and homeland, and practices of homemaking, on two registers. Within liberal political theory, Kotef demonstrates how the household constitutes the basic analytical unit of Lockean possessive individualism, functioning as the tip of the spear in the ideological justification of settler colonial expansion. And in the context of Israel/Palestine, she illuminates how both liberal and rightwing Israelis make themselves at home in landscapes of ruination, and specifically in the ruins of Palestinian homes, demonstrating how homes become tools of destruction and expulsion.

This is a book about how settler colonialism is sustained rather than how it ends. Yet I want to take the scattered remarks that Kotef makes on this latter subject as the point of departure for this review of recent works that address settler colonialism across different geographies and genres. About halfway through her book, Kotef startles the reader with a parenthetical caveat: 'I do not call here for killing all settlers or so many others whose social positions, security, and prosperity generate a world of insecurity for others', she says (131). The comment seems to speak to the café conversation in some way, even if only to pre-empt its obvious antithesis. If the settler wants to eliminate the native, as Patrick Wolfe tells us, it seems logical and even defensible for the native to want to eliminate the settler for reasons of sheer self-preservation. Yet Kotef does not want us to go there, or at least cautions against interpreting elimination in its most corporeal sense. In doing so, she enters into conversation with a number of texts including Lorraine Hansberry's celebrated play *Les Blancs* and the field of settler colonial studies more generally.

Set amidst the throes of decolonisation in an unnamed African settler colony, Hansberry's *Les Blancs* is a masterful study of the complexity but also the illusion of moral, political and psychic choice available to settlers and natives. The play generated extreme and racially polarised responses when it was first performed on Broadway in 1970, with *Playboy* arguing that it 'advocated genocide of non-blacks as a solution to the race problem.' Yet a more careful reading suggests that it is a text preoccupied with shades of grey in both settler and native society and with the impossibility of perceiving these shades under the shadow of settler colonial rule. The natives' choices are represented by the contrasting paths taken by three brothers: Eric, who is most firmly committed to violent insurgency against the settlers; Abioseh, who in becoming a priest chooses the path of assimilation; and Tshembe Matoseh, a figure of quintessential postcolonial hybridity. Educated at the Christian medical Mission that is the site on which most of the play's action unfolds, Tshembe travels extensively, spending time in Europe where he marries a white woman and fathers a child. On his return to his native country he rises to a position of influence in the political leadership of the independence movement, but is torn between his loyalties to his family in Britain and his people in Africa, and between the violent and nonviolent strands of the movement. Interestingly Palestinian writer Tareq Baconi begins his book *Hamas Contained: The Rise and Pacification of Palestinian Resistance* with a brief meditation on the profound influence that *Les Blancs* had on him. For Baconi, it is Tshembe's dilemmas – the strain under which his dedication to non-violence is placed by the apparent futility of peaceful protest – as well as the play's illumination of the fratricidal nature of liberation struggles that supplies a point of entry into his own subject matter.

Kotef is more interested in the settlers in the play. They occupy a range of ethical and political positions even as the play relentlessly interrogates whether their professed scruples amount to very much at all under conditions of settler colonialism, conjuring up but also questioning putative distinctions between 'good' and 'bad' settlers. For Kotef, it is Major Rice – who exhibits the typically heavy handed and racially supremacist attitudes of a colonial military man and repeatedly asserts that the colony is his home – who best exemplifies the forging of the settler self and home through an attachment to violence and a recognisably Lockean justification for it: 'Men like myself had the ambition, the energy and the ability to come here and make this country into something... *They* had it for centuries and did nothing with it. It isn't a question of empire, you see. It is our home' (Hansberry, 81). We learn about life in the Mission through the eyes of Charlie Morris, an American journalist who visits to write a story about its good works, but who gradually becomes jaded with the entire enterprise. However, it is in two other settler figures that the unforgiving limits of ethical action under settler colonialism are most acutely represented. One of these is Dr. DeKoven, who confesses to Morris that although he came to the Mission to help alleviate suffering, he has participated in the very institutions that help sustain it. Arguing that colonial subjects die mainly from 'a way of life' that his work as a medical doctor has reinforced, he concludes with a stunning self-indictment: 'I have helped provide the rationale for genocide.' Towards the end of the play, DeKoven has a premonition of how things will end, seeing a future in which the settlers will be murdered and the world press will condemn this as 'bestial absurdity'. Importantly, he does not see things in this way, arguing that

> The sun really *is* starting to rise in the world, so we might just as well stop pretending it is the middle of the night. *They* are quite prepared to die to be allowed to bring it to Africa. It is *we* who are not prepared. To allow it *or* to die (Hansberry, 197).

Kotef reads this as framing the ethico-political choice for the settler as one of leaving or dying; or more pressingly as being prepared '*both* to allow decolonization to take place *and* to die, to allow it *by* dying' (134). The notion of the settler 'allowing' decolonisation to take place can seem oxymoronic, even offensive, in its possible insinuation that decolonisation takes place because the settler colonist has allowed it rather than because the native has fought for it. Yet this framing of choices is not an account of how decolonisation happens so much as one about what it would mean to act ethically as a settler in a settler colonial context. In this argument, the only good settler is the settler who ceases to be one by leaving or dying. The choice is similarly framed by Madame Neilsen, wife of the Mission's founder, who is alone among the settlers in having established a relationship with the natives that approaches something resembling friendship. She teaches but also learns from them, becoming proficient in their language, foraging techniques and ways of life. When Tshembe asks her whether she intends to stay on in the Mission as the insurgency threatens to engulf it, she replies, 'At my age, one goes home only to die. I am already home' (Hansberry, 208). Yet despite feeling at home in the colony, she does not speak of it in the proprietary terms that the other settlers do. Like Tshembe, with whom she has the closest relationship, she is caught between places, feeling at home in a country that she knows she does not own. Most importantly, she is unambiguous in her support for the resistance. Sensing Tshembe's ambivalence, she stiffens his resolve: 'Our country needs *warriors*, Tshembe Matoseh. Africa needs warriors' (Hansberry, 211). Because Madame Neilsen will not leave, as a good settler she must die, which she does – not heroically but caught in the crossfire, a casualty of the impossibility of the subject position of good settlerhood.

In the immediate aftermath of the Hamas-led attack of 7 October 2023, which killed nearly 1200 Israelis in an unprecedented incursion across the Gaza border, many news reports underscored the irony of its targeting of the kibbutzim which are regarded as some of the most left-leaning communities in Israel. There is something morally incoherent about this critique. If the prohibition on killing civilians is absolute as these reports implied, then the political views of those civilians must be irrelevant. Yet there is another aspect of this discourse that is curious, one at which the Tunisian Jewish writer Albert Memmi might have looked askance. In his book *The Colonizer and the Colonized* – which anticipates many of the themes of postcolonial and settler colonial studies – Memmi describes the figure of the 'left-wing colonizer' as an impossibility. Estranged from their fellow colonisers on account of their sympathies with struggles for national liberation, left-wing colonisers are also potentially ideologically alienated from those very struggles on account of their use of terror and religious zeal. Structurally they are part of the oppressing group whether they accept this or not, sharing in its bounty and collective responsibility. Moreover, there is something delusional about their positionality in the way they dream of an end to the colonial situation without appreciating that this would entail their own overthrow. Under these circumstances, Memmi argues, the only real options for the left-wing coloniser are silence or departure. He might have been writing about himself. As a Tunisian Jew, Memmi had always found himself in a liminal position – a 'native' of the French settler colony but part of a community that was marginally more privileged than the Arab Muslim majority and that sought assimilation within dominant French culture. He would take his own advice, supporting the liberation of Tunisia from French rule but emigrating to France soon after this was accomplished.

In the shortest but most arresting section of her book entitled 'A Brief Reflection on Death and Decolonization', Kotef unpacks the (im)possibilities for ethical action on the part of the settler offered by these texts and is troubled by all of them in the context of Israel/Palestine. She expresses her opposition to 'individual, collective, or political suicide' (Memmi's silence) as well as to the killing of settlers. She does not consider 'leaving' a valid solution. Here she ignores a small but significant Israeli literature on emigration from Israel as a form of resistance to Zionism, exemplified by Hila Amit's *A Queer Way Out: The Politics of Queer Emigration from Israel*. Kotef notes, not unreasonably, that leaving is the privilege of those with 'economic and ethnic advantages' (134) but in doing so neglects the potentials of elite protest. Instead she yearns for the possibility of alliances, shared futures and horizons, affiliating her hopes with Edward Said's vision of peaceful coexistence between Israelis and Palestinians, and gesturing at a future in which the settler remains – not as a settler, but transformed in some substantial way so as to enjoy no more or less of a claim on the state than its native inhabitants.

Lorenzo Veracini has offered a useful aphorism for this transformation, arguing that decolonisation in settler colonial contexts would require one to 'Kill the Settler in Him and Save the Man'. The aphorism inverts the more well-known 'Kill the Indian, save the man', which described the vision of forced assimilation of Native Americans popularised by the nineteenth century US military officer Richard Henry Pratt who founded the infamous Carlisle Indian Industrial School, the flagship Indian boarding school in the United States. Veracini proposes turning the settler colonial logic of elimination of the native (in part through assimilation) against the settler. The call to 'kill the settler, save the man' invites us to think about what it would take for the settler to be able to remain on indigenous lands yet no longer as a settler. Veracini is clear that this would have to be an indigenous-led process if it is not to reiterate the historic injustice of settlers unilaterally setting the terms of relation. But there are other challenges. Kotef is sympathetic to the justice of the demand but sceptical of its feasibility: 'To kill the settler in the man is to kill so much of the man himself that the distinction becomes questionable' (132). Here she is with Memmi, who laments that 'it is too much to ask one's imagination to visualise one's own end, even if it be in order to be reborn another' (Memmi, 84). Yet unlike Memmi who embraces the radical implications of his argument, Kotef shies away from doing so. Having portrayed with considerable acuity the settler colonising self's attachment to violence and particularly to homemaking in spaces of violence, Kotef then problematises all possible avenues for dismantling settler colonialism, illuminating an impasse from which there is apparently so little possibility of escape that her own argument frustratingly and irresponsibly tails off: 'Here I stop writing. I do not know how one writes dead ends or how one writes themselves out of history' (134). While leftwing settlers agonise over their responsibility, the Israeli state certainly knows how to write others out of history. In July 2024, Rasha Khatib, Martin McKee and Salim Yusuf wrote in *The Lancet* that on a conservative estimate, the death toll from Israel's genocidal actions in Gaza since October 2023 may amount to 186,000 people or 8% of the population, once indirect killing through the decimation of the territory's healthcare, food systems, water supplies and housing is also taken into account.

I

In the months since the Hamas-led attack of 7 October 2023, many have turned to Frantz Fanon to evaluate the legitimacy of violent resistance to settler colonial occupation. In an essay published in the *London Review of Books* a month after the attack, Adam Shatz sought to reclaim Fanon from what he described as the 'ethno tribalist fantasies' of those parts of the decolonial left that celebrated the action. Homing in on the first chapter of *The Wretched of the Earth*, the text in which Fanon makes a case for anticolonial violence, Shatz argued that Fanon's description of violence as having a 'cleansing' force had been mistranslated from the original French, in which he speaks instead of its 'disintoxicating' effect. There is of course a great deal else in the chapter that is more difficult to explain away or water down: Fanon's insistence on the necessity of violence against colonialism, which is 'not a thinking machine … [but] will only yield when confronted with greater violence', its positive role in mobilising and bringing the nation into being, and its emancipatory effects in freeing the native 'from his inferiority complex and from his despair and inaction' (Fanon, 61, 94). Instead Shatz places more emphasis on Fanon's preoccupation with the corrosive effects of violence, evident in the case notes that he maintained as a psychiatrist treating both French soldiers and rebels from the Front de Libération Nationale (FLN) in the hospital in which he worked at Blida-Joinville in colonial Algeria. Shatz's Fanon counsels against resentment and revenge and is linked, somewhat inexplicably, to the spirituality of Martin Luther King. Moreover the title of Shatz's *LRB* essay – 'vengeful pathologies' – evinces a disinclination to unpack the military, political and diplomatic logics of the October 7 attacks. In a powerful critique, Abdaljawad Omar rightly notes that Shatz purports to decode Palestinian violence by beginning to explore its contexts but consistently 'circles back to the instinctual desire for vengeance'. When settlers are actually killed, no explanations are possible or permitted beyond the requisite ritualised condemnations.

Reading Shatz's recent biography of Fanon makes clearer how this skewed portrait of the twentieth century's arch theorist of anticolonial violence becomes possible. Early in the book, Shatz acknowledges that much of the power of Fanon's writing 'resides in the tension, which he never quite resolved, between his work as a doctor and his obligations as a militant, between his commitment to healing and his belief in violence' (9). Shatz tells us a great deal about both dimensions of Fanon, locating him as a political thinker in relation to the leading lights of Négritude, existentialism and psychoanalysis, and tracing his development and practice as a psychiatrist through his work in France, Algeria and Tunisia. His book also does much to illuminate Fanon's position in the Algerian liberation struggle as a representative of and ambassador for the FLN, but one who always fit more comfortably within its increasingly marginalised secular Marxist wing.

There is something troubling about Shatz's framing of Fanon as a figure split between a militant 'belief in violence' and a medical 'commitment to healing'. Responding to Hannah Arendt's infamous critique of Fanon as glorifying 'violence for its own sake', David Macey argues in his biography of Fanon that it is almost absurd to criticise Fanon for his advocacy of violence. He did not need to advocate it given its sheer omnipresence and its stranglehold on the unconscious in colonial Algeria. Macey depicts Fanon less as a figure who developed a normative position on violence than as one who theorised its pervasiveness and inescapability in the settler colony. In contrast, beginning with the more conventional view of Fanon as someone who 'believed' in violence, Shatz contorts himself into a number of peculiar positions in an attempt to resolve an ambivalence that he believes he has discovered in his subject.

Sometimes this takes the form of his elevation of one Fanon above another, evident in a series of normatively charged dichotomies that are littered through the text. Shatz contrasts the 'starry-eyed agrarian radicalism' (277) of the political Fanon with the 'mature thought' (381) of the psychiatric Fanon in the clinic. He believes that 'psychiatry enabled Fanon to step away from his grandstanding polemical positions and write with sensitivity and grace about the "mental disorders" produced by the war' (265). And when he notes Fanon's partiality to the 'angry didacticism' in the early fiction of Richard Wright over the 'inquisitive and probing literary journalism that questioned many orthodoxies, including those of the anti-colonial left' later in Wright's oeuvre, this sounds like a reverse projection of Shatz's own preferences (261).

These preferences are less than persuasive when they are grounded in potential misreadings of Fanon. For example, in an attempt to resolve the tension between Fanon's views on violence in the first chapter of *The Wretched of the Earth* and his account of its dehumanising effects in its last substantive chapter, Shatz seems to suggest that Fanon envisaged a temporal sequence in which an inevitably violent opening phase of the struggle for decolonisation characterised by the 'primitive Manichaeism' of settler colonialism would have to be tempered by the revolutionary leadership, on the understanding that 'not all the settlers are their enemies, and not all the natives are their allies' (322). It is true that in the crucial third chapter of the text, entitled 'The Pitfalls of National Consciousness', Fanon presciently warned about the limits of a form of political independence in which the nationalist bourgeoisie took over the reins of government from departing white colonists and serviced the neocolonial arrangements that resulted from such transfers of power. To obviate this, he argues powerfully for a transformation of national consciousness into a universalist socioeconomic consciousness that is directed at the depredations of a transnational class constituted by the shared interests of native and colonial elites. Yet far from entailing a reduction in violence, this calls for its redirection against a different set of targets. As Fanon clearly explains,

> violence used in specific ways at the moment of the struggle for freedom does not magically disappear after the ceremony of trooping the national colours. It has all the less reason for disappearing since the reconstruction of the nation continues within the framework of cut-throat competition between capitalism and socialism (Fanon, 75).

At other times rather than attempting to resolve the tension between Fanon the militant and the doctor, Shatz appears to use the latter to undermine the former. Thus he finds Fanon's faith in the redemptive effects of violence unpersuasive, suggesting that this contradicted much of what he had learned in his study and practice of psychiatry. Shatz even argues that the final chapter of *The Wretched of the Earth* on 'Colonial Warfare and Mental Disorders' implicitly rebuts the opening chapter of the text, which underscores the necessity for violence against the settler (328–329). In fact, Fanon is as categorical about the need for violence at the end of the book as he is at the start, noting that 'armed conflict alone can really drive out these falsehoods created in man which force into inferiority the most lively minds among us and which, literally, mutilate us' (Fanon, 294).

Through all this, Shatz does not consider what it might mean to read Fanon as clinging tenaciously and with equal intensity to both a belief in the inescapability of violence under settler colonialism and an awareness of its destructive effects on those swept up by its all-consuming force. Among the many patients whom Fanon describes in his case notes is an Algerian militant who reports a range of distressing symptoms on the anniversary of his planting of a bomb that killed ten people. It is difficult to miss the note of admiration in Fanon's account of the patient, who he says 'never for a single moment thought of repudiating his past action, realiz[ing] very clearly the manner in which he himself had to pay the price of national independence' (Fanon, 253). Edward Said – himself caught in a double bind between a recognition of the necessity for Palestinian nationalism as a vehicle for the liberation of a colonised people and of its invariably authoritarian and coercive logics – described such conundrums as inhabiting the genre of tragedy. What if, rather than setting the first and last chapters of Fanon's pre-eminent text against one another, we were to read the last chapter as bolstering the authority of the first. After all, someone who so unflinchingly chronicled the traumas of impotence, homicidal impulses, anxiety psychosis, depression, stupor, suicidal ideation and other psychic illnesses of the patients from both sides of the settler colonial divide who visited his clinic, could hardly be accused of demonstrating the irresponsibility of a keyboard warrior or tankie when he – in the same breath – called for violent resistance against the settler colonial machine.

If there is ever a moment of resolution of the tension between Fanon the doctor and the militant – albeit one that was forced on him by circumstances – it is in his 1956 letter of resignation from his post at the hospital in Blida-Joinville. Thwarted in his psychiatric practice by the oppressive political context in which he and his staff were forced to work, Fanon the doctor lays down arms, so to speak: 'if psychiatry is the medical technique that aims to enable man no longer to be a stranger to his environment, I owe it to myself to affirm that the Arab, permanently an alien in his own country, lives in a state of absolute depersonalization ... The social structure existing in Algeria was hostile to any attempt to put the individual back where he belonged.' Even though Fanon continued to practice in Tunisia, as Nigel C. Gibson and Roberto Beneduce note in *Frantz Fanon, Psychiatry and Politics*, from this point onwards psychiatry ceased to be his primary occupation or preoccupation. If resignation offers a resolution of sorts to the tensions between his political and psychiatric praxis, sometimes Fanon can barely restrain himself from suggesting that it might have helped his patients as well. Commenting on the case of a police inspector who understood that his mental disorders were the direct result of his work as an interrogator, Fanon remarks with some incredulity: 'As he could not see his way to stopping torturing people (that made nonsense to him for in that case he would have to resign) he asked me without beating about the bush to help him to go on torturing Algerian patriots without any prickings of conscience, without any behavior problems, and with complete equanimity' (Fanon, 269–270). Perhaps the obverse of Memmi's impossible left-wing coloniser is Fanon's equanimous torturer.

Shatz's book concludes with a magisterial epilogue mapping Fanon's influence over space, time and disciplinary fields in the decades since his death. When laid out in this fashion, the scope of his impact is stunning to behold. Yet one is left with the suspicion that many of Fanon's most hard-nosed followers in this impressive roster – in the Palestinian Liberation Organisation or the Black Panthers, for example – were influenced precisely by the dimensions of Fanon that Shatz disparages as didactic and grandstanding.

II

In contrast to the Manichaeism of a worldview in which natives confront settlers, in *Neither Settler Nor Native* Mahmood Mamdani looks forward to a future in which both settler and native identities will cease to have political relevance in decolonised states. This ambitious book locates settler colonialism within a larger genealogy of political modernity in which colonial governmentalities birth nation-states marked by the politicisation of racial and ethnic identities whereby majorities invariably oppress minorities. Central to Mamdani's concerns is the question of how permanent minorities – fashioned on the basis of identity – might be undone by shifting interest-based configurations emerging out of the give-and-take of democratic politics.

Sprawling in geographical scope with its case studies straddling four continents, this is nonetheless not a work in the classic comparativist mould of side-by-side juxtaposition but one that offers a more connective history. Mamdani's story begins in the United States, which in his view pioneers the technologies of settler colonialism as a response to the settler state's problem of what to do with surviving natives. In studying the US management of the 'Indian Question', we are introduced to the entire panoply of weapons that stock the settler colonial arsenal: internal colonies euphemised as reservations that are accorded the dubious prerogatives of tribal sovereignty and second-class citizenship; dualistic legal systems that misrecognise indigenous relationships with the land as a prelude to appropriating it; and a range of methods – from genocide to cultural assimilation – by which the native presence is sought to be eliminated. These techniques would inform and inspire other projects of mass atrocity including Nazism, apartheid and Zionism, each of which are dealt with in separate chapters.

Not all of the case studies in the book are straightforwardly settler colonial. Thus Mamdani makes clear in a chapter on Sudan that distinctions of settler and native there were inventions and impositions by British colonial authorities, mapped respectively onto 'Arabs' in the North and 'Africans' in the South, with the latter being further subdivided into 'tribes' through the mechanism of indirect chiefly rule. While serving the colonial purpose of divide and rule – or what Mamdani memorably calls 'define and rule' (13) – these governmentalities leave deep and lasting legacies, evident in the conflict that has wracked Sudan, the secession of what is now South Sudan and the internecine warfare that has marked the latter's short history.

Nadine Fraczkowski

The chapter on Israel/Palestine – the longest in the book – also complicates the settler colonial paradigm, distinguishing native Jews who had always lived in historic Palestine from those who came as immigrants prepared to live under Ottoman rule in the first wave of Aliyah, and those who arrived as settlers determined to impose an exclusivist Jewish state that was premised on the expulsion of Arab Palestinians. Here we might note parenthetically how a number of scholars have further complicated the conceptualisation of Israel/Palestine as a case of settler colonialism. Yuval Evri and Kotef argue in their article 'When does a native become a settler?' that natives can become settlers without moving, through an account of how Arabic-speaking native Jews of Palestine were conscripted into early waves of the Zionist project as useful intermediaries in land purchases. In a related piece entitled 'When does a Settler Become a Native?', to which Evri and Kotef refer, Raef Zreik notes the dual character of Zionism as a settler colonial and national project. The duality does not make Zionism less violent, in his view, but more sophisticated in allowing Zionists to feel victimised even as they dispossess Palestinians. Zreik insists that Zionism is settler colonialism in its techniques even if not in its self-imagination, something that is all too evident in its conquest of a land that is constructed as empty, its unrelenting expansion of frontiers, and its dream of the disappearance of the native. In their introduction to a landmark collection of essays seeking to place Israel/Palestine more squarely within the field of settler colonial studies, Omar Jabary Salamanca, Mezna Qato, Kareem Rabie and Sobhi Samour go further in insisting that while Israel's tactics have often been described as settler colonial, they are underpinned by a settler colonial structure that must be centred in any analysis.

While Mamdani spends considerable time describing the making of settler colonial polities, he is equally invested in the question of how they might be unmade. Central to his account of how states and societies cope with mass atrocity is a distinction between conceptualisations of violence as criminal and as political, reminiscent of Walter Benjamin's distinction between law-preserving and law-making violence. The criminal approach to violence regards it as an aberration and responds to it by seeking to identify and punish individual perpetrators. The political approach to violence regards it as a diagnostic of grievance around questions of belonging and focuses more on the underlying issues that drive it. Recognising that political violence relies not only on perpetrators but also supporters and that the latter tend to be mobilised around issues rather than (or perhaps as much as) personalities, its remedial measures are addressed to this wider constituency. While the criminal approach can come across as more severe and as having greater deterrent effect than the political approach, Mamdani effectively suggests that the latter is more ambitious in casting a wider net and seeking a wholesale reconfiguration of dichotomous political identities such as majority/minority, perpetrator/victim, settler/native into the singular category of what he calls 'survivors'. The suggestion is evocative of the scene described by Fanon in which two of his patients from either side of the colonial divide – torturer and tortured – encounter one another by chance on the grounds of the hospital at which he worked. Fanon reminds us of how traumatic the encounter was for both: while the former has an anxiety crisis, the latter attempts suicide in a toilet.

For Mamdani, the Nuremberg trials following the Second World War offer the paradigmatic example of the criminal approach to mass violence and of everything that is wrong with it. Nazism was reduced to an accumulation of individual crimes rather than a political project. Denazification correspondingly became a punitive effort to identify and root out individual perpetrators rather than a transformative political process. Even this criminal approach turned out to be half-hearted and abbreviated as geopolitical considerations, such as the need for German economic recovery in the face of the looming Soviet threat, trumped imperatives of justice. In this context, zealous West German support for the new state of Israel – powerfully on display these days as support for Israel is endlessly declared to be a unified Germany's *Staatsräson* – became an alibi for incomplete denazification, with devastating consequences for Palestinians. Meanwhile nationalism and racial supremacism were never on trial at Nuremberg. They could hardly be, given that – as Aimé Césaire famously reminds us – Hitler's crime had been to apply in Europe 'colonialist procedures which until then had been reserved exclusively for the Arabs of Algeria, the coolies of India, and the blacks of Africa' (Césaire, 14). The hegemony of these political ideologies and procedures would only be reinforced by the creation of Israel as a state for the Jews supported and bankrolled by Western imperialism.

In contrast, South Africa's transition out of apartheid supplies Mamdani with the paradigmatic example of a political approach to the aftermath of mass atrocity. The transition admittedly contained elements of the criminalising approach in the form of the Truth and Reconciliation Commission (TRC). Despite its granting of amnesty rather than punishment to truthtellers, Mamdani argues that its focus on individual perpetrators, its neglect of a wider constituency of beneficiaries of apartheid and its narrow understanding of suffering partially reinscribed the logic of Nuremberg in the South African transition. Nonetheless, in his reading of this process the TRC's importance was vastly outweighed by that of the Convention for a Democratic South Africa (CODESA), which dismantled juridical apartheid and enabled the introduction of majority rule electoral politics. Crucial here is his attention to the social forces that laid the groundwork for a reconfiguration of political identities in ways that broke from the racial categories defined by apartheid: the Black Consciousness movement's reimagination of an expansive political Blackness, as well as solidaristic organising by radical white students and migrant and township labour activists. As he explains, in 'redefining the enemy as not settlers but the settler state, not whites but white power ... South Africa's liberation movements eased whites into the idea of a nonracial democracy' (176). Yet this easing came at a substantial cost – the reform and retention of the apartheid state, amnesty for perpetrators, protection of private property and the consequent entrenchment of white economic privilege, and guarantees of native 'tribal' and white political representation through consociational arrangements at local government levels. Given the place that South Africa occupies in Mamdani's argument as the most successful example of the renegotiation of settler and native identities, it is imperative to examine the price of the political alchemy that he describes.

At times Mamdani appears to present the South African compromise as *inevitable* – the best that could have been expected in a situation of stalemate between the white National Party and the African National Congress (ANC). As he puts it, 'the anti-apartheid movement had fostered a crisis, not a victory' (174) necessitating compromise in which the warring parties agreed to view one another as political adversaries rather than enemies. At other junctures, he presents the South African transition out of settler colonialism as *preferable* to any other imaginable alternative on account of its avoidance of mass bloodshed. This is evident particularly in his separation and sequencing of political and social reform, a move that is elevated almost to an article of faith. At the very outset of the book he proclaims that the political precedes the social, arguing that 'the first question at independence is not "how do we distribute wealth?" but "who belongs?"' (34). Yet he does not take seriously enough the prospect that the price of negotiating universal belonging might be an agreement *never* to redistribute wealth. It is not as if Mamdani is unaware of the critiques, although it is striking – given his evident admiration of apartheid-era student movements – that he does not see fit to mention student movements in South Africa today. Since 2015, movements such as Rhodes Must Fall and Fees Must Fall calling for the decolonisation of the university, the reduction of fees and the reversal of privatisation have been among the fiercest critics of what they see as the post-apartheid ANC government's betrayal of many of its promises of liberation especially vis-à-vis poor black South Africans. Rather, his argument is held up by the forlorn hope that political reform has given South Africans the tools with which to solve problems of social justice.

This sequencing of political reform as a necessary if insufficient prerequisite for social justice results in his oft-reiterated call for a 'decolonization of the political', a process that he argues would entail upsetting the permanent majority and minority identities that characterise the nation-state (or the settler and native identities that structure the settler-colonial relationship) by transmuting both into a common category of citizenship. The focus on citizenship seems symptomatic of a divide, even impasse, between settler colonial and indigenous studies as cognate but distinct fields. Even as indigenous scholars redirect our attention to questions of land ownership and use, settler colonial studies more typically fetishises citizenship as the transformative mechanism through which settler colonialism might be dismantled. Mamdani's 'decolonization of the political' reprises the old liberal ruse that purports to manage inequality by demarcating the political from the social, positing equality in the former while bracketing and deferring questions of hierarchy and difference within the latter. This is the kind of narrative that seems to regard the transformation of the settler colony into a polity that suffers the 'ordinary' problems of liberal democracy as a kind of progress. Envisaged as the first step in a dynamic process, it nonetheless threatens to deliver the truncated decolonisation that Fanon famously associated with the native bourgeoisie.

III

If there was ever a time in which we risked idealising the South African transition out of settler colonialism, it is now. The country's ANC government has justifiably won global admiration on account of its leadership of the Palestine solidarity movement in intergovernmental structures, particularly the International Court of Justice where South Africa has spoken for the global majority in charging Israel with genocide in Gaza. Impossible to fathom as the future of Palestine may be, South Africa glimmers on the horizon as a possible model because Israel enacts a form of apartheid in Palestine today and because the call for boycott, divestment and sanctions against Israel is inspired by and seeks to emulate the historic anti-apartheid movement. More than ever, it seems imperative to better understand the process of South Africa's transition out of apartheid and the extent to which it has been able to dismantle the legacies of white minority rule. Jonny Steinberg's *Winnie & Nelson* helps us to do some of the former through an intertwined biography of the anti-apartheid movement's two largest protagonists. Biography necessarily offers a highly individualised and stylised entry point into large scale social, political and historical processes. Yet Steinberg – like Shatz – is adept at situating his narrative amidst the turbulence of its setting, so that his story is not only one about two individuals but also about contrasting modes of fighting apartheid.

Nelson Mandela's life – or at least a sanctified version of it – is certainly the better known, not least through his own autobiography. Steinberg takes us quickly through the early political milestones – the Defiance Campaign of 1952, the writing of the Freedom Charter in 1955 committing the anti-apartheid movement to a multiracial vision of South Africa, the Treason Trial of 1956 and the Sharpeville massacre of 1960 which precipitated the movement's turn to violence through the creation of uMkhonto we Sizwe (Spear of the Nation; hereafter MK), which would wage a campaign of sabotage of government installations. Shortly after the onset of the campaign (coincidentally, days after Fanon's death in 1961), Nelson would travel abroad to mobilise weapons, materiel and training for the military campaign. Steinberg suggests that he took away from his meetings with FLN officials in Rabat a more sobering assessment of guerrilla warfare as being useful only insofar as it pressured the enemy to negotiate, and of political mobilisation at home and abroad as more consequential for the struggle.

It was in the wake of Nelson's incarceration, first in 1962 and then under a life sentence following the Rivonia trial, that Winnie Mandela emerged as a public figure and indeed as the face of the ANC. A magnetic personality and powerful speaker, she plunged headlong into the struggle, building a singular relationship with the black masses of South Africa especially in urban townships and nowhere more so than in Soweto. Her tempestuous personal life, marked by a succession of unstable love triangles, and the aura of glamour and sex appeal that she radiated, kept her permanently in the news. Subject on multiple occasions to banning orders, arrest, incarceration and torture, she seemed to embody the suffering of ordinary black South Africans and won their unqualified adulation as mother of the nation. Yet her vision of how apartheid would end was distinct from that of her husband, hewing more closely to that of a faction of the ANC that envisaged a Cuban-style guerrilla campaign as bringing about the end of white minority rule. She gave effect to this vision through initiatives that were as brazen as they were militarily amateurish, recruiting the youth of Soweto into what she hoped might become a trained corps of saboteurs who would engage in spectacular acts of violence, and finding routes into exile for others to join the ranks of MK.

Even as the jailed Nelson's star rose – the imperative of his release being taken up by a galaxy of prominent political and cultural figures at the UN, through global musical extravaganzas and birthday celebrations and even in the UK Labour Party – Winnie became ever more deeply mired in the trenches of South Africa's increasingly violent struggle against apartheid. Steinberg usefully reminds us that nearly 20,000 people were killed in the violence that engulfed South Africa in the last decade of apartheid. Much of this violence was a legacy of the structures of indirect rule that Mamdani illuminates. The insurrections of the mid-1980s were protests against hikes in rent and service charges imposed by black local government authorities that the apartheid government of P. W. Botha had installed. They were also a response to the attempted incorporation of black residential areas of Natal into the KwaZulu Bantustan, a decision that triggered ethnic separatist violence between Zulus and non-Zulus which also mapped uneasily onto tensions between the Zulu Inkatha party and the ANC. It seemed as if what had begun as a revolt against apartheid was morphing into an internecine war among black people. Winnie's own role at the time was centred around the infamous Mandela United Football Club, which she established ostensibly to take young people off the streets of Soweto and channel them into revolutionary activities while also giving herself a modicum of protection. In short order, club members went on to perpetrate terrifying acts of vigilante justice against those perceived to be sellouts, informers and spies, with Winnie personally overseeing and participating in some of these acts of violence. Her actions polarised the internal resistance movement, some feeling repelled and wanting to distance themselves from her and others alleging conspiratorially that the club had been infiltrated and directed by the apartheid state to sow disunity and to discredit the Mandelas. A 1991 conviction for kidnapping and assault proved to be the final straw, prompting her resignation from all political positions in the ANC and her eventual divorce from Nelson.

Among Steinberg's many achievements in this book, two stand out. First, his success in illuminating a political partnership and a marriage whose protagonists barely cohabited and who communicated largely through heavily censored letters and supervised visits (to make matters more complicated, much of Winnie's side of the correspondence has yet to be made publicly available). Second, his ability to make intelligible, without ever endorsing, the violence of Winnie and her milieu. Unlike Shatz, Steinberg is less interested in passing judgment on his subjects. Perhaps he feels no need to, given that an entire nation has imagined itself through the process of continuously doing so. Instead he helps readers to view the world through their eyes, partly with reference to their words and those of their closest interlocutors, but also through an acute reading of political and psychic formation under apartheid. In a 1984 interview with documentary filmmaker Peter Davis, Winnie confesses to having been made through her experience of torture, which taught her the hatred that white South Africans – embodied in the figure of her torturer – felt for the black people of the country, a hatred that she internalised and turned back on him (322). Speaking later in life about her role in the struggle as an uncompromising enforcer of social and political norms in the resistance, she explained that black South Africans who had become accustomed to life under apartheid had to be made more frightened of her than of the apartheid regime if they were to rise up against it (351). And in an afterword to her prison diary written shortly before Nelson's death, reflecting on what she knew to be the world's divergent verdicts on the two Mandelas, she writes:

> They wonder why I am like I am ... [T]hey have a nerve to say, 'Oh, Madiba is such a peaceful person, you know. We wonder how he had a wife who is so violent?' The leadership on Robben Island was never touched; the leadership on Robben Island had no idea what it was like to engage the enemy physically. The leadership was removed and cushioned behind prison walls... They did not know what we were talking about and when we were reported to be so violent, engaged in the physical struggle, fighting the Boers underground, they did not understand that because none of them had ever been subjected to that, not even Madiba himself. They never touched him, they would not have dared (464).

Steinberg's gloss on this is instructive: Winnie does not say it in so many words but her implication is that 'what her husband was locked away from all those years was the experience of being black; so thoroughly and, indeed, for so long that it had become puzzling to him' (464).

Nelson and Winnie may have divorced, but their legacies are harder to disentangle. It would be too pat to suggest that either ever had such a dialectic in mind, but as things turned out, Winnie's politics helped to create the crisis of ungovernability to which the apartheid government regarded Nelson's release as the only solution. Yet in bringing this about, she came to personify the underbelly of the struggle, distilling in herself the excesses of every revolution that devours its own children. In this reading, Winnie is a kind of scapegoat, allowing Nelson's ascension to sainthood in the eyes of a global and especially a white public, free of the taint of murderous retribution that is associated with his wife. Yet posterity is a fickle judge. Even before Nelson died in 2013, the rumbles of discontent with his legacy were audible. The avowedly Marxist Economic Freedom Fighters broke away from the ANC that year, alleging its betrayal of the anti-apartheid struggle's more radical promises. Two years later, South Africa's first 'born free' generations rose up in revolt in student movements such as Rhodes Must Fall and Fees Must Fall, their antipathy directed not only at the persistence of the legacies of apartheid in the academy but also at the failure of their elders to dismantle those legacies – a failure for which Nelson's politics of compromise and reconciliation bore significant responsibility. Conversely, Winnie has become a talisman for the frustrations and hopes of radical young black South Africans, her politics presaging the more redistributive futures for which they yearn. Post-apartheid South Africa remains the country of Nelson *and* Winnie Mandela, a reminder – if one were needed – of the troubling inseparability of violence and non-violence in every story of how settler colonialism ends.

If it is difficult to think of any historical examples in which settler colonialism ends non-violently, then liberal condemnations of the violence of the colonised express a kind of fantasy that demands analysis. Moreover, the ideological imperative to join this chorus of condemnation enjoins universal participation in this fantasy. In their determination to read the relationship between violence and non-violence as contrast rather than dialectic, liberal critics fantasise about forms of political action that are both effective and morally pure. In this, they are fellow travellers of Memmi's left-wing coloniser, desirous of a place on the right side of history but with no sacrifice or disruption of their way of life. So it is salutary to recall Memmi's critique of this fantasy: shut up or get out.

Other texts cited:
Abdaljawad Omar, 'Hopeful pathologies in the war for Palestine: a reply to Adam Shatz', *Mondoweiss*, 8 November 2023, https://mondoweiss.net/2023/11/hopeful-pathologies-in-the-war-for-palestine-a-reply-to-adam-shatz/.
Adam Shatz, 'Vengeful Pathologies', *London Review of Books* 45:21 (2 November 2023), https://www.lrb.co.uk/the-paper/v45/n21/adam-shatz/vengeful-pathologies.
Aimé Césaire, *Discourse on Colonialism*, trans. Joan Pinkham (New York: Monthly Review Press, 1972).
Albert Memmi, *The Colonizer and the Colonized* (London: Earthscan, 2003 [1957]).
David Macey, *Frantz Fanon: A Biography* (London: Verso, 2012).
Frantz Fanon, *The Wretched of the Earth*, trans. Constance Farrington (New York: Grove Press, 1963 [1961]).
Hila Amit, *A Queer Way Out: The Politics of Queer Emigration from Israel* (New York: SUNY Press, 2019).
Lorenzo Veracini, 'Decolonizing Settler Colonialism: Kill the Settler in Him and Save the Man', *American Indian Culture and Research Journal* 41:1 (2017), 1–18.
Lorraine Hansberry, *The Collected Last Plays* (New York: Vintage, 1994).
Nigel C. Gibson and Roberto Beneduce, *Frantz Fanon, Psychiatry and Politics* (London: Rowman & Littlefield, 2017).
Omar Jabary Salamanca, Mezna Qato, Kareem Rabie and Sobhi Samour, 'Past is Present: Settler Colonialism in Palestine', *Settler Colonial Studies* 2:1 (2012), 1–8.
Patrick Wolfe, 'Settler colonialism and the elimination of the native', *Journal of Genocide Research* 8:4 (2006), 387–409.
Raef Zreik, 'When does a Settler Become a Native? (With Apologies to Mamdani), *Constellations* 23:3 (2016), 351–364.
Rasha Khatib, Martin McKee and Salim Yusuf, 'Counting the dead in Gaza: difficult but essential', *The Lancet*, 5 July 2024, https://doi.org/10.1016/S0140-6736(24)01169-3.
Tareq Baconi, *Hamas Contained: The Rise and Pacification of Palestinian Resistance* (Stanford: Stanford University Press, 2018).
Yuval Evri and Hagar Kotef, 'When does a native become a settler? (With apologies to Zreik and Mamdani)', *Constellations* 29 (2022), 3–18.

Rahul Rao

Rahul Rao is a member of the Radical Philosophy collective.

Saving liberalism from itself

Samuel Moyn, *Liberalism against Itself: Cold War Intellectuals and the Making of Our Times* (New Haven: Yale University Press, 2023). 240pp., £25.00 hb., 978 0 30026 621 4

In a typically provocative tone, Samuel Moyn opens his latest book *Liberalism against Itself: Cold War Intellectuals and the Making of Our Time* with the striking claim: 'Cold War liberalism was a catastrophe – for liberalism'. Moyn's book contributes to a veritable cottage-industry of books on the dire fortunes of contemporary liberalism but his central argument is that liberalism's wounds were largely self-inflicted. In a series of tightly-argued chapters, Moyn argues that, in the aftermath of the Second World War and the Holocaust, liberals abandoned an optimistic belief in human perfectibility and progress in favour of an anxious and minimalist attempt to secure freedom in a dangerous world. Moyn's indictment is scathing: in their desire to protect individual liberty from tyranny, he argues that Cold War liberals rejected utopianism and demands for greater economic equality, and in their fear of mass politics they turned against democracy itself. The Cold War is long over, at least in its first iteration, but Moyn suggests that contemporary liberals have failed to notice. Liberalism, as he frames it, has become a minimalist and fearful creed that struggles to articulate any reason for its existence – except that the alternatives are worse.

The book is devoted to six twentieth-century intellectuals: political theorist Judith Shklar, political philosopher Isaiah Berlin, philosopher of science Karl Popper, historian Gertrude Himmelfarb, political theorist Hannah Arendt and literary critic Lionel Trilling. The rationale for this cast of characters is not articulated in the book and it includes several figures who are not generally understood (primarily) as Cold War liberals: Popper, for instance, came of age in the Austrian milieu of neoliberal economists Friedrich Hayek and Ludwig von Mises, and was a member of the neoliberal Mont Pelerin Society, raising the question of the criteria by which he is defined as a Cold War liberal rather than a neoliberal. Arendt always denied being a liberal, and even Moyn seems unsure whether to characterise her as one, preferring to describe her as a 'fellow traveller'. And Himmelfarb, who was married to Irving Kristol and was the mother of Bill Kristol, is often understood as a central figure in the rise of neoconservatism.

If Moyn excoriates Cold War liberalism, it is in part because his picture of the liberalism it eclipsed is so rosy: 'Emancipatory and futuristic before the Cold War, committed most of all to free and equal self-creation, accepting of democracy and welfare (though never enough to date)', he writes, 'liberalism can be something other than the Cold War liberalism we have known.' This claim blends past and future to affirm that, if liberalism *has been* something else, it can dispense with its anxious minimalism once again. Liberalism's past, however, largely remains in the background and must therefore be pieced together from scattered remarks. These do not always support the contention that Cold War liberalism marked a rupture with an emancipatory liberalism that it succeeded. 'Before the Cold War', Moyn notes, 'liberalism largely served as an apologia for laissez-faire economic policies and it was entangled in imperialist expansion and racist hierarchy around the world'. Throughout the book Moyn stresses the progressivist, emancipatory and futuristic aspects of nineteenth-century liberalism rather than the radically laissez-faire ideology of a figure like Herbert Spencer or the racial hierarchies that animate the progressivism of numerous nineteenth-century liberals (on which, more below.) And yet the Cold War re-inventors of liberalism found no shortage of material in the liberal tradition with which to fashion a pessimistic and deeply anti-democratic creed.

Moyn distinguishes Cold War liberalism not only from an earlier nineteenth-century liberalism but also from another re-orientation of liberalism that became hegemonic in the late twentieth-century: neoliberalism. Cold War liberalism and neoliberalism were distinct, he argues, and 'both sides understood the differences that kept them apart'. Yet those differences are not always clear. In the book's introduction, Moyn depicts both neoliberalism and neoconservatism as 'successor movements' to Cold War liberalism, which was condemned to 'give birth to monsters'. Yet immediately afterwards, he notes the striking proximity of the Cold War liberals to 'the neoliberalism of Friedrich Hayek and others, invented across the same decades'. Moyn's critique draws on the much earlier critique of 'conservative liberalism' penned by a young Judith Shklar before her own transition to Cold War liberalism. Yet, while Moyn describes Shklar's first book *After Utopia* – originally published in 1957 and re-issued in 2020 with a foreword by him – as 'a composite survey of Cold War liberalism', Shklar attributed liberalism's conservative turn to a very different cast of characters. It was in the German Ordoliberalism of Walter Eucken, Alexandre Rüstow and Wilhelm Röpke, the Austrian School of Friedrich Hayek and Ludwig von Mises, and in the French philosopher Bertrand de Jouvenel and the British-Hungarian polymath Michael Polanyi that Shklar identified liberalism's conservative turn. Not only did these authors 'share a real community of opinion', as she noted. They were also almost all members of the neoliberal Mont Pelerin Society, founded by Hayek in 1947 to revive liberalism in the face of widespread support for socialism, social democracy and economic planning and they all became central figures in the rise of neoliberalism (as I argue in *The Morals of the Market: Human Rights and the Rise of Neoliberalism*, and as Quinn Slobodian also shows in *Globalists: The End of Empire and the Birth*).

Shklar was influenced by her Harvard advisor Carl Friedrich who published a prescient critique of 'The Political Thought of Neo-Liberalism' in the *American Political Science Review* in 1955. In contrast to those who (still) conceive neoliberalism as an anti-statist revival of laissez-faire, Friedrich recognised that neo-liberalism stressed the need for a strong state to protect the market from the interference of sectional interests, notably trade unions. The motto of neo-liberalism, as Friedrich saw it, came from the nineteenth-century liberal Benjamin Constant: 'The government beyond its proper sphere ought not to have any power; within its sphere, it cannot have enough of it.' Although these figures were, to various extents, invested in the Cold War, their animus was aimed much more centrally at what they saw as the deterioration of 'Western civilisation' caused by the rise of socialism and social democracy and the rationalist belief in economic planning. Although Moyn does not devote extensive space to economic questions, he faults the Cold War liberals for failing to defend the welfare state, and so leaving it 'unguarded' in the face of neoliberal attacks. And his critique of Cold War liberalism appears to be animated by his strong critique, developed in his 2018 book *Not Enough: Human Rights in an Unequal World,* of the liberal abandonment of a concern for economic equality.

Yet nothing is less certain than the belief that a return to the liberalism of the nineteenth century is the best way to challenge the neoliberal destruction of the welfare state or to revive a robust conception of economic equality. Moyn's recognition that earlier liberalism was also an apologetics for laissez-faire and the racial hierarchies of European colonialism appears to undercut his argument that Cold War liberalism marked a rupture with the emancipatory liberalism that preceded it. On his account, earlier liberals – such as John Stuart Mill, Alexis de Tocqueville, Benjamin Constant and T.H. Greene – were inspired by the Enlightenment and saw creative agency and free human self-realisation as the highest good and history as a forum in which to pursue it. In contrast, the Cold War liberals turned away from the Enlightenment and from optimistic belief in progress and perfectibility, and purged liberalism of the influence of Jean-Jacques Rousseau, G.W.F. Hegel and Karl Marx. In doing so, they cut off liberalism from ideas of collective self-determination, the ethical state, progress and human perfectibility. In positing a clean break between Cold War liberalism and its precursors, Moyn takes his distance from Shklar, who depicted nineteenth-century liberalism as balanced precariously between anti-Jacobinism and fear of conservatism. Liberalism's conservative turn, she insisted in 1957, 'has not been the work of one day.' In contrast Moyn – who has devoted much of his career to identifying breaks and ruptures in history, notably that between the modern rights of man and contemporary human rights – contends that Shklar's account of continuity understates the extent to which the Cold War utterly transformed liberalism, rendering it unrecognisable.

When Moyn concretises this earlier emancipatory liberalism, it is in a surprising place: Palestine. While Cold War liberals were usually suspicious of collective and national projects, he argues that they made an exception for Zionism. 'In an age when it is common to condemn Zionism', he contends, 'perhaps the deepest problem with Cold War liberalism is that it wasn't Zionist enough'. Moyn's account of Zionism is radically romanticised. It was in their Zionism, he argues, that 'Cold

War liberals did challenge Eurocentrism' by supporting a 'statist liberation movement' aimed at 'postcolonial emancipation'. Casting Zionism as the repository of the older emancipatory liberalism he seeks to redeem, he argues that it was only in the Cold War liberals' accounts of Zionism that 'earlier forms of liberalism, with their activism and statism, were allowed to survive'. To the extent Moyn criticises the Cold War liberals, it is not for their Zionism but for their refusal to extend the same support to the struggles against European colonialism that raged across Africa and Asia throughout the Cold War. In Arendt's *On Violence,* for instance, he identifies what he calls 'flagrant tensions between her enthusiasm for "Jewish self-emancipation" and her skepticism of decolonization'. And he identifies what he sees as a deep inconsistency between Berlin's 'Zionism and his far less indulgent attitude towards other new states after WWII'. What is striking here is Moyn's own assumption that consistency would require support for both Zionism and struggles against European colonialism, and his underlying framing of Israel as a post-colonial state.

Moyn does not grapple with those critics who have understood Zionism as a colonial project built on the racial hierarchies that sustained European colonialism, aligned with the ends of the British and then the US empires, and unified by what the late Palestinian scholar Edward Said called the negation of Palestinians. In his pioneering 1979 essay 'Zionism from the Perspective of its victims', Said suggested that, for Palestinians, Zionism is simply the most successful of the European attempts, stretching back to the Middle Ages, to colonise Palestine. By examining it 'as it was inscribed in the lives of the native Palestinians', Said characterised Zionism as a movement committed to the eradication of Palestinian reality in the name of a '"higher" cause'. In what Moyn depicts as Zionism's progressivist, emancipatory, violent, self-assertion, Said saw a continuation of the European colonial assumption that native peoples and cultures are inferior and can therefore be eradicated to make way for a higher or more civilised form of life. Far from re-

jecting Eurocentrism, Zionism, from this perspective, is 'an essentially Western ideology' that framed itself as 'bringing civilization to a barbaric and/or empty locale' (Herzl's 'outpost of civilization as opposed to barbarism') and then as 'a movement bringing Western democracy to the East'. As Said notes, this latter framing appealed to American liberals like Reinhold Niebuhr, Edmund Wilson and Eleanor Roosevelt. From this perspective, Cold War liberals' support for Zionism appears quite consistent with their broader commitment to 'Western civilisation' and US empire.

Moyn does, at one point, characterise Israel as 'a kind of postcolonial state (however much it was simultaneously a settler colony)'. This position is in line with Derek Penslar's argument that 'a nation can engage in both settler-colonial and anticolonial practices'. But Penslar's analogy between Zionist settlers in mandate Palestine and Afrikaners in South Africa, neither of whom 'identified as scions of the colonizing power', is a long way from Moyn's analogy between Zionism and the successful struggles by non-European peoples against European colonialism in the second half of the twentieth century. And neither adequately capture the fact that the British Empire, as Areej Sabbagh-Khoury argues in *Colonizing Palestine: The Zionist Left and the Making of the Palestinian Nakba*, 'enabled and protected Jewish immigration, Zionist land acquisition and settlement' in Palestine. As Rashid Khalidi has stressed, it was only once the post-World War II decolonisation made colonialism suspect, that Zionists stopped referring to their project as one of colonising Palestine and rebranded Zionism as 'an anticolonial movement.'

In relegating settler colonialism to brackets, Moyn is consistent with much scholarship on liberalism, which, even as it has begun to probe liberalism's intimate relationship to colonialism, has tended to focus on Britain's overseas extraction colonies, with a particular focus on India. More recent scholarship has begun to examine the foundational role of settler colonialism in liberal thought and highlighted the extent to which liberals viewed settler colonies as what Duncan Bell has called 'spaces of political freedom' that were preferable to the despotic, alien rule practiced in India. Moyn is aware that early liberalism was, in his words, 'entangled from the start with global domination' and animated by civilisational and racial hierarchies. And indeed, the earlier liberals to whom he refers for inspiration – figures like Mill or Tocqueville – were often deeply involved in the European colonial project and enthusiastic advocates of settler-colonialism. Tocqueville called for a war of colonisation in Algeria that would 'ravage the country'. And Mill defended the colonisation of what is now Australia by arguing that, as a whole society would be transplanted there from Britain, 'this colony will be a civilized country from the very commencement'. Whether this entanglement was contingent or constitutive of their liberalism is a question Moyn does not pose but answering it has significant implications for whether liberalism can, or should, be re-invented in the present.

Moyn's Cold War liberal protagonists inherited from their liberal precursors a sanitised account of settler colonialism, which directly influenced their understanding of Israel's founding. Berlin, for instance, declared that he was willing to defend to the death the claim that Zionism was not in any way racist. The 'hatred of Arabs' that does exist in Israel, he argued, 'has nothing to do with the Nazis, much more with the Spanish versus Indians.' Arendt was far more critical of Zionism and characterised the demand for a Jewish nation-state as an extension of German nationalism. But she too romanticised settler colonialism throughout her work, most notably in *On Revolution*, where she claimed the 'colonization of North America and the republican government of the United States constitute perhaps the greatest, certainly the boldest, enterprises of European mankind.'

Rather than criticising this aspect of their thought, Moyn criticises the Cold War liberals for something quite different: while early liberals were committed to civilisational hierarchies and 'entangled' with European colonialism, he argues that 'Cold War liberalism did something much worse. Not only did they take sides in a global conflict that wrought enormous damage to the people of the former colonies, having 'been global imperialists', he writes, 'many liberals lost global interest'. Moyn never quite explains why this abandonment of the belief in 'global liberty' and their role in bringing it about was *worse* than the active role of liberals like Mill or Tocqueville in European colonialism, or indeed than the distinctly American conception of freedom that Aziz Rana has termed 'settler empire' in which the prerogatives of settler freedom, and the subordination that accompanied it, are expanded to the world. As applied to our own time, this indictment is perplexing. 'Liberals have not yet figured out how to spread freedom without empire', he writes. 'The forlorn Cold War liberals counselled them not to try.' But not only did the Cold War liberals see themselves as engaged in a great global struggle of freedom against totalitarianism, their inheritors took up this pose to defend what Moyn has elsewhere called the United States' 'forever wars'.

Those Moyn depicts as the contemporary heirs of Cold War liberalism – Anne Applebaum, Timothy Garton, Paul Berman, Michael Ignatieff, Tony Judt, Leon Wieseltier – were almost all fervent defenders of the Iraq War, which they depicted as a crusade for freedom. While Garton expressed some 'tortured liberal ambivalence' in the lead-up to the invasion, Judt was alone in criticising both the wars and 'Bush's useful idiots' for defending them. After decades of endless US wars, many around the world would be forgiven for thinking that if US liberals have still not 'worked out how to spread freedom without empire' it would be far better if they abandoned their self-appointed role of bringing freedom to the world. If there is anything to retrieve from Cold War liberalism it is the chastened recognition of the early Cold War liberals that US militarism abroad risked catastrophe. As a new Cold War looms, the inheritors of Cold War liberalism have combined the worst of liberalism's past: the anti-democratic foreclosure of alternatives is accompanied by a war-mongering commitment to spread their values to the world.

Jessica Whyte is Scientia Fellow (Philosophy and Law) and Associate Professor of Philosophy in the School of Humanities Languages / Faculty of Arts Social Sciences at UNSW Sydney

Jessica Whyte

Cyberstructure

Bernard Geoghegan *Code: From Information Theory to French Theory* (New Haven, CT: Duke University Press, 2023). 272pp., £25.00 hb., 978 1 47801 9 008

In 1969 George Boulanger, president of the International Association of Cybernetics, asked:

> But after all what is cybernetics? Or rather what is it not, for paradoxically the more people talk about cybernetics the less they seem to agree on a definition.

For the general public he proposed that cybernetics 'conjures up visions of some fantastic world of the future peopled by robots and electronic brains!', but added various of his own interpretations: theories of mathematical control, automation and communication, a study of analogies between humans and machines, and a philosophy of life. Cybernetics may be all of those things. At its height it was something more like a movement than a method or a branch of science. It involved a collection of thinkers from various branches of the natural and social sciences as well as the humanities, who worked together on shared concepts and theories – primarily control, information and communication – which were discussed and disputed at a series of conferences. Much of the work was funded by private bodies, and generated both serious and passing interest within certain areas of the academy (including amongst prominent philosophers in Germany and France), and a buzz in the press. It began to decline in the 1970s, however, and is of greatly reduced significance today. (James Baldwin's identification of a 'cybernetics craze' may have been more accurate than Heidegger's prophecy that 'the sciences now establishing themselves will soon be determined and guided by the new fundamental science which is called cybernetics'.)

The diversity of projects under the umbrella of cybernetics, alongside a lack of a unifying theory or method, almost necessitates a historical approach, which has been taken by various books to date. Bernard Geoghegan's *Code: From Information Theory to French Theory* follows this tendency but makes its own contribution in attending to the politics of cybernetics, particularly as it related to humane disciplines or the socio-cultural stream of cybernetic research. Geoghegan focuses on work which was funded by 'robber baron philanthropies' – primarily the Rockefeller Foundation and the Josiah Macy Jr.

Foundation – and undertaken by North American anthropologists and by Russian and French structuralists. He emphasises the technocracy of both philanthropic institutions and socio-cultural cybernetic research, or the sense in which they likened 'social conflict to mechanical failures, suitable for impartial redress by technical experts'. A major contention, in this regard, is that the jargon of technical problem-solving thus served to dissimulate the politics and ethics of these research projects whilst also diffusing 'social struggle'. Throughout, the text follows a technocratic imperative as it travelled from philanthropic bodies into the research that they funded, highlighting both the concrete oppressive circumstances in which researchers and their subjects found themselves, and the ways in which this was concealed in the name of technical redress.

Three strands of argument run through the book, fruitfully woven into the particular stories told in each chapter. One details a drive for data collection and processing, or 'datafication', whereby humans are rendered objects from which data can be gathered. This is made possible by what Geoghegan calls 'enclosures', partially-closed spaces in which data can be gathered. A second emphasises the historical oppressions that went along with these cybernetic and information theoretical research programs: primarily, colonialism, mental illness and the holocaust; each with an associated enclosure: colony, asylum and death camp. Third is the technocratic imperative of research funders – primarily, the Josiah Macy Foundation and the Rockefeller Foundation – as it permeated cybernetic research. These three strands are presented as mutually reinforcing, such that the abstraction of data and the language of code serves to obscure political circumstances, support apolitical machinic analogies, meeting the technocratic demands of institutions and securing their financial support.

These argumentative strands – data production, historical political circumstances, the technocracy of funders and research projects – are explored in five chapters, focusing on anthropological research conducted primarily by North American thinkers Margaret Mead and Gregory Bateson, followed by discussion of structuralist projects undertaken in the US under the banner of cybernetics and information theory, and funded by the philanthropic institutions in question – primarily those of Roman Jakobson, Claude Lévi-Strauss, and Jacques Lacan.

In large part the argument is expressed through presentation of historical and theoretical material, such as the discussion of Mead's ethnographic study of indigenous Balinese culture from 1936-39. Her claim was that whilst both indigenous Balinese and Americans were affected by schizophrenia, the former had a means to resist it which the latter lacked. One of the aims of the research was to produce data which could be used for comparative analysis of schizophrenia in Bali and the USA, which is what Mead did upon returning to America, where she turned her attention to mental health and suburban family life, claiming that Americans lacked both codes common amongst family members and harmonious and repetitive activity from which Balinese tribespeople benefitted.

Geoghegan argues that Mead's approach in this regard was apolitical and technocratic. Bali was a Dutch colony at the time, but this was seemingly ignored and suppressed by Mead, who failed, extraordinarily, to acknowledge the Dutch policy of 'Balinization', which aimed to preserve its own view of traditional Balinese culture, including effectively imposing poverty and malnourishment on the population. Mead was seemingly unaffected by this, and a lead research assistant attested that she never mentioned the Dutch colonial authorities or 'broached a political discourse'. Geoghegan also contends that her project was technocratic, as it ignored the political situation in Bali and the US, approaching the latter as a series of problems requiring technical redress (through techniques inspired by cybernetic conceptions of communication) rather than broader socio-cultural change.

The concrete circumstances in Bali and suburban America suburbia were thus disappeared in Mead's research, according to Geoghegan, through the very practice of datafication and encoding, where the translation of research findings into analogical concepts or self-identical data made an obscuration of the political possible:

> Faced with the unimaginably destructive forces of disease, colonialism, nationalism, and pogroms, midcentury cultural theorists distilled cultural analysis into a kind of acid wash for recording culture as semiotic chains, remote from the crude chauvinisms of racial and totalitarian reasoning.

The 'acid wash' was provided by cybernetic and information theoretical concepts of information, communication and game theory, and the practice of translating the discursive into the numerical and the humane into the scientific. In this regard the three analytical threads are effective in illuminating the historical material selected, particularly with regard to the sense in which analogical anthropological reasoning served as a means to make abstractions which obscured certain aspects of political circumstances.

One of the successes of the text is a blending of political history, personal biography and particular theoretical interests and projects, in a way that is both technically precise and highly readable. Perhaps the finest example is the chapter on Roman Jakobson, which combines his early interest in Russian futurism and folklore, and fear of the latter's decline, with his discovery of Saussure's structural method, the political contexts of his various forced flights and migrations, and his work completed after moving to the US. Jakobson's particular structuralism is thus explained in part through a fear that Russian language and poetry was being destroyed by Bolshevism, from which he fled to Prague in his early twenties, along with his parents. When German troops arrived in Prague, Jakobson was forced to flee again, this time through Scandinavia, eventually arriving in New York in 1941. There he managed to secure a professorship at the École libre des hautes études, hosted by the New School for Social Research and funded and part-vetted by the Rockefeller Foundation. Here Jakobson reformulated Saussure's linguistics to accommodate media technologies such as the telephone, radio and amplified loudspeakers, which, as Geoghegan emphasises, was very much to the taste of the Rockefeller Foundation at the time. When many fellow refugees returned to their home countries in the late 1940s, Jakobson stayed in the US, where he was given a professorship in Slavic studies at Harvard in 1949 and received further funding from the Rockefeller Foundation for an exhaustive analysis of contemporary Russian on the promise that it would better that the Soviets.

Geoghegan carefully details both the significance of cybernetics and information theory and an anti-Soviet political agenda in the construction of Jakobson's work, and identifies them as key to US government and philanthropic agendas. But interestingly, whilst Jacobson's work was closely engaged in cybernetic themes and concepts, Geoghegan contends that his Rockefeller project culminated in an analytical subversion of communication theory through recourse to poetics. Whilst communication theory stabilises discourse, poetics does the opposite. Discourse may build equations from verbal terms such that the metalanguage of communication theory tends towards semantic stability, but poetics proceeds 'in an essentially indeterminate manner that countervails' the stability of communication theory, as a necessary aspect of language that is ungraspable by communication theory. For Geoghegan, then, a remnant of Jakobson's early interest in poetics and futurist poetry is put to use in subverting any dreams of total control or enclosure which communication theory may harbour.

Jakobson's resistant poetics is something of an anomaly, though, and much of the book emphasises the technocratic and apolitical aspects of cybernetics and structuralism – including a complaint that the latter takes over from existentialism as part of a depoliticising tendency in French thought. There are some obvious examples which run counter to this who are given scant attention, however, such as Althusser (and his *Reading Capital* companions) and Norbert Wiener. The latter, for example, was deeply involved with cybernetics and information theory, but refused to allow his work to be used for military purposes after World War II, worried about handing over the successes of cybernetics to 'the world of Belsen and Hiroshima', and defended his MIT colleague Dirk Struik, accused of teaching Marxism, leading the president of MIT to assure the Rockefeller Foundation that Wiener had not 'himself been involved in any Communist or Communist front activities'.

Sometimes, too, earnest interest in cybernetics is somewhat underestimated on the part of thinkers in favour of an emphasis on engagements for the purposes of achieving funding or developing careers. Jakobson's work on information theory and cybernetics, for example, is presented as being motivated by his desire to remain in the US, made possible by institutions keen to support the former. Lévi-Strauss' engagement with cybernetics is presented similarly (though less sympathetically) as an attempt to secure financial support for research; thus, his cybernetic reading of Mauss is described as a 'maneuver' to curry favour with funders. This is a welcome identification of the constitutive impact of material demands in understanding the engagements of various thinkers with cybernetics, and one which counterbalances overemphasis on concepts or a tendency for hagiolatry in histories of French thought. Little room is left, however, for the possibility that engagement with cybernetics and information theory may have been borne out of genuine interest in what appeared to many to be developing into a crucial scientific endeavour – similar to the recent successes of relativistic and quantum physics. Greater discussion of these and other factors would have offered a more complex picture of the overdetermination of research projects, with room for cybernetics and information theory as both funding strategy and intellectual conviction.

A more significant lacunae pertains to Geoghegan's critical engagement with the actual work produced by the thinkers in question. Indeed, whilst the claim that funding bodies demanded technocratic research projects is well argued, there is little critical discussion of the political and scientific (or philosophical) status of the work produced. Geoghegan offers admirably clear glosses of major texts, thoughtfully highlighting the role of cybernetics and information theory therein, but the political critique of conditions, that is, funding institutions, is not carried over to the result: the work produced. Whilst the ideology surrounding and supporting work is well identified, its claims to science or truth are not evaluated in as much depth. Instead, there is a tendency to criticise funding institutions and to endorse moments when thinkers subvert cybernetics and information theory – such as Jakobson's poetics or Barthes' reading of code – whilst shying away from thorough criticism of the work itself.

An interesting moment thus arises when Geoghegan notes a criticism of Levi-Strauss by Maxime Rodinson, who proposes that the former's work is 'little more than US imperialism dressed up as French social theory' (in Geoghegan's gloss). Lévi-Strauss responds: 'But should we not distinguish scientific findings, strictly speaking, from the political and ideological uses to which they are put, all too frequently, in the United States and elsewhere?', before responding to Rodinson's other criticisms in turn. For Geoghegan, Lévi-Strauss 'demurs' before Rodinson's criticisms, 'preferring to turn the inquiry to finer details' of anthropological theory. It may be true that Lévi-Strauss evades the depth of his own question, but, ironically, Geoghegan follows a similar path. Indeed, throughout the text criticism is (rightly) made of both the political imperatives for funding research and their willing acceptance by researchers, and the political circumstances that went undisturbed or else obscured by research. But it does not necessarily follow that this work was unscientific or unphilosophical as a result (or indeed technocratically or politically effective). One wonders, for example, whether Jakobson's engagement with information theory is less truthful than his work on poetics, or whether the latter is affirmed primarily because information theory is associated with reprehensible political institutions. In a more complex way, we might agree that Mead's ignorance of colonial policy in Bali – intentional or otherwise – was an astonishing oversight, both ethically and scientifically, without concluding that this invalidates her claim that indigenous Balinese people were better able to cope with schizophrenia than suburban Americans, and hence provided a potential medical model. If Mead was in fact wrong in her understanding of Balinese resistance to schizophrenia, and if this were a result of her ignorance of colonial policy, then this would be an interesting argument, but the link is not made.

Lévi-Strauss's response to Rodin may be a rather empty self-defence, but it nonetheless points towards a distinction between truth and its conditions which is more delicate. With regard to Geoghegan's text we might reverse his question and ask about conditions for 'scientific findings' rather than 'uses' to which they are put: should scientific findings be distinguished from the political and ideological imperatives associated with funders in the US and elsewhere? Can this distinction be made at all? Geoghegan's text is rich in its analysis of the political conditions for research and convincing in its presentation of the apolitical and technocratic hue of cybernetics and information theory of the period. One is left wondering, though, to what extent all of this research or its 'findings' lacked science, and without a connection rigorously identified between the two, what to make of Lévi Strauss' distinction between politics and science.

Gus Hewlett

Uncaged optimism

Ruth Wilson Gilmore, *Abolition Geography: Essays Towards Liberation*, edited by Brenna Bhandar and Alberto Toscano (London/Brooklyn: Verso, 2022), 506 pp. £12.99 pb., 978 1 83976 170 6.

Ruth Wilson Gilmore is a dialectician who embodies optimism without naivete, demonstrates dexterity in moving between universal, particular and individual dimensions, and describes contemporary conditions and past history with an eye to revolutionising the future, while contextualising everything with care and urgency. She is already justly famous for her massive contributions to the Prison Abolition movement, and these essays enrich our understanding of how her mind radiates outward to the whole world. Confining her brilliance to a single issue would obfuscate her dialectic prowess and far-ranging intellect. The essays and interviews collected in *Abolition Geography: Essays Towards Liberation* reveal, both individually and in their totality, how Gilmore holds together a material analysis of contemporary capitalism, a geographer's sense of place, and her continued optimism for transformation rooted in resistance.

Abolition Geography occupies a particular space and time. The pieces date from between 1991-2018; this time span includes Gilmore's career as an activist and teacher prior to her PhD in Geography, through her writing of *Golden Gulag: Prisons, Surplus, Crisis, and Opposition in Globalizing California* in 2007, extending up to the opening years of the Trump presidency. It does mean that the book does not contain the seismic shifts of 2020 – COVID, the response to George Floyd's murder by the police, the disputed election. As frustrating as it can be to lack Gilmore's commentary on each of our current crises, the essays as a collection enable the astute reader to see how her dialectical approach holds prognosticatory power.

'Abolition geography starts from the homely premise that freedom is a place'. In this book, the places in question are primarily in California, in particular Los Angeles and the Central Valley. She notes how communities that 'appear to lack the power to resist toxic incinerators or prisons' are the ones that get them (e.g. California's Central Valley). That specific geography then connects to how 'people from the hyperpoliced poorest urban areas are locked away in rural prisons' precisely because 'they appear to lack the power to resist mass incarceration that they are arrested and imprisoned'. Thus she forms a grounded, living connection between the environmental movements and prison abolition movements, asking what might happen if the differences created and exploited by late capitalism to divide people – like race/citizenship, innocence/guilt – could dissolve in our imaginations 'in favor of other things, like the right to water, the right to air, the right to the countryside, the right to the city'. Opposition to environmental destruction and the carceral state are both opposition to callous disregard for life, and the resistance embodied in the anti-prison and environmental movements call for 'and use and local democracy' as imperative.

The localisation and specificity in her dialectic does not mean that Gilmore's viewpoint is ever parochial. She announces that her 'interest is in proliferating, rather than concentrating, ways of thinking'. She establishes a few touchstone categories in regards to our age – the forces of 'organized abandonment' that deem 'some people as parasitic and unnecessary', with racism playing a key role in this abdication of any pretense of shared human community. Late capitalism is thus in her now famous phrase 'a machine for producing and exploiting group-differentiated vulnerability to premature death.'

Compromise with a death-dealing machine doesn't alter the fundamental purpose of its destructive intent. Thus she disposes of the use of 'innocence' as a gradualist method for dismantling prisons, because arguing that some types of people (like mothers, or 'people who didn't hurt anyone') shouldn't be in cages, we 'establish as a hard fact that some people should be in cages'. Instead the questions should be what does it mean to put any person, ever, in a cage, and why are more people being put in cages than ever before, on a massively unprecedented scale? The dialectical answers to those questions can be found in the larger political economy, where, as she writes in an article co-written with Craig Gilmore, 'the "free trade" of the globalization era' brought 'with it massive increases in cages for the unfree'. The answer can also be found in reframing the question from one of 'innocence' to a more graphic synonym for 'organized abandonment':

> Human sacrifice rather than innocence is the central problem that organizes the carceral geographies of the prison-industrial complex. Indeed, for abolition, to insist on innocence is to surrender politically because "innocence" evades a problem abolition is compelled to confront: how to diminish and remedy harm as against finding better forms of punishment.

The 'anti-state state' is another key category in Gilmore's analysis, particularly important in her 2007 article 'In the Shadow of the Shadow State'. The 'anti-state state' describes the phenomenon of those ideologues who want to shrink the state to facilitate the free movement of capital, but once these 'anti-state state actors...gain state power by denouncing state power...they spend a lot of money even as they claim they're 'shrinking government',' especially on 'prisons, policing, court and the military' until it seems normal and natural to be 'locking people in cages or bombing civilians or sending generation after generation off to kill somebody else's children'. If these destructive actions become the central priorities for government in the hands of anti-state state actors, then the non-profit sector's attempts at amelioration of these anti-human policies are co-opted in a sleight-of-hand, in which anti-state actors with state power use non-profits to facilitate the 'organized abandonment' of those they deem to be expendable people. Non-profit groups find themselves increasingly taking 'responsibility for persons who are in the throes of abandonment rather than responsibility for persons progressing toward full incorporation' into society. The 'anti-state state actors welcome nonprofits under the rhetoric of efficiency (read: meager budgets) and accountability (read: contracts could be pulled if anybody stepped out of line),' which leads to nonprofits having 'become highly professionalized by their relationship with the state'. Those groups that are more grassroots are hemmed in to a 'mission impossible' if they seek grants, due to funders 'sternly specific funding rubrics' and the fact that grant money is almost always project-specific rather than assisting with 'core operations'. But rather than be wholly discouraging, Gilmore ends the article reminding those working in grassroots organizations that 'the purpose of the work is to gain liberation, not to guarantee the organization's longevity,' such that 'grassroots organizations can be the voices of history and the future to assemble the disparate and sometimes desperate nonprofits who labor in the shadow of the shadow state'.

An example of her dialectic feminism comes in the earlier article from 1993, 'Public Enemies and Private Intellectuals: Apartheid USA'. Gilmore's blend of a wry optimism and clear-sighted analysis emerges in the opening statement that 'capitalism hasn't won, but not for lack of trying'. She analyses these attempts at total victory for capitalism as an unequal partnership of state and business:

> through production of public enemies, the state safeguards the unequal distribution of resources and reinforces the logic of scarcity by deflecting attention from the real thieves and criminals—the transnationals that are making off with profits which even the state can no longer lay significant partial claim to through tax tribute.

Uncovering these structures takes her back to Audre Lorde's poetically prismatic insight: 'The master's tools will never dismantle the master's house'. Gilmore unpacks Lorde's quote as a commentary on capitalism, racism, the means of production, and the goals of liberation. 'Tools' points us to consider 'fundamental orderings in political economy' and understand that if the master loses control of the his 'tools' – the means of production - he remains a human being, but he is no longer the 'master.' The metaphor of the house, meanwhile, 'guides our attention' to think about 'institutions and luxury', the master's house being, by definition, a well-apportioned dwelling that remains ostentatiously present over generations. It is these luxuries and institutions that 'must be dismantled so that we can recycle the materials…to produce new and liberating work'. What makes this analysis compelling emerges from both its inherent logic (poets like Lorde don't pick words like 'tools' and 'house' accidently, after all) and the fact that Gilmore was not just talking about this, but was also 'walking the talk' of Oppositional work. As she notes (and details elegantly in later essays in this collection), she sees Oppositional work '[e]verywhere I turn in Los Angeles today, Salvadoran garment workers, African American and Chicana Mothers ROC, ex-gangsters trying to maintain the truce against the unwavering interests of the police for it to fail'. Can we intellectuals who are also trying to be on the side of liberation, be ready to assist these struggles – then and now? If we are teachers, is our teaching up to that challenge? Are we preparing students to comprehend what is at stake? She rejects the 'dour' and defeatist logic of the Frankfurt School, and the 'pampered and paternalized' hijacking of a cultural movement like the Harlem Renaissance, both of which have proved wanting to answer the depth of the transformation needed. We have to find our own way out.

One important theme throughout these essays is Gilmore's self-conscious understanding of her own positionality and family history as part of the dialectic, or, to invoke Gramsci, how she posits herself 'as an element of the contradictions and elevates this element to a principle of knowledge and therefore of action.' The oldest article in the collection, 1991's 'Decorative Beasts: Dogging the Academy in the Late 20th Century', references her father, 'lifelong New Haven activist Courtland Seymour Wilson' for his perspicacity and persistence. She also highlights a horrifying yet instructive retelling of the 1969 murder of her cousin John Higgins along with another Black Panther comrade at an early meeting for the UCLA Black Studies program. The implicit question was whether or not Black Studies would become 'decorative displacement' or whether this newest branch of the university might take up the totality, seeing race and capitalism as connected, and thus forward the real concern of liberation. To my eye as a reader, there is a red thread from this piece to the most recent in the collection, the concluding 2018 'Abolition Geography and the Problem of Innocence,' understanding the personal as the political, and the individual and particular as also being part of the universal:

> The Black Radical Tradition is a constantly evolving accumulation of structures of feeling whose individual and collective narrative arcs persistently tend toward freedom. It is a way of mindful action that is constantly renewed and refreshed over time but maintains strength, speed, stamina, agility, flexibility, balance…If, then, the structures of feeling for the Black Radical Tradition are, age upon age, shaped by energetically expectant consciousness of and direction toward unboundedness, then the tradition is, inexactly, movement away from partition and exclusion—indeed, its inverse.

Here we see what she means when describing the project of Abolition Geography as taking 'feeling and agency to be constitutive of, no less than constrained by, structure' – people are making history, and making our lives more possible, under circumstances not of our own choosing, but if we can 'tend toward freedom' we can pivot from despair to a grounded and gritty sense of confidence with 'stamina, agility, flexibility.'

Indeed, in her stubbornly ontological understanding of the term "Abolition" Gilmore specifically says that abolitionists (of all eras) 'are, first and foremost, committed to the possibility of full and rich lives for everybody'.

Thus, 'Abolition is a totality and it is ontological…but it is not struggle's *form*. *To have form,* we have to organize'. Understood this way, Abolition is a potent example of the negation of the negation, 'abolition is a fleshly and material presence of social life lived differently…figuring out how to work with people to make something rather than figuring out how to erase something. It's about making things'. Her insistence that there are more human possible futures is rooted in what 'dialectics requires us to recognize[:] that the negation of the negation is always abundantly possible *and* hasn't a fixed direction or secure end. It can change direction, and thereby not revive old history but calibrate power differentials anew'.

There is no easy way to summarise Ruth Wilson Gilmore's thought, and that is why volumes like this, that enable us to follow her train of thought, are so valuable. The book's co-editors – Brenna Bhandar and Alberto Toscano – have done a tremendous favour for activists and thinkers worldwide by uniting these pieces, previously scattered across an array of journals and media. The editors' thematic arrangement of the essays is nearly made superfluous by the connective threads weaving through Gilmore's thought, yet there are some especially instructive editorial choices, such as opening with 'What Is To Be Done' from 2011, and the placement of the sparkling transcribed interviews near the end, after a reader has gained familiarity with Gilmore's patterns of thought and theoretical categories. The editors' introduction contains a strong outline of Gilmore's work and themes, and could be read before, during, and after contemplating Gilmore's own words. The index, while good, is incomplete on some key entries, and it would help with the dialectic specificity of the essays to have printed the year of their initial publication somewhere on each entry's initial page. But these are minor complaints. The editors' labor is too often invisible and thankless, but deserves to be made visible and applauded.

One lesson that I have learned from reading, studying, and listening to Ruth Wilson Gilmore, is that a world and life of scarcity is not our fate, but a construct foisted on us by those who are hoarding the resources. The fact that those same hoarders would put us in cages, or murderously attack enemies to be 'hurled into eternity' became the central theme of her work. But what emerges in *Abolition Geography* is that the opposite, the negation of the negation, a world in which life and creativity are valued, is 'always abundantly possible,' and we can catch glimpses of it in our own activity. It is her 'stamina, agility, flexibility' that lead me to conclude that Gilmore is the Steph Curry of dialectics. I can watch a highlight reel of Curry three-pointers, analyze them, see how he did it and understand it. But what is astounding is not the physics itself, but the actual doing of it, in real time. Gilmore does this in analyzing contemporary movements for freedom, as the currents and flows shift around us, at great speed. It inspires more than awe – it leads to the shock of recognition in our own lives, bodies, and places, as we ask what are the transformations in which we participate. Read the book, think and make change.

Jennifer Rycenga

Feminist snap

Sara Ahmed, *The Feminist Killjoy Handbook* (London: Penguin, 2023). 336pp., £10.99, 978 0 24161 953 7

For a few years I taught an undergraduate module called Feminist Killjoys, a title I took from the work of theorist Sara Ahmed. The figure of the 'feminist killjoy' has since come to define Ahmed's intellectual project and gives her name to Ahmed's latest work, *The Feminist Killjoy Handbook*. The feminist killjoy is a willing troublemaker who refuses to let social norms or institutional pressures get in the way of doing what is right. Ahmed repurposes this insult as a badge of honour, mirroring earlier reclamations of queer and crip. Each year my students adopted the name with pride, finding in Ahmed's words a new way to reframe difficult and painful experiences, and delighting in telling their horrified families what they were studying at university. They found the appeal of the killjoy hard to resist.

As a fellow killjoy, but more importantly, as an overworked university teacher, I loved this class. It had that magical combination of revelation and reliability: it sparked conversation like nothing else, created bonds that sustained us through some tricky texts, and always worked. But last year, teaching in Ireland, it didn't. While my English students had embraced Ahmed's call to snap social bonds that harm, my Irish ones were more hesitant to speak out at the family table, more cautious about this form of conflict and more sceptical of its efficacy. Mulling it over, I grumbled about Irish cultural conservatism and feminine socialisation. No doubt my students were inhibited by Ireland's housing crisis; most lived with their families, unlike my students in England. I thought about Ireland's communal fractures: the colonial and sectarian violence since papered over by neoliberalism, and more recently, two bitterly-fought referenda on abortion and equal marriage. The context pushed me to think about what happens next. I asked: what comes after the killjoy?

The Feminist Killjoy Handbook is published with Penguin's imprint Allen Lane, rather than Ahmed's usual Duke University Press. The switch indicates her desire to reach a wider audience, as does the title, which echoes the post-Brexit and post-BLM trend for politicised self-help books. The success of Ahmed's 2017 *Living a Feminist Life* suggested the potential for a crossover hit. It inadvertently rode the wave of the post-#MeToo popular feminist revival and was ubiquitous at the time on social media. Every self-respecting feminist academic snapped a photo of its cover next to a latte and a pen to show she meant business. The rainbow-coloured *Handbook* is finely-tuned to look good on an Instagram grid, and Ahmed has promoted the book on a lengthy tour. Having heard her speak a number of times, I went to the Edinburgh date, hosted in a packed lecture theatre by Lighthouse Books. The atmosphere was like no other academic talk I have ever attended. It felt more like a gig by an indie band about to break the mainstream, or, perhaps, a sermon at an evangelical church. The audience whooped; Ahmed grinned. In the Q&A, voices quivered as they shared painful stories, seeking solace and advice.

It's hard to begrudge Ahmed – or her fans – some joy. In 2016, she publicly resigned her professorial post at Goldsmiths over the university's failure to tackle staff harassment of students. Her most significant treatment of this experience appears in her 2021 book *Complaint!*, which describes how she subsequently became a 'listening ear' for other survivors of harassment and abuse in the sector who sought her out to tell their stories. Ahmed has also spoken out prominently on her blog about a range of lightning rod issues that few scholars want to touch, from trigger warnings in universities to transphobia in British culture. These entries often appear reworked in later books. Ahmed has always done intellectual work in public, although refashioning herself as a public intellectual has presumably become more pressing since she became an independent scholar.

The Feminist Killjoy Handbook is not a book that tries to persuade the unconvinced. It addresses a reader who has internalised the epithet as a source of pride and wants to be bolstered in their conviction. Ahmed urges her readers to continue being feminist killjoys and acknowledges the challenges of doing so, notably the reactions of others. She offers a mantra that will be familiar to her readers: 'If you expose a problem, you pose a problem; if you pose a problem, you become the problem'. This is a 'killjoy truth', the 'core truth' of them all. These 'truths' appear in bold throughout, alongside 'killjoy maxims', 'killjoy commitments' and 'killjoy equations', reproduced at the end in a handy list. The book begins with chapters on 'Introducing the Feminist Killjoy' and 'Surviving as a Feminist Killjoy' – the latter including 'killjoy survival tips' in bold – before chapters on the feminist killjoy's roles as cultural critic, philosopher, poet and activist. It ends with a reading list of books primarily by Black and women of colour scholars and activists, and reading group discussion questions. The questions remind us that one of Ahmed's goals is to generate killjoy solidarity to sustain us when we become depleted. Though she doesn't note it here, Ahmed's project is in the second-wave tradition of consciousness-raising. The second wave, and anti-social queer theory, helps Ahmed hold on to negativity. As she writes elsewhere, drawing on Betty Friedan, making women happy is not the point of feminism. Instead, Ahmed urges us: stay unhappy with this world!

Ahmed's first book explicitly aimed at a popular audience is a culmination of her broader intellectual project in topic and method. Her method might be described as distillation. Ahmed returns to the same themes, and often the same phrases, anecdotes and even literary analyses, in a distinctive style characterised by repetition, rhyme and paradox. As she turns over words and phrases to show them from unexpected angles, her method exemplifies the core message: don't move on, don't let go. At its best, the difficulty of Ahmed's style intensifies her points, embodying her injunction that we have to become what we are judged as being. At other times, it frustrates. Her wordplay can feel like shuffling cards, a trick that thrills the first few times but leaves us wanting. That said, more densely theoretical texts like *Willful Subjects* (2014) reveal the origins of concepts later refined to the point of truism in a detailed, if sometimes slightly motivated, reading of the Western philosophical canon. For instance, Ahmed's notion of the 'feminist snap', the breaking point, derives from Lucretius' notion of the atom that swerves to 'snap the bonds of fate', while her account of the invisibility of forces that align with our will draws on Heidegger's hammer and Schopenhauer's stream. Ahmed, who once wrote a book citing no white men, may raise an eyebrow or roll an eye at my restoration of the white men cited in her earlier work to defend the seriousness of her later work.

The new book cleaves closely to Ahmed's earlier works, with chunks that are recognisable from elsewhere. She adds references to topical issues and newer films, from the politics of commemorating empire to *Everybody's Talking about Jamie* (2021). A new feature is fan mail: readers who have written to Ahmed to say how her writing has changed her life that suggest to the reader: it might change yours. The style is less poetic, perhaps a necessity in writing for a trade press, but not necessarily more direct. Ahmed formulates generalisable maxims, yet in spite of references to her personal life and wider culture, her body of evidence comes most substantially from the university, and her research on diversity work and university complaints procedures. The modern university is certainly worthy of sustained investigation. Its overuse of non-disclosure agreements against staff and students who disclose harassment and discrimination, protection of superstar abusers, and persistent use of casualised contracts, among other things, ruins lives and corrupts any claim it might make to being committed to the noble goal of education. The 1752 Group, which campaigns on these issues, was founded at Goldsmiths the same year Ahmed resigned. Their name is a reference to the £1752 allocated by Goldsmiths for a 2015 conference on staff-student sexual harassment, by which the university hoped to make the problem go away.

Activists outside the academy may wonder about the broader relevance of Ahmed's insights. The university is a distinctive space, with quasi-judicial systems of laws and regulations for which Ahmed elsewhere developed her own language of walls, doors and corridors. Activists have safe spaces policies (often), accountability processes (sometimes), and transformative justice practices (rarely). The rest of society – poor them – has the civil and criminal justice systems, which occasionally, invited or not, enter into these worlds. Unions, too, operate across these spaces, but for all her praise for complaint collectives, Ahmed always gives this one short shrift. She says little about the relationships between the different systems through which a complaint might pass, and as a result, it's rarely apparent in her work what she wants to happen, or if she thinks change is possible at all. Ahmed entreats her readers to join her in declaring: 'When critique causes damage, I am willing to cause damage.' 'I am willing to snap a bond that is damaging to others'. The subtitle of Ahmed's blog is 'killing joy as a world-building project'. But activists committed to social justice may wonder what kind of world is being created here, as we righteously kill someone else's joy, while accepting the inevitable fact that we will have our own killed joy in turn. In earlier work Ahmed anticipates, but never fully dispels, a concern derived from Wendy Brown that she makes a fetish of the wound.

The Feminist Killjoy Handbook is notable for what I think is the first mention of the police in Ahmed's work. This comes in the context of Black feminist Kirsten West Savali's comments on the Women's March NYC after the election of Trump. White attendees in their pussy hats snapped photos with cops, and organisers celebrated afterwards that no arrests were made. Ahmed, paraphrasing Savali, notes that 'a positive relation to the police as protectors is only possible for white women', before claiming that killjoy politics necessitates police abolitionism. This came as a surprise, since what should be done with racists, abusers and others who say and do bad things has long felt like an open question in Ahmed's work. Abolition does not seem implied by her earlier books on diversity policy so some dots needed to be joined here for regular readers. For the women in academia who wear Ahmed's mantras on t-shirts and pin badges as they insist that their cleaner address them as 'Dr', this radical position will also come out of the blue. In this brief section, Ahmed includes a lengthy quote from

Angela Davis, Gina Dent, Erica Meiners and Beth Richie's *Abolition. Feminism. Now* (2022). But abolitionist politics invites a more difficult question than Ahmed seems prepared to address: what are the killjoy's responsibilities to the people whose joy they kill?

This section comes in Ahmed's chapter on 'The Feminist Killjoy as Activist', and seems prompted in part by the need to address topical issues in a popular book. The chapter is the closest Ahmed gets to solutions, which she has long refused to be drawn on. Perhaps this is right; a political movement, least of all feminism, should not expect answers to be handed down from a sage on the stage, as some desperate people at the talk I attended seemed to hope. Still, this feels a little like false advertising in a handbook. One wonders whether Ahmed's promised *Complainer's Handbook*, which she is currently writing, will follow the same path. Ahmed may refuse the model of an instructor, yet her reading group questions do little to destabilise her authority. They are primarily exegetical, asking the readers to interpret their experiences in the light of her concept, or to find more evidence. Nowhere in the list does Ahmed ask her readers: what will you do now? Or: what did I get wrong? The list ends with an invitation for readers to email her their stories. To her credit, even in a popular book, Ahmed still makes time to listen to people who have not otherwise been heard.

The killjoy, the complainer; before this, the unhappy queer, the melancholic migrant. Ahmed has moved increasingly towards figures. This has led over time to a more celebratory style that irons out the interesting and instructive hesitation of her earlier work. In *Willful Subjects*, she warns that the book is not a mere celebration of the will and wilfulness; in *The Promise of Happiness*, she notes the 'risk [of] overemphasising the problems with happiness by presenting happiness as a problem'. *The Feminist Killjoy Handbook* comes with some caveats, notably that we can't always assume we're the killjoy, and therefore right, because we have been in the past. This shapes Ahmed's discussion of transphobia in feminism.

Ahmed is keen to stress that transphobes are not feminist killjoys, even if they, too, believe themselves to be 'difficult women' speaking against the grain. For Ahmed, they have in fact 'taken the place of the patriarchal father'. Yet there seems little in the concept that prevents it from being claimed by transphobes, should they wish to. Ahmed even uses Mary Daly's description of the 'hag' to define the feminist killjoy. Daly is author of *Gyn/Ecology* (1978), which is most politely described as doing what it says on the tin. Without a strong theoretical scaffolding to guide us, we're left with one arbiter of who is or isn't a feminist killjoy: Ahmed.

Hannah Boast

Real movement

Karl Marx, *Critique of the Gotha Program: New Translation* (Oakland: PM Press, 2023). 99pp., £10.99, 978 1 62963 916 1

Why republish Karl Marx's *Critique of the Gotha Program* today? In the introduction to this new translation, Peter Hudis gives two reasons: the new translation contributes to our understanding of Marx's views on post-capitalist society and it is intended as a political intervention. Providing a clearer understanding of what communism would look like is vital for struggles today.

The Gotha program was the unifying document of the two main working-class parties in Germany. In 1863 the former collaborator of Marx and Fredrich Engels, Ferdinand Lassalle, founded the General Union of German Workers (ADAV). Marx had fallen out with Lassalle in 1862 due to political and theoretical differences, specifically Lassalle's efforts to form an alliance with the dictatorship of Otto von Bismarck. Wilhelm Liebknecht, a former member of the ADAV and August Bebel, both supporters of Marx, founded the Social-Democratic Party (SDAP) in 1869. Both parties were around the same size in 1875 when Liebknecht and Bebel enter negotiations to unify with the ADAV without consulting Marx and Engels. The Gotha program was the founding document of what was now called the Socialist Workers Party of Germany (SAPD). Marx and Engels originally saw the event as a retrospective capitulation by Liebknecht and Bebel's party to the views of Lassalle, who had died in 1864. What later became known as the *Critique of the Gotha Program* was an internal letter Marx sent to Liebknecht, Bebel, Ignaz Auer and August Geib.

Reading the *Critique of the Gotha Program* is vital for any understanding of Marx's conception of communism. It demolishes numerous myths related to Marx's views that have developed since his death and that have since grown into dogma. Firstly, the idea that Marx's contention that communism is a living movement embedded in the self-activity of the working class, and made possible by the contradictions within capitalism, meant that he rejected all forms of speculation about a future communist society is only true up to a certain point. Marx discussed the outlines of a communist society throughout his career to a greater extent than is usually acknowledged. While acknowledging the early contributions of those grouped together as 'Utopian Socialists', including Saint-Simon, Charles Fourier and Robert Owen, Marx in *the Communist Manifesto* explicitly rejects prescribed plans for a future communist society which lack or have defective strategies for arriving at their end goal. In the letter that contained his *Critique of the Gotha Program*, Marx declares: 'every step of real movement is more important than a dozen programs'. Nonetheless, Marx believed a correct theoretical understanding of the communist goal directly influenced the effectiveness of parties. He was hardly benevolent towards rival tendencies, spending large amounts of his time producing works like *The Poverty of Philosophy*, a critique of the anarchist Pierre Proudhon. As Hudis points out it was often in his more directly political interventions that his positions on communism were outlined.

Secondly, Marx rejected the 'iron law of wages', the idea supported by Lassalle among others that wages would be driven to subsistence levels under capitalism. Marx outlined in *Wage Labour and Capital and Value, Price and Profit* that his notions of immiseration should be measured against the expanding wealth within capitalism. In contemporary terms, he was discussing relative poverty over absolute poverty (of course both are a feature of capitalism). Marx was particularly annoyed that the Gotha program contained support for the 'iron law of wages', potentially alienating trade unionists struggling for higher wages.

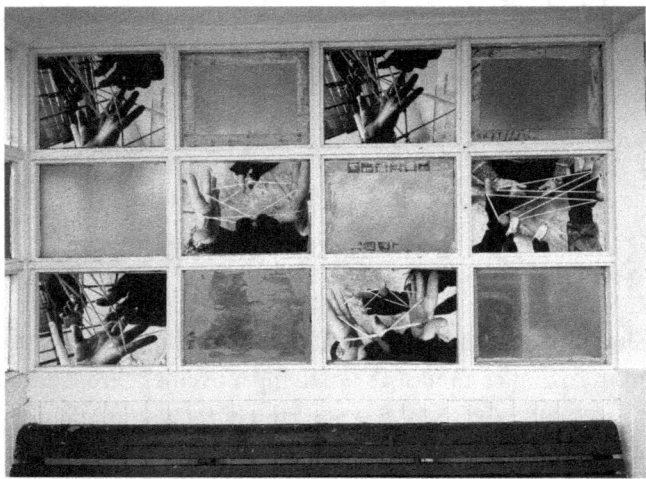

Thirdly, the notion that Marx's conception of communism relies on ignoring individual differences in skill, effort and disposition in production is refuted in *Critique of the Gotha Program*. Marx specifically discusses how in the 'first phase of communism' workers will be paid in tokens relative to the time they work. This formal equality is based on a real inequality as some workers will be more skilled, more productive than others and yet will receive the same amount in payment. The 'second phase of communism' will abolish this inequality to the effect that consumption will be based on human need. Despite various conservative stereotypes to the contrary, Marx makes it clear that collective ownership of the means of production does not mean that individual consumption items are held in common once distributed.

Up until the Paris Commune in 1871, Marx's statements were ambiguous on the question of the state. As Hudis points out, Marx learned from the Paris Commune that the capitalist state needs to be smashed rather than taken over. Marx's only revision to the *Communist Manifesto* and his updates to the French Edition of *Capital Volume 1* revolve around this insight. Marx's understanding of the relationship between the state and the construction of communism requires careful delimitation and the new translation of the *Critique of the Gotha Program* makes an invaluable contribution to our understanding of this issue.

A common understanding of Marx's vision of a post-capitalist society follows the schema of the smashing of the capitalist state, the creation of the dictatorship of the proletariat, a transitional state for the suppression of the capitalist minority, a socialist period with a nationalised economy followed by communism. The term 'dictatorship of the proletariat' is often thought to have originated with August Blanqui although there is no evidence of this. As Hudis points out, this schema is not fully aligned with what Marx describes in *Critique of the Gotha Program*. Marx does describe a 'political transition period' of the 'revolutionary dictatorship of the proletariat' which would essentially be a state democratically controlled by the workers for the suppression of the bourgeoisie. There is no mention of a socialist phase – as Hudis notes Marx tended to use the word's socialism and communism interchangeably. Both the first and second phase of communism described by Marx do not mention the existence of a state. As communism is premised on the abolition of social classes and the state's function is described as being for the suppression of one class by another, the state does not exist in any form of communism according to Marx. The difference between first and second phases of communism is based on the shift from consumption being based on hours worked to consumption based on human need. The division of labour and the division between mental and physical labour is abolished in the second phase of communism. Confusion on this issue has been created by previous translations in which the word *Staatsfunktiomen* has been translated as state rather than state functions. Marx asks: 'what transformation will the body politic (staatswesen) undergo in Communist society? In other words, what social functions analogous to present state functions (staatsfunktiomen) will remain at that juncture?'

Previous translations imply the state's existence under communism, whereas the new translation has a greater consistency with the overall arguments put forward by Marx in the text. Hudis incorrectly describes Vladmir Ilyich Lenin as reading into *Critique of the Gotha Program* a distinction between socialism and communism. But in *State and Revolution* Lenin is clear that Marx only discusses the first and second phases of communism while the distinction between socialism and communism is described is being based on Engels's preface to *Internationales aus dem Volkstaat* written in 1894. Engels notes that the name social democrat may 'pass muster' but is 'inexact' for a party whose goal is 'not merely socialist in general, but downright communist'.

Why do these past debates matter? The new translation is described by Hudis as an intervention in present day struggles that are often characterised by an ethos of anti-capitalism without having an 'adequate conception of our goal'. Rising hopes captured by Syriza, Podemos and Corbynism (among others) in Europe produced the real prospect of left governments between 2014 and 2017; correspondingly a spate of predominantly left accelerationist writings on what a post-capitalist society might look like were published. Whether influenced by the early work of Nick Land or a specific reading of the Operaismo tradition, the work of Nick Srnicek and Alex Williams, Antonio Negri and Michel Hardt (prior to the publication of *Assembly*) have focussed on linking technological shifts in contemporary capitalism to the development of a communist future. The destructive aspects of class struggle are neglected in this approach, while the line between the future use of technology under communism and a celebration of current productive practices are frequently blurred. The weakness of these approaches, regardless of intention, is that they have given agency to technological advances over the struggles of the exploited and oppressed.

The defeat of radical left electoral projects and the continued rise of the far right and fascism have led to a renewed theoretical emphasis on defining capitalism itself. Yanis Varoufakis has repurposed for the radical left the originally conservative concept of 'techno-feudalism' coined by Glen Wely and Eric Posner, Cedric Robinson's conception of 'racial capitalism' is increasingly discussed and deployed, Maurizio Lazzarato's concept of 'political capitalism' has restated the role of violence and state repression in the continued reproduction of capitalism. Maintaining a link between adequately defining capitalism and an orientation towards existing struggles is vital.

Hudis points out that Marx in *Critique of the Gotha Program* puts the emphasis on the self-activity of workers in creating a communist society. Marx criticises the Gotha program for demanding that the state fund cooperative societies. He declares that the '*only*' value of cooperative societies is if they are the 'independent creations of the workers', not protégés of the capitalist state. If Lenin once described socialism as Soviets plus electricity, the emphasis needs to swing back towards the Soviet pole of that formulation. Peter Linbaugh in the afterword to *Critique of the Gotha Program* concisely declares Marx does not 'paint pictures', he takes 'photographs'. Marx generalises his theoretical concepts by learning from workers struggles rather than abstract model building. Hudis correctly points out that discussing and understanding what we are fighting for is crucial to guiding the struggles of today. What requires further elaboration is the missing link between ongoing struggles and a future communist society: that is, strategy.

Chris Newlove

Spectres of value

Christopher J. Arthur *The Spectre of Capital: Idea and Reality* (Leiden: Brill, 2022). 449pp., £148.00 hb., 978 9 00451 517 8

Christopher J. Arthur's latest, perhaps most significant book to date, *The Spectre of Capital: Idea and Reality,* presents his distinctive approach to value form theory and Hegelian Marxism. The culmination of a career in Marxian philosophy, *The Spectre of Capital* recapitulates earlier theoretical innovations – the dialectics of sociation, dissociation and association, a renewed articulation of the labour theory of value, Arthur's 'homology' thesis – within a more comprehensive theory, the systematicity of which derives from a newly foregrounded proposition: capital should be conceived as 'spectre'. (See also his earlier essay, 'The Spectral Ontology of Value', in *RP* 107 (2001).) *The Spectre of Capital* is a systematically dialectical reconstruction of Marx's *Capital*, expounding a dualistic method to grasp the reality of economic form. Capital, Arthur argues, ought to be elucidated in relation to a concrete other that retains an unsystematisable ontology. Here, value forms are understood as 'simply logical' and the ontology of capital as Idea. History, in this account, has engendered a bleak idealism of pure forms, whereby Hegel is inverted and capital is not being but nothingness. The truth, for Arthur, is not in the whole; the whole is emphatically false. *The Spectre of Capital* considers the dominance of abstract social forms in a manner that is irreducible to the arguments of either Hegel or Marx. Exceeding the writings of both, the book is neither a philological exercise nor a contribution to intellectual history. Arthur instead formulates a distinctive theory of capitalist modernity that demands to be read on its own terms. But what is Arthurism? And what politics does it possess?

Spanning nearly 400 pages – including instructive appendices that outline the relation of Hegel's logic to the logic of the value forms (establishing technical details of Arthur's own architectonic, as well as clarifying terminology) and including tables outlining logical categories –*The Spectre of Capital* offers a detailed and overarching overview of Arthur's value form theory. Echoing the *Communist Manifesto's* 'spectre of communism', the term 'spectre' is used to illuminate the dialectical reality of capital: a social form that inverts the concrete communist movement. The play on the manifesto highlights Arthur's construal of capital's identity as both spectral yet ever-present in form and real in social power – hence the subtitle of the book: *Idea and Reality*.

The thesis that capital is a 'spectre' requires a thoroughgoing critique to explicate its genesis. Arthur sets about doing so through a unique presentation of the value form's dialectical development. This book length presentation is separated into two parts. *Part 1: Object and Method* provides a justification for the value theoretical approach to the critique of political economy. *Part 2: The Ideal Constitution of Capital* (which encapsulates the bulk of the book) systematically presents the dialectical ontology of capital's forms. Within these pages, Arthur identifies various shortcomings in Marx and Hegel to which, he claims, theory is obliged to respond.

Arthur judges Hegel's logic as incapable of approaching ontological truth but as sufficient for reflecting the logic of modernity's social form: capital's abstraction. Hegelianism, in this regard, is able to depict an inverted false ontology of pure form only. Dialectical innovations in *The Spectre of Capital* stem from Arthur's insistence that the relevance of Hegelian logic to the concept of capital is not based on method; rather, Hegel's systematic logic of categories underpins the false ontology of capital, where value-forms gain priority over their material bearers. The philosophical upshot is that the absolute should be considered a false totality. The result of Arthur's reckoning with Hegel is a conclusion that the Idea of capital is determined by a logical tendency toward completion through immanent development. Capital posits its own presupposition, making the concept of capital self-grounding, self-determining and – most politically stifling – self-reproducing.

The (re)reading of Hegelian systemic dialectic feeds into a reworking of corresponding inadequacies perceived in Marx. Arthur's analysis thus departs from Marx on a number of key theoretical points, four of which will be identified here. The first is that the sequential development of value-forms is re-ordered. The second follows: the discussion of the labour theory of value does not take place until a general form of capital is established. Building from this, in a third deviation, Arthur provides a political theory of the source of value in labour. The fourth is Arthur's solution to the transformation problem termed the 'transformation procedure.'

The deficiencies Arthur locates in Marx stem from the presentational order of the commodity form's development. Arthur's insistence is that labour, or production for that matter, should not appear within the presentation of *Capital* until the logic of commodity exchange has acquired immanent self-sufficiency as a general form of capital; that is, until it can self-reproduce. While production based on the commodification of labour – generalised commodity production – is necessary for the systematic generalisation of commodity exchange, the category of labour is not logically necessary to depict exchange's logic. Arthur insists that incorporating labour and production into the presentation too early inhibits comprehension of the logic of exchange in terms of pure social form exercising a determinative power over its material bearer. Arthur's claim is that capitalist form determines its content. The strong sense in which this is meant cannot be gleaned from Marx's *Capital,* where labour is presented as that which all commodities have in common. And the precedence given to labour in Marx leads to the misrecognition of the political possibilities that lie within labour, which is dictated by pure formal abstraction, despite its role as a basis for value forms. Arthur, here, revises Marx further: the capital relation is not a capital-labour relation, he argues, but instead 'the capital relation', which then *develops into* a class relation. For Arthur, waged labour, in yielding value and surplus value, negates itself: it is internal to capital's concept and is a category of capital. Building from this, Arthur intuits 'a political theory of the source of value.' Arthur's systemic dialectic does not dispute that living labour is both in and against capital. However, for Arthur, until history realises a 'consciously organised anti-systemic movement', capital merely atomises the working class and labour. A counter subject, in this regard, remains merely 'virtual.'

The final section of the book's second half, *Division III: The System of Capital*, offers a glimpse into the more concrete implications of the theory, with capital's social forms considered in relation to circulation, production and social reproduction. Here, Arthur departs from a narrower focus on systematic presentation and situates the ideal movement of capital within the realm of material process. The move establishes the basis for Arthur's own 'transformation procedure', worked out in Chapter 14: The Dual Ontology of Capital. The dual ontology is in reference to the ontological distinction between the material and ideal 'levels of reality'. Far from an affirmation of conventionally dualistic philosophy, this ontological dualism is symptomatic of capitalist modernity, where the idealist ontology of capital as a pure social form is the synthetic result of historical process. Giving the transformation of values into prices an ontological base, rather than one based on quantity – that in effect results in a naturalisation of the value form – enables Arthur to abandon a quagmire of traditional Marxist debate. The distinction between value and price, for Arthur, is the distinction between two distinct ontological realms: that of the ideal movement of capital and that of material process. What Arthur refers to as the 'transformation procedure' requires comprehension of these two opposed systems of determination. So undertaken, there is no 'problem' as such. Instead, it becomes clear that price can only be derived through looking at the reproduction of capital as a system – which includes both capitalist and non-capitalist social relations – that in turn distorts the abstract capital relation.

The dual ontology of Arthur's systematic dialectic is where the potential to undermine the political limits of Hegelian logical forms can be found. This is where Arthur departs from other value-form theorists, such as Moishe Postone. However, despite recognising the necessary double ontology required to grasp the mediation between the abstract and the concrete, it is not clear how Arthur might conceive the concrete as a distinct ontology. While this exclusion enables what is perhaps the most robust study of the concept of capital within Hegelian Marxism to date, neglecting scrutiny of the ontological basis for non-capitalist objects, or 'capital's other', renders the form of power exercised by capital obscure. What philosophy of nature, life and the material can illuminate the 'other' upon which capital acts?

Perhaps these are challenges with which the reader and future scholarship is intended to grapple. The necessity of doing so is negatively manifest in a book as intentionally limited in focus as Arthur's. Collective scholarship that integrates the systematicity of pure form with concrete epistemology – giving philosophical meaning to non-capitalist materiality – is needed not only to piece together the enormity of global capitalism but to interpret where room for capital's counter-subject can be affirmed. Without so doing, theory risks disregarding the impartial, uneven (and political) ways that value forms determine concrete life. While we need a robust concept of capital to delineate the specific abstract power unique to the capitalist mode of production, we also need something akin to Marx's unsystematic address thereof. This is because the concrete 'other' of capital, which functions as its conditions of possibility and medium of reproduction, contains distinct ontological compulsions of its own, resisting and morphing value's forms of appearance. Extensions to the Arthurist project should turn their attention this way.

While Arthur's analysis eschews 'application' to the empirical and historical contexts of abstract forms and their concrete bearers, Arthur does point to where possibility lies within the dynamic of the self-reproduction of the pure forms of capital. Arthur's philosophically systematic theory of 'pure form' could be construed as the insistence that we must fully understand the social form of capital if we are to achieve conscious understanding of the historical material realm and act strategically. For Arthur, doing so necessitates that one interprets capital as a social ontology, where abstract social forms mediate the concrete world asymmetrically to pursue their own self-reproduction at the expense of life and the natural world.

The Spectre of Capital provides scholarship with a philosophical lens adequate to capital's abstract forms.

Self-restricted to 'pure theory', Arthur addresses the principles of capital's social form in abstraction from their empirical history. What results, however, offers up a epistemic resource for historically informed empirical study. So framed, 'Arthurism' might enable analysis to grasp the underpinning form of power behind historical development all the better. In this sense, the theoretical basis Arthur ventures establishes the groundwork for a political analysis and practice more fully aware of its opponent, granting insight into capital's compulsions, determinations and preconditions. Without better understanding capital's reproduction of social forms – and, correlatively, the question of why human agents continue to act as personifications of capital – actors, theoretical and practical, will fail to see the stakes of particular actions. Empirical analysis, as such, requires a robust understanding of abstract logical forms both to grasp the present and to envisage social life's reproduction without capital. *The Spectre of Capital* is an imperative contribution to this ongoing project.

Rebecca Carson

Exiled sounds

Sam Dolbear and Esther Leslie, *Dissonant Waves: Ernst Schoen and Experimental Sound in the 20th century* (London: Goldsmiths Press, 2023). 320pp. £32.00 hb., 978 1 91338 056 4

Sam Dolbear and Esther Leslie's book on the life and work of Ernst Schoen confronts two not dissimilar problems of memory and writing. How to write about radio, a form not reducible to denotation? And, how to depict a life of which the record is limited and partial?

As far as an analysis of Schoen's main medium is concerned, Dolbear and Leslie's task is aided by the fact that Schoen's unpublished manuscript *Broadcasting: How It Came About* has been preserved along with magazines and programmes from the station that employed him, even if recordings for so many of the programmes he produced have not.

As for the second problem concerning limited biographical source material, this may be addressed through the use of conjecture and supposition. But there are manifold risks to such an endeavour; the biographer is pulled between loyalty to the presentation of experience in all its erratic messiness and the neat linearity of narrative. These dilemmas are all the more likely to confront those who document people and events at the fringes of official history. In *Wayward Lives, Beautiful Experiments*, her account of black feminist rebellions in New York and Philadelphia in the early twentieth century, Sadiya Hartman insists that studies of those made marginal to history must confront the boundaries of the archive and exclusivity of documentary records. The historian must, Hartman argues, press 'at the limits of the case file and the document, speculate about what might have been, imagined things whispered in dark bedrooms and amplified moments of withholding, escape and possibility.'

In their study of Schoen, Dolbear and Leslie opt for a different biographical strategy, which they call, borrowing from Theodor Adorno's study of 'Radio Physiognomics', the 'hear-stripe.' Adorno was referring to the background static one hears in radio reception that, in his view, generates a continuously moving sonic canvas upon which music is projected and by which it loses its own dynamism and reality. As Dolbear and Leslie deploy it, though, the hear-stripe refers to the foregrounding of archival gaps and silences, themselves products of world-historical events which bear scrutiny in their own right (in Schoen's case: the rise of German fascism, the Second World War and migration-cum-destitution). Equally, surviving ephemera that might otherwise be overlooked takes on new significance, from fairground photographs to dream journals. In this way, a life is reconstructed alongside the material and historical forces which shaped it without pretences to neat linearity nor comprehensiveness.

Born in 1894, among the most formative events in Schoen's early life was the 'dramatic' reading circle he formed as an adolescent in Berlin in 1910 alongside his friends Walter Benjamin and Alfred Cohn. This was a fecund period of scholarship and learning, including periods of study with composers Edgard Varèse and Ferruccio Busconi, and it lasted until 1916 when Schoen joined the infantry reserves. 'War's communicative armoury was being adapted for its aftermath', Dolbear and Leslie write and, indeed, following a period of work in a POW camp, Schoen entered a burgeoning media industry upon his return to Berlin in 1918. This included spells as a writer for a cultural newspaper, as an editor for a press agency, and as a press officer for the imperial coal concession, all between 1918 and 1922. It was a period when Schoen orbited a group of artists and writers at the intersection of dada and constructivism: Raoul Hausmann, Werner Graeff, Tristan Tzara, John Heartfield and, of course, his old friend Walter Benjamin.

From 1924, the year that radio for entertainment purposes emerges in earnest in Germany, Schoen joined the SÜWRAG station in Frankfurt as a programme assistant and was quickly promoted to lead its programming department. It was in this period lasting up to Hitler's rise to power that, searching out the possibilities inherent to a medium still in its infancy, Schoen conducted his most important work. This included the aforementioned book on broadcasting, as well as an early radio play produced alongside SÜWRAG director Hans Flesch and for which Schoen composed the music. Adventurous in its reflections on the new medium itself, the play drew complaints from listeners befuddled by its setting in a radio station and uncertain if they were hearing a work of fiction. Schoen might also be credited with the invention of the now customary short introductory lecture designed to present new pieces of music to audiences.

This was also a period where Schoen intervened in national cultural debates, including a controversy around the teaching of jazz in conservatories in 1927 which, for its detractors, amounted to an attack on Germanness. It's noteworthy that Schoen's position was more or less opposed to that of Adorno who, in a series of infamous essays published a few years later, would describe jazz as a pathological reflection of chattel slavery and discern in its rhythms the discipline of industrial society. Conversely, Schoen views jazz as a uniquely American form which should be celebrated for its revitalisation of European music with new techniques and instruments.

Where Schoen's name is known today, however, it's primarily for the work he did alongside Walter Benjamin around radio programming for children. The parlour games and sing-a-longs they aired renewed something of the mass dialogical possibilities of the medium. Radio could also function as a means of transgressing the borders by which children are segregated from adult worlds. Characteristically adult themes of crime or catastrophe were often the subject of Benjamin's stories for children while other plays commissioned by Schoen sought mischievously to lay bare the mechanisms of the studio. Along similar lines, Schoen's musical compositions for children unstiffened the severity of atonal music while refusing the uncomplicated melodies typically reserved for the young.

Dolbear and Leslie present Schoen as committed to the possibilities inherent to a then still open, virtual technology; the site of new forms, genres and styles against the 'bourgeois laws of inertia', as he once put it. But this period of experimentation was fated to be short-lived. By 1929 pro-government content was increasingly being imposed upon broadcasters and by 1932 growing state control led to increasingly centralised programming. By 1933 Hitler's speeches clogged the airwaves and Schoen had been dismissed. 'Radio was captured', in Dolbear and Leslie's words.

From this moment on, the Schoen archive gets especially patchy. In 1933 he is accused of having tried to cut transmissions of a speech of Hitler's and promptly arrested. He escaped but was detained a second time for programming socialists and Jews and was only released by virtue of a heroic act by his wife, Joanna Schoen, with whom he fled to England in May of 1934.

The Schoens' exile in London marks a period of hardship that would persist off and on for the rest of Ernst's life. Despite a few publications in the BBC Radio Times – one on opera, another on radio and others still on Webern and on Krenek – paid jobs were few and far between, and the frustrations of economic insecurity were compounded by the failure to get his history of broadcasting published. More or less steady work only arrived in 1940 when Schoen gained a post as a translator in the German section of the BBC External Services Department. This, in turn, led to his being sent by the BBC to Germany in 1947 to report on the post-war state of cultural institutions there. But to his great disappointment and despite his production of a programme for German Youth Radio, Schoen was mainly excluded from the cultural reconstruction of his native country. His proposal to the BBC for radio programming in the British Occupied Zones was ignored and he returned to Britain broke and frustrated.

Schoen returned a final time to Germany in 1952, never to leave again, after being made formally redundant by the BBC, though work there had already long dried up. This final period of his life is characterised by fruitless pursuits of both steady work and compensation from the German government. He eked out a precarious existence mainly as an archivist for the Deutches Theatre and as a translator of British literature until his death in 1960. The implication is partly that, as Dolbear and Leslie have it, there was no place for Schoen's ilk in the post-war world.

In this regard, it is useful to contrast Schoen with Adorno who, aside from Benjamin, was probably his most significant interlocutor, although 'frenemy' might be a more apt term. When Schoen sought publication of his study of broadcasting at the Frankfurt School, Adorno wrote to Horkheimer advising against it. In his letter Adorno called the work 'quite schematic and empty' and described Schoen as not being 'theoretically gifted.' Around the same period, in a letter to a friend Schoen described Adorno's theory of music as both replete with conceptual shortcuts and blunders and 'almost schizophrenic in its snobbism.' Whether or not these accusations were justified, Adorno's sustained obliviousness to the hardships faced by Schoen after 1933 comes off as insensitive at best; a sentiment underscored by his response to Schoen's decision to turn down a request to

help collate Benjamin's writings. Schoen wrote to Adorno that he felt 'separated from [Benjamin's texts] by an abyss, out of which we try to climb today only with endless efforts, a struggle which will, I suppose hang over us for the rest of our lives.' Upon receiving Schoen's letter Adorno reported to Gershom Scholem that Schoen had declined, he suspected, because they hadn't chosen an East German publisher for Benjamin's works.

The theory of radio is another point of discord between Adorno and Schoen and we can piece together the outlines of a riposte to Adorno's unrelenting pessimism vis-a-vis music's technological mediation. Radio, for Adorno, marks a final stage in the capitalist corruption of musical culture whereby the intensity of the musical statement is lost to the acoustic conditions of small domestic spaces and to its integration into quotidian time. Authoritarianism pervades where programming standardises experience into a schedule and where voices are disembodied. To broadcast symphonic works is to atomise them, especially for the new listener lacking musical education or context. Musical colour and texture are lost by mechanical reproduction and this, in turn, makes music's culinary consumption all the easier.

In contrast, Schoen adopts the expediency of the programmer and so, operating in an altogether different theoretical register, retains radio as a site of possibility. Schoen's argument aligns with Adorno's insofar as he holds that the remediation of earlier forms for radio, whether opera or theatre music, can't simply entail their reproduction. This would 'disable' the listener lacking visual cues or a sense of wider context. Radio must, therefore, strive for a form 'that is essentially original and its own.' But the constitution of a new listening subject will demand a new pedagogy too, and this will involve careful selection of works and historical explication, demonstrations of how light forms are derived from high art, and so on.

Music in industrial society can become more than mere adornment, Schoen holds, but only if a social need for it can be construed. I have already mentioned the use of parlour games, sing-a-longs and quizzes and, in this light, we should discern these Brechtian gestures bending radio away from uni-directional transmission as attempts to interrupt audience passivity. But Schoen also insists that one needs to recognise the social situation whereby radio is consumed by the worker exhausted at the end of his shift: low standards are imposed on him which he must be equipped to resist.

Friedrich Kittler once characterised the emergence of radio networks as a result of efforts to retain control over mass communication against the nearly two hundred thousand demobilised German radio operators who kept their equipment after World War I and put it to 'anarchistic abuse.' With Schoen we encounter something like a continuity of this abuse of a technology and, given Dolbear and Leslie's presentation of his life, we confront a thought arrested by the terrors of war and its aftermath.

Paul Rekret

Tourists of the world, unite!

Hiroki Azuma, *Philosophy of the Tourist* (Falmouth: Urbanomic, 2022). Translated by John D. Person. 256pp., £25.00 pb., 978 1 91510 300 0

In *The Case against Travel*, Agnes Callard writes that tourism turns us into the worst version of ourselves. Far away from 'home' – any metropolis in the Global North – the tourist does silly things nobody wants to hear about; writing postcards or taking photos of animals. Taking her own experience at a falcon hospital in Abu Dhabi as an example, she writes:

I took a photo with a falcon on my arm. I have no interest in falconry or falcons, and a generalized dislike of encounters with nonhuman animals. But the falcon hospital was one of the answers to the question, 'What does one do in Abu Dhabi?' So I went.

She found the trip 'dehumanizing'. Back home, her life contained 'zero falconry' just as before. If the birds were not transformative, they taught her something about tourism: 'we already know what we will be like when we return.' Tourism 'prevents us from feeling the presence of those we have travelled such great distances to be near.' In short, tourism is an experience of total alienation.

Callard is not alone in loathing tourism. Everyone hates tourists: they exploit economic disparity, culturally appropriate, turn cities into Airbnbs and pollute the planet. Recently, a tourist carved his girlfriend's initials into the 2,000-year-old Colosseum. 'Tourists, go home!' graffiti is found in most tourist towns. In the Mediterranean, tourist hot spots are often focal points of the refugee crisis. Last summer, a fishing boat in Greece packed with migrants sank just a few miles from tourists sunbathing.

Not an easy terrain for Japanese cultural critic Hiroki Azuma to launch his *Philosophy of the Tourist*. Azuma's book is an unashamed love letter to the tourist. Why the tourist? The tourist is a hybrid Other: unlike the villager or the nomad, the tourist belongs to one community but sometimes visits others. The tourist is the flâneur of our time: an indifferent, potentially happy consumer-subject who traverses the local and the global. For Azuma, no radical political vision of the twenty-first century can ignore the tourist. Together with the falcons, the tourist embarks on a journey towards multispecies solidarity.

The founder of *Genron*, Tokyo's forum for critical theory, Azuma also runs a 'dark tourism' company that organises trips to Chernobyl (they published a *Chernobyl Dark Tourism Guide*). Azuma became controversial for envisioning Fukushima as 'a 'mecca' for dark tourism, on the model of Hiroshima and Auschwitz'. He defends this shady project from the perspective of the tourist: to know the 'original' Fukushima – and otherwise uneventful prefecture – one has to see the 'derivative' one: an accident site contaminated by radiation.

Azuma's style is effortless: Disney and Dubai meet Derrida and Deleuze. Although the prose is lucid, the structure is messy. Azuma takes his readers on a wild ride from eighteenth-century philosophy, *The Brothers Karamazov*, network theory, manga, Chernobyl, *Neuromancer*, Hegel, Kojève and Lacan to terrorism. Azuma himself admits that the book is unpolished. The original appeared at the height of a tourism boom in the 2010s before COVID-19 briefly stopped leisure trips. However, in his preface to the English edition, Azuma proclaims the resurrection of the tourist.

The book is divided into two parts, 'Philosophy of the tourist' and 'Philosophy of the family (an introduction)'. The first chapter 'Tourism' sketches some goals: first, to build a framework to think anew about globalism; second, to think about people in terms of contingency; third, to develop a form of philosophical discourse that transcends the serious/frivolous distinction. If we want to understand the world, we have to explore it as tourists: to visit random places on a whim to see people we don't need to see. That makes the tourist an unpredictable subject open to chance encounters:

> For the tourist, everything at their destination is a commodity and an exhibit that is the object of their neutral, passive – that is to say, contingent – gaze. The tourist gaze is none other than a gaze that views the entire world as an arcade or shopping mall.

The tourist's interest is purely consumptive and without direction. Like the flâneur, the tourist is *drifting*: they view the world with a 'chance gaze'. Sometimes, and this is crucial, tourists see things that locals don't want them to see. Therefore, the tourist deconstructs Callard's simplistic antagonism between real and false experience. This, for Azuma, is a valuable 'misdelivery'. However, tourists are not the reasonable subject of philosophers. These frivolous drifters are in fact the enemy of twentieth-century philosophy in its entirety:

> Tourists are the masses. They are labourers and they are consumers. The tourist is a private being and does not take on any public role. Tourists are anonymous, and they do not deliberate with locals at their destination. They do not participate in the history of their destination either, nor in its politics. Tourists simply use money. They ignore national boundaries as they fly across the surface of the planet. They don't make friends or enemies.

We should not read Azuma too literally here – he is a provocateur. There is no moral signalling in *Philosophy of the Tourist*. Of course, you can only be a tourist if you happen to hold certain passports and have enough money to travel. And you don't become a political agent just by using money or taking a flight. However, what Azuma is interested in is a novel form of subjectivity. The tourist teaches us that there is no self to which we can come home. Azuma deliberately creates friction to carve out an ambivalent subject in-between the familiar and the uncanny.

One of the key ideas to understand the tourist is the postal metaphor of misdelivery – a transformative potentiality of contingent communication. For Azuma, drawing on Derrida, misdelivery is one of the few principles that support solidarity with the Other. Like a letter reaching the wrong destination, the American tourist in Abu Dhabi has some misfired communication with the falcons. And this misdelivery is all that matters. Even if we fail to build solidarity with falcons, we have to keep on trying – the very failure of solidarity creates an effect *that makes it seem as if it exists*'. Therefore, we must actively expose ourselves to misdelivery: we have to become tourists.

A critical reading of Kojève is at the heart of the second chapter 'Politics and Its Outside.' Here, Azuma expands the philosophy of the tourist into a radical alternative to post-Enlightenment political theory. Azuma's vision relies on Kojève's concept of the End of History – itself the product of the philosopher's touristic trips to Japan in the 1950s. Taking hundreds of photos of zen gardens, Kojève proclaimed that history has ended. All that remains are derivative simulacra and empty rituals. 'In other words', Azuma asks, 'is not the world itself becoming a theme park?'

Azuma retraces the first appearance of dark tourism to Voltaire's *Candide* (1759) which lets the protagonist travel the world to realise its shortcomings. Another precursor is Kant's *Perpetual Peace* (1795) which grounds universal peace in tourism. The Kantian tourist neither represents their civil society nor the foreign policy of their states. Tourists are 'guided only by their own interests and by the commercial spirit of travel agencies'. And yet, they '*are contributing to peace independently of the state system*'. Once again, we have to take Azuma with a pinch of salt: he does not say that booking a holiday creates world peace.

However, Azuma's tourist provides an alternative circuit to becoming a global citizen. Unlike Hegel's maturing from family member to citizen, everyone is always already a *potential* tourist – even people who never leave their countries. In that sense, tourists are a political force beyond politics. Therefore, tourism should be the right even of members of 'rogue states' like Russia. Azuma insists that the principle of perpetual peace erodes if we ban Russian tourists. This is of course a problematic demand. Do some tourists not also support their rogue government? And is the tourist really an apolitical agent? These issues become more severe when it comes to the relation between the refugee and the tourist. However, with Azuma we have to expose ourselves to these misdeliveries too.

Azuma sharply criticises Kojève's vision of a world after history. His posthumanism differs from both Kojève's animalisation and Arendt's *animal laborans*. Having neither friends nor states, the tourist is not an animal but an ambiguous hybrid: 'invited to consume like animals while being human, and simultaneously forced to speak about politics like humans while being animals'. The tourist is both a face and a number. Following Masachi Ōsawa, Azuma detects a similar 'split' between the national and the global. These two conflicting orders make up our 'stratified world' (nisō kōzō). Drawing on 1970s Japanese manga, Azuma describes reality as 'an amorphous monster that is neither organism nor machine, with countless independent 'faces". We live in a two-layered world: our human layer (thought) is disconnected while our animal layer (desire) is connected – to capital.

Azuma finds the seeds of a radical politics of the tourist in libertarianism and the 'multitude'. Azuma's criticism of Hardt and Negri's *Empire* is one of the pearls of the book. He convincingly shows why their concept of multitude is ultimately mystical. For Azuma, Hardt and Negri's 'guerilla solidarity' has no content beyond faith. In short, their multitude relies on negative theology. But how can the multitude attain sovereignty *in reality*?

This question guides the fourth chapter, 'Toward a Postal Multitude'. If *Empire* proposed a self-circulating monism, the philosophy of the tourist draws on a multi-layered, stratified system. A billion tourists dispatched around the world, who 'indulge in consumption without regard for any ideology', are a *postal* multitude. Their mob mobility creates countless situations of misdelivery. The fact that tourists not interested in art still visit the Louvre is a misdelivery 'linked to a type of enlightenment'. Even if they don't *understand* the painting, there is communication – a condition for postal solidarity. This solidarity is unintentional and accidental:

> Where the multitude go to demonstrations, the tourist goes on junkets. Where the former builds solidarity without communication, the latter communicates without solidarity... Although the tourist doesn't deliberately build solidarity, they do exchange words with people they happen to meet. Whereas demonstrations always have an enemy, tours have no enemies.

The tourist is an immature subject in a network generated by chance. A crowd of tourists is nothing more than 'customers purchasing gas from the same utility company, or passengers riding on the same bus'. And yet, for Azuma, it is precisely this random association of individuals that makes up society. To illustrate the ways in which individuals are linked through clusters, Azuma delves into network theory. The tourist is a transformative node in the network of human society; if a stranger 'rewires' a closed set of connections, 'that new encounter (short cut) is precisely what all of a sudden makes the world small'. The tourist shifts from one scale to the other, traversing the national and the global.

The unfinished second part of the book is an attempt to apply the philosophy of the tourist. However, large parts of it are unrelated to tourism. Readers who expect some concrete guidelines of the politics of the tourist will be disappointed. The fifth chapter, 'The Family', describes postal solitary as *familial* – not in the sense of the bourgeois, nuclear family but in the way in which pets can become our family. Family resemblances (Wittgenstein) give a vague sense of cohesion to this 'accidental' family. We don't really know why a dog's face can look similar to his owner but we call it a *face* regardless. If Callard felt dehumanised by the falcons, Azuma dreams of multispecies solidarity.

Misdeliveries between birds and humans build a family. Azuma's philosophy of the family turns Heidegger on his head; it starts not with death but from the contingency of birth, or what Derrida called *dissemination*:

> Dissemination refers to the discharge of sperm. The massive numbers of sperms create our contingent nature. A new philosophy born out of the relativity of birth and the contingency of the family, a philosophy that could be counterposed to Heideggerian philosophy born out of the absoluteness of death and the necessity of fate...

A child is born like a letter sent by mistake. Once the letter is there, its sender becomes irrelevant.

Drawing on Lacanian subject theory, the sixth chapter, 'The Uncanny', tries to develop a new view on the information society – maybe too far a stretch. Exploring notions of the uncanny in sci-fi, Azuma explores cyberspace as another touristic landscape. Tourists decipher the world as if it is a code. While the tourist shortcuts the network, the 'database animal' is estranged by the internet. For both subjects, reality is *another* world of simulacra and misdeliveries.

The book closes with an exploration of terrorism in Dostoevsky; key themes are the killing of the father and the Tsar. Azuma finds forerunners of the tourist in Dostoevsky's protagonists: the terrorist, the sadist and the *Underground Man*, all 'impotent subjects surrounded by children'. Azuma's speculations in 'Dostoevsky's Final Subject' are refreshing but only vaguely related to tourism.

Philosophy of the Tourist is a thought experiment. The tourist can teach us that the human did not yet disappear: it has a hundred faces now and moves around the world.

Isabel Jacobs

Tailors of taste

Nick Seaver, *Computing Taste: Algorithms and the Makers of Music Recommendation* (Chicago: University of Chicago Press, 2022). 224pp., $99.00 hb., $20.00 pb., 978 0 226 70226 1 hb., 978 0 226 82297 6 pb.

The cultivation of musical taste has long been subject to critical reflection. Plato deemed music crucial for human flourishing because it reaches the innermost depths of our souls. Absent the harmony the best music imparts and disarray in our personal lives and dissonance in our societies was said to follow. Given the stakes, guidance from knowledgeable intermediaries in the form of philosopher kings was essential. Nick Seaver presents a similar narrative regarding intermediaries of music recommendation services in his new book *Computing Taste: Algorithms and the Makers of Music Recommendation*. Scientists, engineers, programmers and product managers in the industry share a common creation myth where algorithms help to overcome obstacles to tailored taste. Novel internet technology and the rise of digital distribution in the mid-1990s provided a cornucopia of options that unleashed music from the grasp of cultural gatekeepers. Record store clerks, critics and DJs no longer had a monopoly on legitimate taste, but in their absence, listeners were faced with too much unfiltered music. As exciting as the endless possibilities for musical exploration were, people needed new forms of guidance. And so, the makers of music recommendation ushered in a new age of music appreciation aided by predictive algorithms.

We should be skeptical about the details of the music recommendation origin story, Seaver warns. Nonetheless, he argues that much can be learned from understanding how people in the industry, such as those who work for Spotify or Apple Music, make sense of their trade. The people Seaver studies work with algorithms to recommend music to listeners, but it is an imprecise undertaking. As a data scientist he interviewed acknowledged, while taste makers aspire to tap into a 'platonic ideal' that aligns music to the chords of our souls, the actual process is 'not so pure'. Rather than using predictive algorithms to access some heretofore unknown but true form of why people like the music they like, Seaver finds unsettled images of taste. How makers of music recommendation understand their input vary and often draw from non-technical narratives to do their work. Recommender systems do not abide by a singular technical logic.

Seaver explains that techniques of music recommendation are justified on the premise of their origin myth: listeners are overwhelmed and in need of guidance. People have always experienced 'filtering' of their music choices based on their parents' tastes, geography and other contexts. Now, with advances in technology and data drawn from a users' ratings, people can experience music without the inherent limitations of such filtering mechanisms. Music recommenders fill the gap with care and an embrace of difference. They describe their work both in opposition to the old guard of gatekeepers and, employing pastoral metaphors, play the role of park rangers, gardeners and farmers, explorers and guides, cartographers and surveyors. Some roles that recommenders identify with are more compassionate than others. Seaver juxtaposes the narratives recommenders espouse about care for listeners with their acknowledgement of structural demands to make profit. He highlights how images of 'traps' and 'hooks' portray listeners as unsuspecting prey that can be kept listening by way of persuasive technologies. Seaver highlights the way recommendation systems are fragmentary, incoherent, and dynamic based on the complex listener data they draw from. He finds that people working with these systems often feel constrained by and in awe of the variety of listeners. The contexts that a listener puts themselves in (exercising versus relaxing), as well as differences between diverse types of listeners (lean forward vs. lean back) make it difficult to categorise listeners.

In the second half of the book, the scope moves from how recommenders view listeners to how they engage with the sound of music, the spatiality in which types of music are mapped and the metaphors recommenders give themselves in tending to the sound and space of music. At least on the surface, how music sounds is irrelevant from the point of view of music recommenders. Music is studied as a kind of information. Computers are no different than brains, and algorithms are like well-trained ears. Nonetheless Seaver finds a gap between which patterns algorithms can find, in something like musical genres, and what intuitively makes sense to the human ear. Often patterns pair music that fans of a genre would not recognise. Programmers, because of this, repeatedly check the patterns of machine learning against their own assessments. The way music is grouped into various genres is both technical and intuitive. Music recommenders navigate a terrain between formal and informal practices. They go back and forth from equations to intuitions. Accordingly, Seaver argues that if one were able to open the much talked about black box, the technical code itself would not be enough to understand music recommendation outputs.

Throughout the book, Seaver is reflexive about his experience conducting research. At times, he provides an intimate look at what it felt like to be an outsider and the emotions he faced while doing fieldwork: joy, frustration, surprise. Although Seaver could be criticised for his minimal treatment of his ethnographic tactics, there are helpful methodological suggestions: it is okay to change one's scope given constraints in the field; much can be learned from how people understand their roles; and often some of the most interesting things happen in interviews just after the recorder is turned off. The epistemic implications are also significant. They corroborate the argument Seaver is making about the subjective nature of music recommendation systems: there is no objective or value-neutral way to recommend taste or study those who do. Emotions, ethical reflections, positionality and context are not brushed to the side, inviting readers to engage with the subject matter and to question the assumptions underlying the research.

The strength of his connection to ethnography is evident as he does more than simple reporting on technical details of science and technology in the music recommendation industry. Seaver brings each aspect of his study into conversation with studies in the ethnographic record. For instance, studies of reindeer pastoralists in Finland, nuclear scientists in the United States, and indigenous trappers in the Western Hemisphere are reflected on respectively to illuminate intriguing ways recommenders try to captivate their subjects without erasing their individuality, the challenges in gaining access to secluded institutions like streaming corporations, and the intricate nature of persuasive technologies used to 'trap' listeners. Making links across disciplines allows Seaver to compare institutions and contextualise those he is studying. Connections to other expert spaces make for a compelling read and serve as a bridge to insights about the continuity of music recommendation spaces. For example, he describes affinities between ethnographic studies of nuclear scientists to music recommendation offices. The self-proclaimed cutting-edge spaces of technology and taste are often found to be conventional.

Those looking for technical details of the industry or insights from the perspective of a musician might be unsatisfied. Seaver's primary focus lies outside of the musician's craft or how listeners engage with music. That is not to say details of this kind are absent from the book. For example, Seaver spends some time talking to a programmer about Djent (a subgenre of metal music) and the process of categorising types of the genre. And there is an enjoyable discussion about the music of Pitbull and Diplo that reflects on the recommendation patterns of both. Instead of a technical snapshot of an industry at a given time, readers are presented with a set of worldviews that continue to shape the way predictive algorithms are used for the cultivation of taste.

Seaver references seminal figures important for taste and science and technology studies including Pierre Bourdieu, Donna Haraway, Michel Foucault and Theodor Adorno but his engagements with these authors are often underdeveloped. By design, he limits his analysis to what his subjects understand themselves to be doing. This approach does not adequately pair beliefs against the material realities of capitalism, unless it is mentioned by the music recommenders themselves. Authors in the traditions he references would each insist on a deeper look at the relationship between technology, ideology and underlying conditions. In addition, a litany of scholarship draws from these traditions to think about predicative algorithms (often even in reference to taste) and an engagement with them would have made for a more nuanced critique of the politics of technology in recommender systems.

Given his light treatment of science and technology studies, Seaver's challenge to critics of technology is not as incisive as it could be. For example, he pushes against critics who he notes often worry about the reductive effects of quantification and how machine learning metaphors, which draw on pastoral metaphors, naturalise and therefore mystify the work they are doing. A more thorough engagement with contemporary critics who draw from Foucault, for example, would reveal a more nuanced set of concerns. For example, Colin Koopman's 2019 book *How We Became Our Data: A Genealogy of the Informational Person* is not referenced but would help strengthen his analysis of power in the corporations he studies. Given that music recommendation companies are a part of a wider informatic world which, as Koopman demonstrates, has a long and often racist history, connecting analysis of recommender worldviews to those histories would help readers understand more deeply what is at stake when corporations present algorithmic curation as wholly new and largely free of human shortcomings like 'bias'. Seaver discusses the impact of human decision making on curation processes often. That these are human, not merely technical processes, is an accomplishment, but he does not incisively examine their relation to broader discourses and histories of power.

That said, the most significant achievement of this work lies in its contribution to critical algorithmic studies. Seaver finds a way to trace encounters between industry techniques and the varied worldviews within. In so doing, he situates his work alongside other scholarship on predictive algorithms that is critical without being totalising. The original ethnographic observation and reflection on algorithmic curation provides readers with a deeper understanding of the mechanisms at play, the narratives embedded in these systems, and their implications for artists and listeners. By delving into unexplored avenues of the music recommendation industry and shedding new light on familiar ideas about the complicated relationship between techniques and cultural imaginaries, *Computing Taste* distinguishes itself as a significant addition to the existing literature on the politics of technology and cultural experiences in the digital age.

Glen Billesbach II